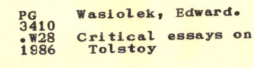

Critical Essays on Tolstoy

Critical Essays on
World Literature

Robert Lecker, General Editor
McGill University

Critical Essays on Tolstoy

Edward Wasiolek

G. K. Hall & Co. • Boston, Massachusetts

Library of Congress Cataloging in Publication Data

Wasiolek, Edward.
  Critical essays on Tolstoy.

  (Critical essays on world literature)
  Includes index.
  1. Tolstoy, Leo, graf, 1828–1910 — Criticism and interpretation —
Addresses, essays, lectures. I. Title. II Series.
PG3410.W28   1986   891.73'3   85-24883
ISBN 0-8161-8827-0

CONTENTS

INTRODUCTION

Every great writer lives more than one life: the life of his own language and literary tradition and his lives abroad. Jack London was a writer of social and philosophical significance for the Russians, a writer of adventure tales for us; Longfellow's *Hiawatha* is something we admire in elementary school; it is a narrative poem of such power and beauty — at least in Bunin's translation — that it has always overridden political and social change in Russia. Even in periods of virulent anti-Americanism, it continues to be popular. Our Chekhov and Dostoevsky have never been Russia's, and theirs have not been ours. Tolstoy might seem to be an exception to these multiple lives. His writing is of such stark simplicity and such blunt directness, so universal in its appeal, so shorn of local pecularities, so pared to reach men everywhere, whatever their station and their nation, that he would seem to have only one life. Yet he has been read and understood in different ways in Russia, England, and America. Russian critical thought was there at the beginning of Tolstoy's career; our beginning came later, so late indeed, that most of his great work had been written, acclaimed, and debated in Russia before our critical consciousness became aware of it. One still winces when reading Matthew Arnold's words of 1887: "The crown of literature is poetry, and the Russians have not yet had a great poet." Our Tolstoy has been, for the most part, the Tolstoy who wrote *War and Peace* and *Anna Karenina*, and for a time in the last decade of the nineteenth century and the first of our century, Tolstoy the prophet: the old Count who ploughed the fields, made his own shoes, and instructed the world how to practice Christianity. Most of all, we know hardly at all the literary tradition of which Tolstoy was a part and the critical tradition in which he was understood and evaluated. It has had its own dynamisms and its own assumptions.

Nothing distinguished nineteenth-century Russian criticism more than its ideological character. The dominant view of the century was that literature and criticism existed to perceive the truth, understand it, and act on it. Criticism and literature existed to have an effect on society. It was not enough to see the truth; one had to infect others with it. Russian criticism assumed that great art and vision and ideas went together, and it

1

assumed further that the task of the critic was to elucidate and exposit the vision and ideas of an author. The critic was more than a passive elucidator of "truths" in the author's work. He could and often did shape the literature that was being produced, on the grounds that the "truth" was not the property of the author alone. Criticism was looked upon as an active and creative force, different in kind from the creative force of the writer, but just as important.

It is easy, after a century of relativism, objectivism, and neutral structuralism, to deride such a position, especially since it continues in Soviet criticism today. But the fact of the matter is that the position conferred on literature, the writer, and the critic was a position of seriousness and importance. Literature was not simply the "invention" of the individual mind (romantic personalism never took root in Russian critical attitudes), nor simply an intellectual construct, but a vehicle for discovering fundamental truths about history, nature, and the nation's soul. The position gave to literature, the writer, and the critic a sacred mission. The stakes were high, and they were never higher than in the 1850s, when Tolstoy first came upon the Russian literary stage.

The ideological temper in the 1850s was white-hot. The aristocratic and gradualist liberalism of the thirties and forties had given way to a new generation of young, angry intellectuals, who were impatient for social and moral change. The most prominent among them were: Chernyshevsky, Dobroliubov, and Pisarev; and the most influential of them was without doubt. Chernyshevsky. He is today enshrined in the hero's hall of pre-Soviet ideological saints, perhaps more for his personal courage and uncompromising opposition to the autocracy than for his ideological stance. It has been noted that these "radicals" were impatient for social change, and not noted enough that they were just as impatient for moral and psychological change. They wanted to transform not only governments, but also, man. They wanted a new man, and the phenomenal popularity of Chernyshevsky's *What Is to Be Done?* attests to this fact. In this immensely influential novel, Chernyshevsky gives us his view of the new man and woman and the social changes that would issue from such a transformation.

Chernyshevsky has often been painted in the West as a crude ideologue, who hated literature and badgered writers into ideological corners. The tenacity with which this view has been held by some distinguished academics in the West has done us very little good. Chernyshevsky's review of Tolstoy's *Childhood* is a subtle piece of exposition: balanced, judicious, perceptive, and fair in its treatment of the novel and of Tolstoy's talent. Rather than belaboring Tolstoy for failing to be socially relevant, he scolds those who would have Tolstoy address contemporary problems: "One really ought to understand that not every artistic conception admits of the instruction of social questions; one ought not forget that the first law of art is the unity of the work, and that therefore in depicting *Childhood* one must write about childhood and not something else, not social questions, not military scenes, not Peter the Great."

Ideology for Chernyshevsky was nothing so crude and shallow as sailing with the winds of the day. He saw that Tolstoy in *Childhood* was ideological in a more profound and significant way. He described how Tolstoy tried to catch and portray psychological processes as they emerged from a young consciousness, before they were caught in an ideological net of old ideas and notions; and as such, to seize the very nature of the mind and the emotions. This is what Chernyshevsky meant by "the purity of moral feeling" (*chistota nravstvennykh chuvstv*). Such feeling was pure because it was not yet sullied with the accumulations of the past and had not yet been shaped by accepted values and ideas. Indeed this was what Tolstoy was attempting to do, and what he would always attempt to do: to uncover beneath the accumulations of civilization's debris that unsullied nature of man. This was not so different from what Chernyshevsky was attempting to do, although Chernyshevsky was more polemical and more convinced that the "dirt" and accumulations would not go away by themselves, that one would have to act to reconstruct man and society.

Chernyshevsky caught something that Bakhtin and his followers have never been able to understand about Tolstoy: that beneath the seeming arrogance, bluntness, and uncompromising insistence on single truths, there is in Tolstoy's craft and cast of mind an unvarying and relentless dissolution of both conventional and personal truths. His thinking and art seemed to be carved in marble, but there is a persistent and subtle modification of the outlines, something like the endless drip of minerals modifying a stalactite. Nothing is easier to see in Tolstoy than his attacks on conventional truths. He knows what is false and he knows what is true, and the world is compounded of falseness: in the way men govern, the way they worship, the way they eat, marry, play, make love, dress, and spend their leisure time. What is less easy to see is that he attacks not only the truths of others, but also his own truths. This is what Chernyshevsky caught in this slight but profound review when he perceived the young Tolstoy's attempt to get at psychological processes — at perception and consciousness — before they were shaped by existing forces. Chernyshevsky saw the social drama in Tolstoy's drama of consciousness. Bakhtin does Tolstoy an immense disservice when he sees only a single voice in Tolstoy's works, and Derrida and his followers could find their predecessor in Tolstoy, as could Lacan and his followers. The self is no firm and unmodifiable entity in Tolstoy's works, or when it is, it is removed from living life.

A contrast of Chernyshevsky's early piece on Tolstoy with Lenin's immensely influential article "Tolstoy in the Mirror of the Revolution" is instructive and tells us something of the ideological temper of Russian and

Soviet literary criticism. After a period of ideological struggle in the early decades of this century, Soviet criticism has come to deify Tolstoy's works. The continuing Soviet bibliography of criticism on Tolstoy since 1917 now lists more than 20,000 items. Lenin's article on Tolstoy, and a few other short pieces, have gone a long way to the deification of Tolstoy. Lenin's piece was written in 1905, more than a decade before the revolution, but it, and a few other pieces he wrote on Tolstoy, have established themselves as canon of Soviet criticism. "Tolstoy in the Mirror of the Revolution" makes a sharp distinction between the "good" Tolstoy and the "poor" Tolstoy. The good Tolstoy is the aristocrat who identified himself with the views, emotions, values, fears, and hopes of the peasantry and articulated what was dumbly in their breasts: hatred of the church, the authorities, and the emerging capitalist exploiters, and fear of the social changes that were sweeping over Russia in the second half of the nineteenth century. Tolstoy, for Lenin, saw what was rotten in Russia and what needed to be changed, but he did not know how to respond to these corruptions. Tolstoy turned away from social solutions and toward moral solutions, and ended up as socially ineffective and irrelevant.

Clearly, this is a one-sided view of Tolstoy, self-serving and limited. But it is not without merit. The view that Tolstoy embodied and articulated those dumbly felt and inchoate fears of social change on the part of the peasantry is a suggestive and compelling thesis. It is a fact that Tolstoy castigated almost every institution of Russian society and contemporary civilization with a wrath reminiscent of Marx and his criticism of Victorian society. It is a fact, too, that Tolstoy had no better institutions to put in their place, or those he proposed—such as his support of Lloyd George's view of ownership of land—were vaguely put forth and unworkable. Tolstoy did turn away from social solutions to moral solutions, from public to personal life, to the confusion and frustration of some of his followers. When Lenin is unfair, and even obtuse, is to grant so little, almost nothing at all, to those matters of moral conscience that Tolstoy raised. They are of great subtlety and importance.

Lenin looked at Tolstoy's works from an intensely ideological point of view, and in this he is both captive and propagator of the nineteenth-century critical tradition. He assumes without questioning that the great writer has a social responsibility. It would never occur to him, nor to Chernyshevsky, nor to that long list of influential critics of the nineteenth century to believe or to accept that a work of art exists only to be "beautiful" or to be a well-made object. There were conservative or "aesthetic" critics in the nineteenth century: Turgenev, Grigoriev, Dostoevsky (in part), Botkin, and Druzhinin, among others. Yet they, too, in various ways assumed that the artwork served man in some active and effective way. Apollon Grigoriev, friend and philosophic counsellor of Dostoevsky, fought viciously with radical critics like Chernyshevsky and

Dobroliubov. He considered their call for social change arbitrary and unreal. Yet throughout the criticism, we get the same insistence on art as something important, serious, sacred, and the artist as a prophet and embodier of significant truths. He believed in a quasi-mystical way that a work of art reveals universal truths that transect historical moments and that feeling, and not reason, is the most important faculty in creating and understanding art.

Dostoevsky gave high praise to the power and art of *Anna Karenina*, but much of the novel outraged his sense of truth. On the most immediate level he was outraged by Levin's and Tolstoy's questioning of the righteousness of the Balkan war of 1877, in which Russia had gone to the support of the Serbians against Turkey. Levin's remarks that he did not feel the patriotic fervor that was sweeping Russia, and his assumption that he, too, represented Russia was taken by Dostoevsky as insufferable egotism, a refusal to humble one's ego before God and the Russian people. Indeed, it is the rationalism of Tolstoy and the sense that man alone can decide what is good and evil that runs across the grain of Dostoevsky's convictions. Dostoevsky believed, as he says in his review of *Anna Karenina*, that there is no one who can judge what is right or wrong for Russia, for history, for himself, and to do so—as he sees Tolstoy and Levin doing—is to arrogate to oneself on the basis of a shallow rationalism what cannot be understood or weighed. Dostoevsky understood Tolstoy correctly, for there is no evil in Tolstoy's world. There are only wise and stupid judgments, the consequences of which we call evil. What is more striking, however, in Dostoevsky's criticism of *Anna Karenina*, and of all criticism, is how thoroughly ideological it is, how quickly art and craft, no matter how honored, are overshadowed by questions of truth, evil, good, and the destiny of Russia. Art and craft are not denigrated. It is assumed throughout that only by way of art can we understand these questions in the most penetrating and profound way. Art is too serious to be craft alone.

The only significant departure from the Russian insistence on artist as ideologue, prophet, seer, and social mover was the Formalist school of criticism of the late teens and the twenties of this century. The Formalists, in their insistence on craft, on art as a linguistic artifact, on the work itself, apart from its sociological or philosophical being, are not without precedence in Russian criticism. They had their predecessors in Veselovsky, Potebnia, Druzhinin, Botkin, and in Pushkin himself. But what is instructive is how tied the departure is to what it has departed from: first, in the shrillness of its revolt, in the extremity of its positions, and finally, in the way it conceived of the integrity of the art object. The art object, for the Formalists, was never separated from history and the literary tradition in which it existed, and it had complex relations with social reality. Leo Tolstoy figured largely in the theory and practice of the Formalists. Boris

Eikhenbaum, one of the foremost exponents of the movement, wrote a series of influential books on Tolstoy. In *The Young Tolstoy* he explored the technical sources of Tolstoy's art. He wanted to explode the romantic myth that art comes from mysterious personal inspiration. Both the ideological critics of the nineteenth century and the Formalists insisted that art was not "invention" and the consequence of personality, but was objective truth. Tolstoy and the Formalists came together, too, in that they saw the function of art as a systematic breakdown of conventional ways of seeing things.

II

Anglo-American criticism on Tolstoy has been, by and large, less varied, historical, and comprehensive than Russian criticism. First of all, there is a lot less of it. Indeed, there was very little Anglo-American criticism of Tolstoy until the twentieth century, and despite the prestige and even awe with which *War and Peace* and *Anna Karenina* have been held in the West, the volume of scholarship and serious criticism on Tolstoy still is in modest quantity. Our criticism has been largely confined to *War and Peace* and *Anna Karenina*, and to a much lesser extent to a few of the later novels: *The Death of Ivan Ilytch*, *The Kreutzer Sonata*, and *Hadji Murad*. There was in the 1890s and the first two decades of the twentieth century, a fairly large literature in England and America on what one could call "the second Tolstoy," that is, that post-conversion Tolstoy, who for a time turned from literature and devoted himself to theological studies, and then to the implementation of his new Christianity in his personal life. This consisted in an ethic of renunciation: of property, luxury, excess of any kind, and finally of sex. Tolstoy's new Christianity caught the imagination of a good part of the civilized and sophisticated world, and his words were propagated in hurriedly edited and published texts in England and America. Tolstoy the prophet, religious leader, overshadowed the writer in the last twenty-five years of his life, but he continued to create, along with his expository writings, creative works of great beauty and significance, and today, it is these creative works that have greatly overshadowed the religious Tolstoy.

If we turn to criticism on *War and Peace* and *Anna Karenina*, where there is a substantial body now in English, one is struck with how narrow a perspective it has taken. Criticism on *War and Peace* in Russian (pre- and post-revolutionary) runs the gamut in kinds: source studies, linguistic analyses, exhaustive editing, historial studies of varied kinds, social, psychological, ideological. *War and Peace* for the Russians has been a universe for them, a gigantic mirror in which they have seen every part of themselves. Anglo-American criticism has churned in a narrow valley, and has occupied itself largely with structural problems and problems of morality and psychology, abstracted from the context in which the novels were written. It is often a criticism of sensitive, intelligent, and perceptive views, but also one that is strikingly ignorant of Russian history, of Tolstoy himself, and of the tradition of Russian literature. Much that has been characteristic of English criticism is already present in Matthew Arnold's very influential article on *Anna Karenina*. Matthew Arnold got his Russian literature by way of French translations, as did many of the original reviewers of Tolstoy's works. Arnold established what might be called the "exclamatory tradition" in English, and to a lesser extent in American, criticism on Tolstoy. When he says "But the truth is we are not to take *Anna Karénine* as a work of art; we are to take it as a piece of life. A piece of life it is," we are at a loss to take this statement literally. *War and Peace* and *Anna Karenina* are works of art and not life. They are conscious imaginings, carefully structured, meticulously crafted and labored over. We must take the statement of Arnold's as an indication of how powerfully he was moved by Tolstoy. It is a statement that has affected greatly a whole tradition of English critics on Tolstoy, for the statement in variation has been repeated by them over and over again. Virginia Woolf says, for example, "Life dominates Tolstoi as the soul dominates Dostoevsky." Even as late as the 1950s Lionel Trilling quotes Matthew Arnold's statement and considers it seriously before putting some distance between himself and the statement. The immediacy, scope, and power of Tolstoy's vision must have seemed, to the English critics, too great to fit into what their conception of art and the norms of the novel were. The phrase and its consequent repetitions register astonishment and awe, and as such they constitute a great tribute to Tolstoy's creative power.

Despite its naivetés, Matthew Arnold's article is a sensitive and penetrating reading of *Anna Karenina*, and he poses questions that are still to be answered today. There is something English in his astonishment that someone as beautiful, sensitive, and intelligent as Anna could be carried away so irretrievably by someone as unprepossessing as Vronsky. Yet it is one of the central questions of the novel. Vronsky is, by contrast with Anna, shallow; he is too small for her love and her passion. The disparity between the two, in the force of their passions, the depth of feeling, and in the fineness of character, suggest that Anna is driven by forces more powerful and certainly more profound than Vronsky's charms. Matthew Arnold, in this early review, sensed much of the complexity and power of the novel, and his remarks still strike one as fresh today. It is a tribute to English criticism on Tolstoy that he is so often referred to.

Henry James is in stark contrast to Arnold's sympathetic and sensitive reading. His unflattering and insensitive remarks about Tolstoy's craft are all the more astonishing, because he was and remains one of our best critics of the novel. It would not be an exaggeration to say that he gave the foundation of novel criticism in America. Tolstoy represented something alien and unfathomable for James. He produced works of indisputable genius, yet he violated every canon that James considered indispensable for the novel. James abhorred the indiscriminate point of view in fiction and championed the restricted point of view, where the authorial presence was hidden or absent. He abhorred overt moralizing and philosophising. A novel was a made thing, and though the author had the responsibility of giving us the sense and feel of actual life, he would never do so by letting life pour in indiscriminately. Yet this was what Tolstoy seemed to do: his authorial presence was overt, shameless, and massive; he moralized and philosophized about every conceivable subject; he seemed to continue that leisurely tradition of multiple plot lines and consequent lack of focus that had characterized the eighteenth-century English tradition and that had continued in some mediocre novelists in the nineteenth century — that shapeless pudding that he objected to in Galsworthy's novels. Among Russians, James vastly preferred Turgenev, who seemed to have that self-consciousness and sense of measure and taste that Tolstoy lamentably did not have. Tolstoy was something of a barbarian or an "elephant," to use James's phrase, an image that gets over Tolstoy's bulk, but also implies clumsiness and force without grace.

James was a critic of considerable subtlety and perception, but he was never more wrong than in his understanding of Tolstoy. He failed utterly to comprehend what was great and different about Tolstoy. Tolstoy was apparently too much of a challenge for him to judge dispassionately. His remarks on Tolstoy were few and short, but they were amplified greatly in Percy Lubbock's *The Craft of Fiction*, where Lubbeck acknowledged Tolstoy's creative power, vision, imagination, but questioned his craft. Lubbock was in the grip of James' conception of what a good novel should be, and Tolstoy could not be fitted into this conception. For Percy Lubbock, then, Tolstoy was wrong and not the conception. Lubbock poses the question of Tolstoy's structural failings sharply when he says: "With one hand he takes up the largest subject in the world, the story to which all other human stories are subordinate [the domestic novel]; and not content with this, in the other hand he produces the drama of a great historic collision, for which a scene is set with no less prodigious a gesture. And there is not a sign in the book to show that he knew what he was doing; apparently he was quite unconscious that he was writing two novels at once." But Tolstoy did know, and the hundreds of pages of rough drafts that have survived, his wife's own testimony that Tolstoy always covered a fresh version of his manuscripts with multiple corrections — all testify to an artistic consciousness that was attentive to the smallest details of the novel.

Lubbock's questioning of the unity of *War and Peace* has focused much of Tolstoy criticism both in England and in America on the problem of unity. This is admittedly an important critical concern, and perhaps it is the most important. But it is not the only problem. Or rather, it depends on how one conceives of the question of unity. It can be conceived in a mechanical way — in the alternation of chapters of war and peace — or it may turn on all manner of binary sets: rationalism and irrationalism, consciousness and unconsciousness, primitivism and sophistication, city and country, and so on. Isaiah Berlin has posed the problem of unity in a provocative and significant way. He is persuaded that among the hundreds of characters, the multiple actions, the different quests, deaths, coincidences, passions, loves, deaths, and hates there lies some common truth to which the good characters strive and from which the bad characters depart. He is persuaded that a center exists, but the center is something that he cannot grasp. He tells us: "What is it that Pierre has learnt, of which Princess Marie's marriage is an acceptance, that Prince Andrey all his life pursued with such agony? Like Augustine, Tolstoy can only say what it is not. His genius is devastatingly destructive. He can only attempt to point towards his goal by exposing the false signposts to it; to isolate the truth by annihilating that which it is not — namely all that can be said in the clear, analytical language that corresponds to the all too clear, but necessarily limited vision of the foxes."[1] Berlin himself, apparently, as this quotation would seem to indicate, decided that Tolstoy had not formulated that center, that there was an irremediable contradiction or fissure in *War and Peace*. The failing is more than Tolstoy's inability to formulate the center that he hints at. There is a contradiction at the core of *War and Peace* that is blatant and persistent, and it is this contradiction that constitutes the thesis of his *The Hedgehog and the Fox*. According to Berlin, Tolstoy gives us a world in which the personal experience is shown to be superior to public life. Tolstoy celebrates personal consciousness, responsibility, freedom and, at the same time demonstrates, with considerable ruthlessness, that such freedom and responsibility are illusions and deceptions. Berlin puts it this way: "And yet the primacy of these private experiences and relationships and virtues presupposes that vision of life, with its sense of personal responsibility, and belief in freedom and possibility of spontaneous action, to which the best pages of *War and Peace* are devoted, and which is the very illusion to be exorcized, if the truth is to be faced." Berlin concludes: "This terrible dilemma is never finally resolved." One can argue that it is Berlin who has not been able to resolve them, and that the contradictions reside only in his understanding of *War and Peace*. Yet, one can acknowledge that he has posed questions about *War and Peace* of a significant nature, and done so with intelligence and sympathy.

The title of *The Hedgehog and the Fox* is a commentary on the dual nature that Berlin saw in Tolstoy's creative personality. It refers to the fact that the fox has many strategems of defense, but the hedgehog only one. Like the fox Tolstoy responded powerfully to the many-sided nature of life; he was able to catch the most delicate nuances and precise particularities of life. At the same time, like the hedgehog, Tolstoy yearned to find not many truths, but a single big truth. With that formulation Berlin joined a long tradition of writers who have formulated the contradictory nature of Tolstoy's personality and creative power. Merezhkovsky, for example, long before Berlin, saw Tolstoy as pitted against himself. Tolstoy had a powerful sensuous nature and an equally powerful intellect and moral sense, which subjected his sensuous nature to merciless scrutiny and condemnation. He was a pagan and a saint. In his youth the pagan held sway, in his middle and late years the moral judgment and analytic intellect gained ascendancy and the saint held sway. Before Merezhkovsky, the Russian critic Mikhaylovsky formulated a different kind of dualism. In "The Right and Left Hands of Tolstoy" (1875), he described Tolstoy as both a bold and radical critic of existing institutions and a timid conservative. Even before Mikhaylovsky, Appolon Grigoriev, a Slavophile critic of mystic tendencies and close friend of Dostoevsky, spoke of Tolstoy's analytic thrust, which threatened to kill the creative side of his talent.

III

It is not enough to ask oneself, as Anglo-American criticism has done persistently, whether Tolstoy's novels have been well made, but to ask oneself what they are made of. What they are made of is a complex literary tradition, a time of crucial change for Russia, and a complex, powerful personality. Once one asks the question, one is led into multiple lanes of criticism. No writer has been more biographical in his works than Tolstoy, and no life has been more massively documented and authenticated. One need not use one's imagination to show what Tolstoy was doing and thinking from day to day. He documented it in thirteen volumes of diaries, and forty-six volumes of letters, and his friends documented it in scores of reminiscences. His novels are in part made from his own being and in whole from the being of his person and the being of his time and place.

We need a biographical criticism that is more than a recitation of public events of his life; we need a criticism that explores how the multiple facts of his complex personality shaped his works and revealed itself in them. Some of this could be done by a sophisticated psychoanalytic criticism. But this is what is missing in American criticism. We have very little psychoanalytic criticism on Tolstoy, and what we have has been devoted in fiction, to *The Kreutzer Sonata*, and in life, to his tortured relations with his wife. It has been assumed, perhaps, that in contrast to Dostoevsky, Tolstoy was too rational, ordered, normal to have a dark underside to his life and art. Yet in many of his novels his characters act on irrational motives, are compulsive, driven, and display all the symptoms of neurotic characters. There is, too, no sophisticated social criticism of

Tolstoy's novels, Marxist or otherwise. Yet Tolstoy's own life, vision, and values were powerfully influenced by his class position, his hatred of the status quo, and his sympathy for the peasant class. *Resurrection*, for example, is a massive and explicit condemnation of the way power was distributed in Russia. *Anna Karenina* is without doubt a powerful and wrenching drama about a woman caught between sin and retribution, a moral drama, to be sure, but it is also a drama in which the movement of Russian contemporary society, with its contradictions, inequities, and especially its shifting power relations, is caught and portrayed. Levin is enmeshed not only in the changing technology, but also in the need to establish his relations with his peasants on a different basis. Novels like *Master and Man* and especially *The Death of Ivan Ilytch* are, whatever the moral and religious and philosophical message, maps of social change in Russia.

Fortunately, there is time to do some of these things and many things we have not conceived of. The history of criticism on Tolstoy will not end, because Tolstoy will not end. Both the man and his work are of such dimension and complexity that they will be there to confront us with what we have to bring to them.

Tolstoy has fared less well in the twentieth century than has his great contemporary, Dostoevsky. Dostoevsky's twisted, dark, and self-destructive view of man seems to answer to our times better than Tolstoy's lucid, rational, and essentially optimistic view. Tolstoy's view of man is sanguine, sane, and healthy. If men act in unhealthy and self-destructive ways, they do so not from nature, but from some distortion of their natures. His optimism is not facile, however. He knows what terrible things men can do to each other and to themselves, but he also knows that they are capable of courage, wisdom, and happiness. The bedrock of his optimism lies in his belief that the nature of things is essentially meaningful, that there is a structure of meanings operative in our world. The world, for Tolstoy, is not chaos; man is not a speck of cosmic dust. He has purpose and meaning and faculties capable of seizing that purpose and meaning. Tolstoy never wavered in his belief that we could make ourselves better, and it is this belief that had a powerful effect on great numbers of people in the nineties and the first decade of this century. And no writer used the weapon of art more powerfully than he did in showing that there was order and purpose in life, that we could go wrong but also go right.

The awe that Tolstoy's art inspired in Matthew Arnold is still with us, and the awe that he inspired as a person — especially in his contemporaries — we can still feel in reading about him as a man. Stanislavsky once said that one felt proud to be living at a time that Tolstoy lived, and Maxim Gorky, who wrote in his reminiscences so sensitively and beautifully about Tolstoy the man, communicated more powerfully than anyone else what Tolstoy meant to him and his contemporaries: Once when he saw him by the sea at Gaspra, like an old magician commanding the waves to fondle his feet, he struck Gorky as someone "who knows the beginnings and ends of things, and reflects on the end of the stones, of the grasses of the earth, of the waters of the sea, and on everything from stone to sun. The sea is part of his soul, and everything about him comes from him and out of him." Gorky left the scene with the happy thought: "I am not an orphan on this earth as long as this man lives." We too are not orphans on this earth, as long as Tolstoy's works are read and his words remembered.

University of Chicago   EDWARD WASIOLEK

Notes

1. Isaiah Berlin, *The Hedgehog and the Fox* (New York: Mentor, 1957), 115.

BIOGRAPHY,
REMINISCENCES,
AND RECEPTION

Tolstoy's Place in European Literature
Edward Garnett*

The justness of the word *great* applied to a nation's writers is perhaps best tested by simply taking each writer in turn from out his Age, and seeing how far our conception of his Age remains unaffected. We may take away hundreds of clever writers, scores of distinguished creators, and the Age remains before our eyes, solidly unaffected by their absence; but touch one or two central figures, and lo! the whole framework of the Age gives in your hands, and you realise that the World's insight into, and understanding of that Age's life has been supplied us by the special interpretation offered by two or three great minds. In fact, every Age seems dwarfed, chaotic, full of confused tendencies and general contradiction till the few great men have arisen, and symbolised in themselves what their nation's growth or strife *signifies*. How many dumb ages are there in which no great writer has appeared, ages to whose inner life in consequence we have no key!

Tolstoy's significance as the great writer of modern Russia can scarcely be augmented in Russian eyes by his exceeding significance to Europe as symbolising the spiritual unrest of the modern world. Yet so inevitably must the main stream of each age's tendency and the main movement of the world's thought be discovered for us by the great writers, whenever they appear, that Russia can no more keep Tolstoy's significance to herself than could Germany keep Goethe's to herself. True it is that Tolstoy, as great novelist, has been absorbed in mirroring the peculiar world of half-feudal, modern Russia, a world strange to Western Europe, but the spirit of analysis with which the creator of *Anna Karènina* and *War and Peace* has confronted the modern world is more truly representative of our Age's outlook than is the spirit of any other of his great contemporaries. Between the days of *Wilhelm Meister* and of *Resurrection* what an extraordinary volume of the rushing tide of modern life has swept by! A century of that "liberation of modern Europe from the old routine" has passed since Goethe stood forth for "the awakening of the modern

*From G. K. Chesterton, G. Perris, and Edward Garnett, *Leo Tolstoy* (New York: Pott, 1903), 26–36.

15

spirit." A century of emancipation, of Science, of unbelief, of incessant shock, change, and Progress all over the face of Europe, and even as Goethe a hundred years ago typified the triumph of the new intelligence of Europe over the shackles of its old institutions, routine, and dogma (as Matthew Arnold affirms), so Tolstoy today stands for the triumph of the European *soul* against civilisation's routine and dogma. The peculiar modernness of Tolstoy's attitude, however, as we shall presently show, is that he is inspired largely by the modern scientific spirit in his searching analysis of modern life. Apparently at war with Science and Progress, his extraordinary fascination for the mind of Europe lies in the fact that he of all great contemporary writers has come nearest to demonstrating, to *realising* what the life of the modern man *is*. He of all the analysts of the civilised man's thoughts, emotions, and actions has least idealised, least beautified, and least distorted the complex daily life of the European world. With a marked moral bias, driven onward in his search for truth by his passionate religious temperament, Tolstoy, in his pictures of life, has constructed a truer *whole*, a human world less bounded by the artist's individual limitations, more mysteriously living in its vast flux and flow than is the world of any writer of the century. *War and Peace* and *Anna Karènina*, those great worlds where the physical environment, mental outlook, emotional aspiration, and moral code of the whole community of Russia are reproduced by his art, as some mighty cunning phantasmagoria of changing life, are superior in the sense of containing a whole nation's life, to the worlds of Goethe, Byron, Scott, Victor Hugo, Balzac, Dickens, Thackeray, Maupassant, or any latter day creator we can name. And not only so, but Tolstoy's analysis of life throws more light on the main currents of thought in our Age, raises deeper problems, and explores more untouched territories of the mind than does any corresponding analysis by his European contemporaries.

It is by Tolstoy's passionate seeking of the life of the soul that the great Russian writer towers above the men of our day, and it is because his hunger for spiritual truth has led him to probe contemporary life, to examine all modern formulas and appearances, to penetrate into the secret thought and emotion of men of all grades in our complex society, that his work is charged with the essence of nearly all that modernity thinks and feels, believes and suffers, hopes and fears as it evolves in more and more complex forms of our terribly complex civilisation. The soul of humanity is, however, always the appeal of men from the life that environs, moulds, and burdens them, to instincts that go beyond and transcend their present life. Tolstoy is the *appeal* of the modern world, the cry of the modern conscience against the blinded fate of its own *progress*. To the eye of science everything is possible in human life, the sacrifice of the innocent for the sake of the progress of the guilty, the crushing and deforming of the weak so that the strong may triumph over them, the evolution of new serf classes at the dictates of a ruling class. All this the nineteenth century has seen accomplished, and not seen alone in Russia. It is Tolstoy's distinction to have combined in his life-work more than any other great artist two main conflicting points of view. He has fused by his art the science that defines *the way* Humanity is forced forward blindly and irresponsibly from century to century by the mere pressure of events, he has fused with this science of our modern world the soul's protest against the earthly fate of man which leads the generations into taking the ceaseless roads of evil which every age unwinds.

Let us cite Tolstoy's treatment of War as an instance of how this great artist symbolises the Age for us and so marks the advance in self-consciousness of the modern mind, and as a nearer approximation to a realisation of what life is. We have only got to compare Tolstoy's "Sebasto-pol" (1856) with any other document on war by other European writers to perceive that Tolstoy alone among artists has *realised* war, his fellows have *idealised* it. To quote a passage from a former article let us say that

"Sebastopol" gives us war under *all* aspects — war as a squalid, honoura-ble, daily affair of mud and glory, of vanity, disease, hard work, stupidity, patriotism, and inhuman agony. Tolstoy gets the complex effects of "Sebastopol" by keenly analysing the effect of the sights and sounds, dangers and pleasures, of war on the brains of a variety of typical men, and by placing a special valuation of his own on these men's actions, thoughts, and emotions, on their courage, altruism, and show of indifference in the face of death. He lifts up, in fact, the veil of appearances conventionally drawn by society over the actualities of the glorious trade of killing men, and he does this chiefly by analysing keenly the insensitiveness and indifference of the average mind, which says of the worst of war's realities, "I felt so and so, and did so and so: but as to what those other thousands may have felt in their agony, that I did not enter into at all." "Sebastopol," therefore, though an exceedingly short and exceedingly simple narrative, is a psychological document on modern war of extraordinary value, for it simply relegates to the lumber-room, as unlife-like and hopelessly limited, all those theatrical glorifications of war which men of letters, romantic poets, and grave historians alike have been busily piling up on humanity's shelves from generation to generation. And more: we feel that in "Sebastopol" we have at last the sceptical modern spirit, absorbed in actual life, demonstrating what war is, and expressing at length the confused sensations of countless men, who have heretofore never found a genius who can make humanity realise what it knows half-consciously and consciously evades. We cannot help, therefore, recognising this man Tolstoy as the most advanced product of our civilisation, and likening him to a great surgeon, who, not deceived by the world's presentation of its own life, penetrates into the essential joy and suffering, health and disease of multitudes of men; a surgeon who, face to face with the strangest of Nature's laws in the constitution of human society, puzzled by all the illusions, fatuities, and conventions of the human mind, resolutely sets himself to lay bare the roots of all its passions, appetites, and incentives in the struggle for life, so that at least human reason may advance farther along the path of self-knowledge in advancing towards a general sociological study of man.

Tolstoy's place in nineteenth-century literature is, therefore, in our view, no less fixed and certain than is Voltaire's place in the eighteenth century. Both of these writers focus for us in a marvellously complete manner the respective methods of analysing life by which the rationalism of the seventeenth and eighteenth centuries, and the science and humanitarianism of the nineteenth century have moulded for us the modern world. All the movements, all the problems, all the speculation, all the agitations of the world of today in contrast with the immense materialistic civilisation that science has hastily built up for us in three or four generations, all the *spirit* of modern life is condensed in the pages of Tolstoy's writings, because, as we have said, he typifies the soul of the modern man gazing, now undaunted, and now in alarm, at the formidable array of the newly-tabulated *cause and effect* of humanity's progress, at the appalling cheapness and waste of human life in Nature's hands. Tolstoy thus stands for *the modern soul's alarm in contact with science.* And just as science's *work* after its first destruction of the past ages' formalism, superstition, and dogma is directed more and more to the examination and amelioration of human life, so Tolstoy's work has been throughout inspired by a passionate love of humanity, and by his ceaseless struggle against conventional religion, dogmatic science, and society's mechanical influence on the minds of its members. To make man more *conscious* of his acts, to show society its real motives and what is *is* feeling, and not cry out in admiration at what it pretends to feel — this has been the great novelist's aim in his delineation of Russia's life. Ever seeking the one truth — to arrive at men's thoughts and sensations under the daily pressure of life — never flinching from his exploration of the dark world of man's animalism and incessant self-deception, Tolstoy's *realism* in art is symbolical of our absorption in the world of fact, in the modern study of natural law, a study of ultimately without loss of spirituality, nay, resulting in immense gain to the spiritual life. The *realism* of the great Russian's novels is, therefore, more in line with the modern tendency and outlook than is the general tendency of other schools of Continental literature. And Tolstoy must be finally looked on, not merely as *the conscience of the Russian world* revolting against the too heavy burden which the Russian people have now to bear in Holy Russia's onward march towards the building-up of her great Asiatic Empire, but also as the soul of the modern world seeking to replace in its love of humanity the life of those old religions which science is destroying day by day. In this sense Tolstoy will stand in European literature as the conscience of the modern world.

[Tolstoy and Craft]   Henry James

It would be too easy to say that Tolstoy was, from the Russian point of view, for home consumption, and Turgenev for foreign: *War and Peace* has probably had more readers in Europe and America than *A House of Gentlefolk* or *On the Eve* or *Smoke*, — a circumstance less detrimental than it may appear to my claim of our having, in the Western world, supremely adopted the author of the latter works. Turgenev is in a peculiar degree what I may call the novelists' novelist — an artistic influence extraordinarily valuable and ineradicably established. The perusal of Tolstoy — a wonderful mass of life — is an immense event, a kind of splendid accident, for each of us: his name represents nevertheless no such eternal spell of method, no such quiet irresistibility of presentation, as shines, close to us and lighting our possible steps, in that of his precursor. Tolstoy is a reflector as vast as a natural lake; a monster harnessed to his great subject — all human life! — as an elephant might be harnessed, for purposes of traction, not to a carriage, but to a coach-house. His own case is prodigious, but his example for others dire: disciples not elephantine he can only mislead and betray.*

A picture without composition slights its most precious chance for beauty, and is moreover not composed at all unless the painter knows *how* that principle of health and safety, working as an absolutely unpremeditated art, has prevailed. There may in its absence be life, incontestably, as *The Newcomes* has life, as *Les Trois Mousquetaires*, as Tolstoy's *Peace and War* [sic], have it; but what do such large loose baggy monsters, with their queer elements of the accidental and the arbitrary, artistically *mean*? . . . There is life and life, and as waste is only life sacrificed and thereby prevented from "counting," I delight in a deep-breathing economy and an organic form.†

Tolstoy and D[ostoyevsky] are fluid pudding, though not tasteless, because the amount of their own minds and souls in solution in the broth gives it savour and flavour, thanks to the strong, rank quality of their genius and their experience.‡

---

*From "Turgenev," Library of World's Best Literature, vol. 25, 1897; reprinted in *The Future of the Novel*, ed. Leon Edel (New York: Vintage, 1956).

†From preface to *The Tragic Muse*; reprinted in *The Art of the Novel*, ed. R. P. Blackmur (New York and London, 1934).

‡From letter to Hugh Walpole, 19 May 1912; published in *Selected Letters*, ed. Leon Edel (New York, 1956).

Leo Tolstoy as the Mirror of the
Russian Revolution
V. I. Lenin*

To see a correspondence between the name of the great artist and the revolution,[1] which he has obviously failed to appreciate, and from which he obviously stands aloof, may at first glance appear strange and contrived. One could hardly call a mirror that which ostensibly does not reflect the phenomenon correctly. But our revolution is an extraordinarily complex phenomenon. Among the masses of those who are directly involved in making and participating in it there are many social elements who have also clearly failed to appreciate what was happening, and who also stood aloof from the real historical tasks with which they saw themselves confronted by the course of events. And if we have before us a really great artist, at least some of the essential aspects of the revolution are bound to have found a reflection in his works.

The authorized Russian press which is saturated with articles, letters, and notices about Tolstoy's eightieth birthday, is least of all interested in an analysis of his works from a point of view that explains how they reflect the character of the Russian revolution and the forces behind it. This entire press is filled to the point of nausea with hypocrisy, a dual kind of hypocrisy: official as well as liberal. The former is the crude hypocrisy of venal hacks who were yesterday ordered to hound Tolstoy, and today are told to look for his patriotism and to try and keep up the proprieties before the eyes of Europe. Everyone knows that hacks of this kind have been paid for their writings and they are incapable of deceiving anyone. Much more refined and therefore much more pernicious and harmful is hypocrisy of the liberal kind. To listen to the Constitutional Democrat Party windbags who publish the *Speech*, one gets the impression that they are fully and fervently in agreement with Tolstoy. In fact, their calculated pronouncements and pompous phrases about the "Great seeker after God" are lies throughout, since a Russian liberal neither believes in Tolstoy's God, nor does he agree with Tolstoy's criticism of the existing order of things. He simply attaches himself to a fashionable name in order to increase his tiny political capital, to pose as a leader of the nationwide opposition, tries, with the thunder and crackle of claptrap, to drown out the demand for a direct and clear answer to the question: what causes the glaring contradictions of "Tolstoyanism," and what shortcomings and weaknesses of our revolution they indicate?

The contradictions in the works, views, doctrines, the school of Tolstoy are glaring indeed. On the one hand we have the brilliant artist who has produced not only incomparable pictures of Russian life but also

*From the *Proletariat* 35 (24 September 1908):11. Translated for this volume by Boris Sorokin.

first-rate works of world literature. On the other hand we have a country squire acting the fool-in-Christ. On the one hand we have a remarkably powerful, direct, and sincere protest against social lies and falsehood, while on the other we have the "Tolstoyan," i.e., the washed-out hysterical sniveller, a gutless species known as the Russian intellectual who publicly beats his breast and cries: "I am vile, I am disgusting, but I am working on my own moral self-improvement: I no longer eat meat and nourish myself with rice patties." On the one hand Tolstoy remorselessly criticizes capitalist exploitation and exposes the violent methods of the government, the farce of the courts and of public administration, reveals the entire extent of the contradictions between the growth of wealth and the achievements of civilization, and the increasing destitution, brutalization, and misery of the working masses; on the other he preaches his feeble-minded doctrine of "nonresistance to evil" by forceful means. On the one hand there is the most sober realism of his works, the tearing away of all and sundry masks; on the other he preaches one of the vilest things on earth — religion — and wants to replace priests who look upon their job as an official function with priests who would do the same from moral conviction, that is, he promotes the far subtler and therefore particularly repulsive form of clericalism. Indeed [one could say with the poet Nekrasov]:

> Indigent and abundant,
> Mighty and impotent
> Is Mother Russia.

It is self-evident that Tolstoy, given such contradictions, could not possibly understand either the labor movement and its role in the struggle for socialism, or the Russian revolution. But the contradictions in Tolstoy's views and doctrines are not accidental; rather, they reveal the contradictory conditions of Russian life in the last third of the nineteenth century. The archaic Russian village, only yesterday freed from serfdom, was literally abandoned to the capitalist and tax collector to be fleeced and plundered. The archaic foundations of peasant economy and peasant life, foundations that had really held for centuries, were demolished with extraordinary speed. And the contradictions in Tolstoy's views must be evaluated not from the point of view of modern labor movement and modern socialism (such an evaluation is, of course, necessary, but it is not enough), but from the point of view of the frantic protest against advancing capitalism, the ruin of the masses and their loss of land, a protest that had to arise in the archaic Russian village. Tolstoy is ridiculous as a prophet who has discovered new prescriptions for the salvation of mankind, and therefore utterly ridiculous are those miserable foreign and Russian "Tolstoyans" who have attempted to make a dogma out of the weakest side of his doctrine. But Tolstoy is great as the spokesman of the ideas and moods that arose among millions of Russian peasants at the time when the bourgeois revolution arrived in Russia. Tolstoy is original, because the aggregate of his views, taken as a whole, represents exactly the peculiarities of our revolution as a *peasant* bourgeois revolution. From this point of view, the contradictions in Tolstoy's views are indeed a mirror of those contradictory conditions in which the peasantry had been placed historically in the context of our revolution. On the one hand, centuries of oppression by serfdom and decades of accelerated ruin after the emancipation piled up mountains of hate, resentment, and desperate determination. The urge to raze to the ground the official church, the landed squirearchy, and government by landed squires, to destroy all old forms of customs and landownership, to clear the land, and to create instead of a class-based police-state a community of free and equal small peasants — this urge follows like a red thread every step in history the peasants have taken in our revolution and, undoubtedly, the ideological content of Tolstoy's writings corresponds much more to this peasant urge than to the abstract "Christian anarchism" as the "system" of his views is sometimes described.

On the other hand, although the peasants desired new forms of community life, they had a very unconscious, archaic, feeble-minded attitude toward the shape this community life was supposed to take, what struggle it would require to actually earn their freedom, what leaders they could have in this struggle, what was the attitude of the bourgeoisie and the bourgeois intelligentsia towards the interests of peasant revolution, and why the violent overthrow of tsarist rule was necessary in order to abolish the ownership of the land by the landlords. The peasants' entire past life taught them to hate the landlord and the official, but it did not, and could not teach them where to look for answers to all these questions. In our revolution a minor part of the peasantry really did fight, did organize to some extent for this purpose; and a very small part rose up in arms to wipe out its enemies, to destroy the tsar's servants and the protectors of the landlords. The majority of the peasants cried and prayed, foolishly argued and dreamed, wrote petitions, and sent petitioners, exactly in the spirit of Leo Nikolaevich Tolstoy. And, as always happens in such cases, the effect of this Tolstoyan appeal to stay away from politics, the Tolstoyan renunciation of politics, this lack of interest in and understanding of politics, was that only a minority followed the lead of the class-conscious revolutionary proletariat, while the majority fell prey to those unprincipled, servile, bourgeois intellectuals who are known as Constitutional Democrats and run back and forth between meetings of laborites and State Minister Stolypin's anteroom, and beg, negotiate, compromise, and promise to reconcile, until they are kicked out with a soldier's jackboot. Tolstoy's ideas are a mirror of the weakness, the shortcomings of our peasant revolt, a reflection of the spinelessness of the archaic village and the ingrained cowardice of the property-oriented small peasant.

Just look at the soldier revolts of 1905–1906. From the point of view of their social background, these men who fought in our revolution were part peasants and part proletarians. The latter were in the minority; therefore the movement in the armed forces does not even approximately show the same degree of nationwide solidarity, party consciousness, as one finds in the proletariat which became Social-Democratic overnight, as if by the wave of a hand, so to speak. On the other hand, there is nothing more erroneous than the opinion that the failure of the soldier revolts was due to lack of leadership from the officer ranks. On the contrary, the enormous progress the revolution has made since the days of the People's Will Party is demonstrated precisely by the fact that this time it were the soldiers, [sometimes referred to as] "the cattle in grey uniforms," who rose up in arms against their superiors and whose [unexpected] self-reliance so thoroughly scared the liberal landowners and the liberal command structure of the armed forces. The common soldier fully sympathized with the peasants' cause; his eyes lit up at the very mention of land. In the armed forces there were many instances when power passed from the command to the rank and file, but there was almost no instance where a determined effort was made to make use of this power; the soldiers wavered; and after a couple of days, sometimes even hours, having killed some hated commanding officer, they would release the rest, enter into negotiations with the authorities and then face the firing squad, bare their backs for the birch, in a word, put back on the yoke, exactly in the spirit of Leo Nikolaevich Tolstoy!

Tolstoy['s works] reflect the pent-up hatred, the ripened desire for a better life, the desire to get rid of the past, as well as the immature dreaming, lack of political skills, and revolutionary spinelessness [of the peasantry]. Historical and economic conditions explain both the inevitability of the beginning revolutionary struggle within the masses, as well as their lack of preparedness for this struggle, their Tolstoyan nonresistance to evil, which was a most serious cause of the defeat of the first revolutionary campaign [of 1905].

It is said that defeated armies learn well. Of course, a comparison between revolutionary classes and armies is accurate only in a very limited sense. The development of capitalism changes and intensifies by the hour the conditions that pushed the millions of peasants into action, united by their hatred of the feudal landlords and their government, to get involved in the revolutionary-democratic struggle. Among the peasants themselves the growth of trade, dominance of the marketplace, and the power of money steadily displace the archaic social structure and the archaic Tolstoyan ideology. But there is one gain from the early years of the revolutionary and the early reverses within the mass revolutionary struggle about which there can be no doubt: a mortal blow has been struck at the old softness and flabbiness of the masses. The lines of demarcation have become sharper. The boundaries between different classes and parties are clearer now. Hardened by the hammer blows of lessons learned under Stolypin's rule, with relentless and consistent agitation by the revolutionary Social-Democrats not only the socialist proletariat but also the democratic masses among the peasants will inevitably advance from their ranks more and more seasoned fighters who will be less and less vulnerable to our historical[ly conditioned] sin of Tolstoyanism!

Notes

1. The revolution referred to is the revolution of 1905.

The Russian Point of View   Virginia Woolf*

There remains the greatest of all novelists — for what else can we call the author of *War and Peace*? Shall we find Tolstoi, too, alien, difficult, a foreigner? Is there some oddity in his angle of vision which, at any rate until we have become disciples and so lost our bearings, keeps us at arm's length in suspicion and bewilderment? From his first words we can be sure of one thing at any rate — here is a man who sees what we see, who proceeds, too, as we are accustomed to proceed, not from the inside outwards, but from the outside inwards. Here is a world in which the postman's knock is heard at eight o'clock, and people go to bed between ten and eleven. Here is a man, too, who is no savage, no child of nature; he is educated; he has had every sort of experience. He is one of those born aristocrats who have used their privileges to the full. He is metropolitan, not suburban. His senses, his intellect, are acute, powerful, and well nourished. There is something proud and superb in the attack of such a mind and such a body upon life. Nothing seems to escape him. Nothing glances off him unrecorded. Nobody, therefore, can so convey the excitement of sport, the beauty of horses, and all the fierce desirability of the world to the senses of a strong young man. Every twig, every feather sticks to his magnet. He notices the blue or red of a child's frock; the way a horse shifts its tail; the sound of a cough; the action of a man trying to put his hands into pockets that have been sewn up. And what his infallible eye reports of a cough or a trick of the hands his infallible brain refers to something hidden in the character so that we know his people, not only by the way they love and their views on politics and the immortality of the soul, but also by the way they sneeze and choke. Even in a translation we feel that we have been set on a mountain-top and had a telescope put into our hands. Everything is astonishly clear and absolutely sharp. Then, suddenly, just as we are exulting, breathing deep, feeling at once braced

*From *The Common Reader* (New York: Harcourt, Brace, 1925), 253–56. Copyright 1925 by Harcourt Brace Jovanovich, Inc.; renewed 1953 by Leonard Woolf. Reprinted by permission of the publisher.

and purified, some detail — perhaps the head of a man — comes at us out of the picture in an alarming way, as if extruded by the very intensity of its life. "Suddenly a strange thing happened to me: first I ceased to see what was around me; then his face seemed to vanish till only the eyes were left, shining over against mine; next the eyes seemed to be in my own head, and then all became confused — I could see nothing and was forced to shut my eyes, in order to break loose from the feeling of pleasure and fear which his gaze was producing in me. . . ." Again and again we share Masha's feelings in *Family Happiness*. One shuts one's eyes to escape the feeling of pleasure and fear. Often it is pleasure that is uppermost. In this very story there are two descriptions, one of a girl walking in a garden at night with her lover, one of a newly married couple prancing down their drawing-room, which so convey the feeling of intense happiness that we shut the book to feel it better. But always there is an element of fear which makes us, like Masha, wish to escape from the gaze which Tolstoi fixes on us. Does it arise from the sense, which in real life might harass us, that such happiness as he describes is too intense to last, that we are on the edge of disaster? Or is it not that the very intensity of our pleasure is somehow questionable and forces us to ask, with Pozdnyshev in the Kreutzer Sonata, "But why live?" Life dominates Tolstoi as the soul dominates Dostoevsky. There is always at the centre of all the brilliant and flashing petals of the flower this scorpion, "Why live?" There is always at the centre of the book some Olenin, or Pierre, or Levin who gathers into himself all experience, turns the world round between his fingers, and never ceases to ask even as he enjoys it, what is the meaning of it, and what should be our aims. It is not the priest who shatters our desires most effectively; it is the man who has known them, and loved them himself. When he derides them, the world indeed turns to dust and ashes beneath our feet. Thus fear mingles with our pleasure, and of three great Russian writers, it is Tolstoi who most enthralls us and most repels.

But the mind takes its bias from the place of its birth, and no doubt, when it strikes upon a literature so alien as the Russian, flies off at a tangent far from the truth.

Leo Tolstoy   Maxim Gorky*

I

What gnaws at his heart more than anything else is the thought of God. At times it seems to be less a thought and more a kind of inner battle. He speaks of God less than he would like, but the thinks of him constantly. It is not a sign of old age or a presentiment of death. Rather, I think it comes from his exquisite human pride. And from a sense of humiliation, too, because being Leo Tolstoy, it is humiliating to submit one's will to some kind of streptococcus. If he were a scientist, he would surely create outstanding hypotheses and make great discoveries.

II

He has remarkable hands: not beautiful, knotted from swollen veins and yet full of special expressiveness and creative strength. Leonardo da Vinci must have had hands like that. You can do everything with hands like that. At times, while speaking, he will gradually close his fingers into a fist, and then suddenly he will open them and at the same time pronounce some apt and profound thought. He resembles a God, not a Sabaoth or Olympian, but a kind of Russian God, who "sits on a maple throne under a golden lime tree," and if not majestic, then perhaps more cunning than the other gods.

VI

"The minority need God because they have everything else. And the majority need him because they have nothing." I would put it differently: most people believe in God from cowardice, and only a few believe in him from the fullness of the heart.

VII

He advised me to read the Buddhist writings. He always talks about Buddhism and Christ sentimentally: he has no enthusiasm, no passion, and not a single spark when he speaks of Christ. I think he sees Christ as naive, pitiful; and although at times he admires him, he hardly loves him. It's as if he were afraid that if Christ came to a Russian village, the peasant girls would laugh at him.

*From "Lev Tolstoy," in *Sobranie sochinenii* (Collected works) (Moscow: 1963), 18:54–93. Translated from the Russian for this volume by Edward Wasiolek.

IX

He reminds me of those itinerant pilgrims with sticks in their hands travelling over the earth their whole life, going thousands of miles from one monastery to another, from one saint's relics to another, terribly homeless and alien to everyone and everything. The earth is not for them, nor is God. They pray to him from habit but in the secret depths of their souls, they hate him. Why does he drive them from one end of the earth to another? People are stumps, roots, stones on the road. You stumble over them and feel pain. One can do without them, but sometimes it's pleasant to impress on men how different they are from him and show how much difference there is between them.

XIII

If he were a fish, he would swim, surely, only in the ocean, never in the inland seas and certainly never in fresh water rivers. Here and there small fish dart about him. What he says is not interesting, not necessary to them, and his silence does not frighten them or make them anxious. He is quiet in a knowing and impressive way, like a real hermit who has left this world. Though he speaks a great deal on dutiful themes, one feels that his silence is greater. Certain things cannot be told to anyone. He certainly has thoughts he is afraid of.

XVII

In his diary, which he gave me to read, I was struck by this strange aphorism: "God is my desire." Today when I gave him back the diary, I asked him what that meant?

"It's an unfinished thought," he said, looking at the page and screwing up his eyes. "I must have wanted to say: God is my desire to know him. No, not that." He began to laugh. He rolled the diary page into a tube and shoved it into the pocket of his blouse. He has many undefined relationships with God. Sometimes their relationship reminds me of "two bears in one den."

XVIII

About science.

"Science is a bar of gold made by a charlatan alchemist. You want to simplify it and make it agreeable to everyone. But in doing so, you will find that you have minted many false coins. When the people discover the true worth of these coins, they won't thank you.

XX

About women he speaks readily and much, like a French novelist, but always with the coarseness of a Russian peasant. This oppressed me earlier. Today in Almond Park, he asked Chekhov:

"You whored a lot when you were young?"

Chekhov smiled in a confused way, pulled at his beard, and said something inaudible, and Tolstoy, looking at the sea, confessed, "I was indefatigable."

He said this in a contrite way, using a salty peasant word at the end of the sentence. I noticed for the first time that he said the word simply, as if there were no others to take its place. And all similar words coming from his shaggy lips, sound simple, and natural and lose whatever soldierly coarseness and filth they might have. I remember the first time I met him and he talked about "Varienka Oliessova" and "Twenty-six Men and a Girl." From an ordinary point of view his conversation was a chain of indecent words. I felt slighted and even insulted then, for it seemed to me that he thought I was at home only with such language. Now I understand that it was stupid to feel insulted.

XXIV

"A woman is more sincere than a man with her body, but her thoughts are false. But when she lies, she does not believe her lies. But Rousseau lied and believed the lies."

XXV

"Dostoevsky wrote about one of his mad characters that he lives and takes vengeance on himself and others because he served a cause he did not believe in. He wrote that about himself, that is, he could have said the same thing about himself."

XXVI

"Some of the words used by the church are astonishingly unclear. What kind of sense is there in the words 'The earth is God's and the fullness thereof'? That is not from the Bible but is some kind of popular scientific materialism. . . ."

XXVII

He likes to pose difficult and cunning questions.

"What do you think of yourself."

"Do you love your wife?"

"Do you think my son Leo has talent?"
"Do you like Sophia Andreevna?"
"You can't lie in his presence. . . .

XXXI

"Dickens said a very wise thing: 'We are given life under the definite condition that we defend it courageously to the very end.' On the whole he was a sentimental and garrulous writer, and not very smart. But he knew how to construct a novel, as no one did, certainly better than Balzac. Someone said: 'Many are seized with passion to write books, but few are ashamed of this afterwards.' Balzac was not ashamed, nor was Dickens, and both wrote quite a bit that was bad. All the same Balzac was a genius, or what you can't find another word for but genius. . . ."

LETTER

Tolstoy is dead.
The telegram used the most ordinary words: he is dead.
My heart was pierced. I cried out with anger and grief. Now half out of my mind I imagine him as I knew and saw him. I am tormented with the desire to talk about him. I imagine him in his coffin: he lies there smooth as a stone, at the bottom of a stream, and in his gray beard there is quietly hidden, unknown to anyone, his cunning smile. His hands are finally quietly folded. They have finished their difficult task.
I remember his sharp eyes; they saw everything through and through; and the movement of his fingers, as if they were sculpting something out of the air. I remember his conversation, his jokes, his favorite peasant words, and his elusive voice. And I saw how much of life this man had embraced, how inhumanly wise and terrifying he had been.
I saw him once as perhaps no one else had seen him. I was walking over to him at Gaspra, at the coast and at Yusupov's estate. I saw his small angular figure in a gray, crumpled suit and crumpled hat on the very shore among the rocks. He was sitting with his head in his hands, with the gray strands of his beard blowing through his fingers. He was looking into the distance, out to sea and small green waves carressed his feet obediently, as if telling something of themselves to the old magician. The day kept changing and the shadows of clouds crawled over the rocks and the old man, like the rocks, kept changing from light to dark. The boulders had huge cracks and were covered with smelly seaweed. There had been a high tide. He too appeared to me like an old stone come to life, who knows the beginnings and ends of things, and reflects on the end of the stones, of the grasses of the earth, of the waters of the sea, and on everything from stone to sun. The sea is part of his soul, and everything about him comes from him and out of him. In the motionless thoughtfulness of the old man, one

felt something prophetic and magical, which went into the darkness under him and stretched into the empty blue over the earth, as if his concentrated will called forth and repelled the waves, controls the movement of the clouds and the shadows, moves the stones to life. And suddenly, in a moment of madness, I felt that—was it possible—he would stand up, wave his hand and the sea would become quiet and smooth like glass, and the stones would awaken and cry out, and everything around would come to life, murmur and begin to speak in various voices about themselves, with him and against him. I cannot put into words what I felt then. I felt triumphant and afraid and then everything blended into one happy thought: "I am not an orphan on this earth as long as this man lives."

Then I walked carefully away so that the pebbles crunching under my feet would not disturb his thoughts. And now I feel myself to be an orphan; I write and I cry. Never in my life did I cry so inconsolably so desperately and so bitterly. I don't know whether or not I love him. But does it matter whether I love or hate him? He always inspired in me huge feelings and passions, phantastic feelings. Even the unpleasant and hostile, which he called forth exploded rather than oppressed the soul; they widened the spirit, made it more sensitive and capacious . . .

He spoke about Dostoevsky reluctantly and in a strained way, as if evading and suppressing something.

"He should have become acquainted with the teachings of Buddhism or Confusionism; that would have quieted him down. What is important for everyone to know about him is that he was a man of rebellious flesh. When he got angry, bumps would hop about on his bald head and his ears would move. He felt a lot, but he thought badly. He learned to think from Butashevich and other Fourrierists and hated them for the rest of his life. He had something Jewish in his blood. He was suspicious, ambitious, difficult, and unhappy. It's strange that he is read so much; I can't understand it. All those Idiots, Adolescents, and Raskolnikovs are wretched and useless. It is not like that, it is simpler and clearer. What a shame that people don't read Leskov. He is a real writer. Have you read him?"

He loved Chekhov and when he looked at him, he seemed almost to stroke Chekhov's face with a tender look. Once Chekhov was walking along a small path with Alexandra L'vovna, and Tolstoy who was sitting on the terrace—he was still ill at the time—more or less stretched out after them and said in a half whisper:

"Ah, what a lovely and beautiful man: modest, quiet, like a girl. He even walks like a girl. He's simply marvelous."

When he wanted to, he could be very nice, sensitive, and soft; his talk could be fascinatingly simple and elegant. But sometimes it was hard and unpleasant. I never liked the way he talked about women. He could be extraordinarily vulgar, and there was something artificial in his words, something insincere, and at the same time something very personal. It was as if he had been hurt once and he could not forget the hurt or forgive.

And suddenly he asked me, as if he were striking me:

"And why don't you believe in God?"

"I don't have faith, Lev Nikolaevich."

"That's not true. You have faith by nature, and you can't do without God. You'll feel that soon. You don't believe from obstinacy, from resentment: the world is not created as you would have it. Some don't believe from shyness. This is true of young people. They adore a woman, but they are afraid to show it, because she won't understand it. They are afraid. You need courage and boldness for faith and for love. You've got to say to yourself: I believe and everything will be all right; it will all come out as you need it, make itself clear, and attract you. You love much, and faith is intensified love. One has to love even more, then love will become faith. When you love a woman, she is the best in the world, and that is already faith; an unbeliever cannot love. He falls in love with one woman today, and in a year with another. The souls of such people are tramps, living without point. That is not good. You were born a believer, and there is no point in fighting it. You speak of beauty? And what is beauty? The highest and the most perfect is God."

Before this he almost never talked to me about this matter, and the importance of the subject and its suddenness overwhelmed me. I remained silent. He was sitting on a couch, with his legs tucked under him; and then smiling through his beard, he said, shaking his finger at me:

"You won't get out of this with silence."

And I who did not believe in God, looked at him for some reason very carefully and a little fearfully; I looked and I thought: "That man is like a God."

EARLY STORIES

Reviews

Tolstoï's *Sebastopol*   Anonymous*

The works of Tolstoï come thick and fast. This makes the second this week. Let them come, great, solid, masterful works that they are, alive with a tremendous vitality, aglow with the heat of a soul kindled by the divine fire!

On the whole we think we prefer that Tolstoï should come to us by way of France rather than direct from Russia. There is something Kamschatkan, jargon-like, about him in the latter case; in the former he is softened, polished, refined a little. Just a little; his native strength and vigor are unabated.

The history of the Crimean War has been written by Kinglake; what we have in Tolstoï's *Sebastopol* is a picture of it; a series of pictures, three, taken respectively in December, 1854, and in May and August, 1855; the first just after the bloody battles of Balaklava and Inkermann, the second just after the terrible first assault on the Malakoff and the Redan, the third at the time of the fall of the famous fortress by the capture of the Malakoff mamelon. Anybody who has visited one of those popular war cycloramas of the day which are planted in our large cities, "The Battle of Gettysburg" in Boston, for example, or "Lookout Mountain" in Kansas City, will understand what this book is like when we say that its words place the reader in the midst—in the very midst—of the Russian bomb-proofs at Sebastopol during the hottest days of siege. The first scene is a picture simply; in the second we follow the daily fortunes of an officer, and some dramatic action with dialogue is introduced; in the third we have the sensations of a youthful ensign, assigned to duty for the first time, receiving his baptism of fire, and falling tragically in the fight.

. . .

His aim is manifest: to depict the horrors—the brutal, bloody, sickening, hardening horrors—of war. But he does it without one word of bitterness, without one gesture of reproach.

*Review of *Sebastopol*, trans. Frank D. Millet. From *Literary World* 18 (23 July 1887):234–35.

"Look! czars, premiers, diplomats, statesmen," he says in effect, "this is War! I simply draw the picture created by your ambitions, prides, jealousies, and selfishnesses, precisely as it is, and ask you just to pause still and look upon it. If you will do so deliberately, reflectively, I am content. I leave you to your own convictions."

More Tales from Tolstoï   Anonymous[*]

The seven stories composing this volume, written between 1852 and 1859, represent Tolstoï at low tide. Probably they would not have been hunted up, translated, published, but for the interest awakened by Tolstoï at high tide. The first period of authorship is obscurity, sometimes merging into oblivion. The second period may be recognition. The third infrequently is fame. When the period of fame is reached, then all the periods that have preceded become matters of interest. We light the lamp and go backward, picking up whatever is to be found. Because of what Tolstoï has written in the eighties we are interested to see what he wrote in the fifties. That, perhaps, is a sufficient excuse for this volume. It is the chief one.

The Tolstoï of 1850 was not the Tolstoï of 1880. The Tolstoï of 1880 is a new creature, living in a new world, moved by new forces, living for a new idea. Yet in Tolstoï's case, as in every other, the child was father of the man, and this literary-wise as well as ethically and spiritually. There are traces in the volume before us of the seed-sowing whose fruitage later volumes have furnished. The long opening tale which gives the book its name, "A Russian Proprietor," is a series of sketches, such as a descriptive reporter might now supply to a metropolitan journal, of the poverty, destitution, squalor, misery, helplessness, inertia, of a group of Russian peasant homes under serfdom, lightened by the single gleam of a humane purpose to better their condition. Here is the dawn of the day we witness in Tolstoï's later writings. The autobiographic element in these pages is visible. "Lucerne" has a similar moral: the portrait of a poor wandering Tyrolese minstrel painted against the rich and showy background of tourist life at the "Schweitzerhof" on the quay at Lucerne; a study of social contrasts with a lesson of equality and fraternity.

In "Albert," a musician's tale, and "Recollections of a Scorer," a gambling history, we have evidently leaves out of Tolstoï's still earlier experience, the days of his wild and irregular life; and the story of the "Two Hussars" belongs in the same category. The teaching here—so far as there is any teaching—is hardly more than the cruelty of fate, the

*Review of *A Russian Proprietor and Other Stories*, trans. Nathan Haskell Dole. From *Literary World* 19 (17 January 1888):10.

pitilessness of retribution. They are powerful cartoons of the working passions.

In "Three Deaths," again, and in "A Prisoner in the Caucasus," we have a simpler and quieter realism, not less effective, but less intense. Through the scenes here depicted the reader will pass with a sense of relief, as if emerging from a somber wood into a clearing, to which some sunshine has access, and where an occasional flower grows.

Articles and Essays

Tolstoy's *Childhood*
N. G. Chernyshevsky*

Tolstoy's attention is turned above all to the way in which one complex of thought-feelings derives from another. He is interested in observing how an emotion, arising spontaneously from a given situation or impression, undergoes an influence from memories, succumbs to them and with similar thoughts supplied by the imagination, merges into other thought-feelings, returns again to its point of departure and wanders on and on along the entire chain of recollections; how a primary sensation becomes a thought-feeling by the process of augmentation: it generates thoughts that carry it on and on, collecting on the way and fusing with dreams, past experiences, anticipations of the future, and reflections of the present. Psychological analysis can move in different directions: one writer is concerned mostly with character outline; another cares about the influence social intercourse and everyday conflicts have on characters; a third pursues the connection between feelings and actions; a fourth analyzes passions; Tolstoy is interested most in the psychic process itself, its forms, its laws, the dialectics of the soul, to coin a definition. . . .

Psychological analysis is perhaps the most essential quality that endows a creative talent with power. Usually, however, it assumes a descriptive character; it takes a certain static feeling and breaks it up into its component parts and produces an anatomical chart. In the works of great poets we note, aside from this aspect, another trend that has a startling effect upon the reader or audience: it is the ability to catch the dramatic changes of one feeling into another, one thought into another. But usually we are presented merely with the two outermost links of this chain, only the beginning and the end of the psychic process, and this is so because the majority of poets who have a dramatic element to their talent are mostly concerned with the results, manifestations of inner life, conflicts among people, action, and not the mysterious process itself, by

*From "*Detstvo i otrochestvo: Voennye rasskazy* grafa L. N. Tolstogo" [*Childhood and Youth: War Stories* by Count L. N. Tolstoy], *Sovremennik* 12 (December 1956). Translated from the Russian for this volume by Boris Sorokin.

39

means of which thoughts and feelings are generated; even in monologues that, apparently, ought mostly to represent this process, express invariably the struggle of emotions, and the noise of this struggle distracts our attention from the laws and transitions according to which conceptual associations occur: we are concerned with their contrast and not the forms in which they occur. Almost invariably monologues, unless they contain a simple dissection of a static feeling, only superficially differ from dialogues: in his famous soliloquies, Hamlet, "splits in two" and argues with himself; his soliloquies belong, in essence, to the same kind of scenes as the dialogues between Dr. Faustus and Mephistopheles, or arguments between the Marquis de Posa and Don Carlos. The essence of Tolstoy's talent consists of his being unwilling to limit himself by the depiction of the results of the psychic process: he is interested in the process itself, and the barely perceptible phenomena of this inner life, that succeed one another with extraordinary speed and inexhaustible variety are masterfully depicted by Tolstoy. There are painters who are celebrated for their special skill in catching the flickering reflection of a ray of sunshine on swiftly rolling waves, the trembling of sunlight on rustling leaves, its play on shifting shapes of clouds. One says of such painters that they know how to capture the life of nature. Tolstoy does something similar with regard to the most mysterious movements of the psychic life. Therein lies, as we imagine, a unique feature of his talent. Of all the remarkable Russian writers he is the only master of this art.

Of course, this ability must be inborn, just as any other talent; yet it would not be enough to provide such an all-too-general explanation: a talent develops only through a deliberate moral effort, and it is in this effort whose extraordinary energy is attested to by the above-mentioned peculiarity of Tolstoy's works, that one must see the foundations of the power acquired by his talent. We are talking about going inside oneself, about the tireless tendency to observe oneself. The laws of human action, play of passions, connection between events, influences between circumstances and relationships we can study by closely observing other people; but all the knowledge acquired in this way will have neither the depth nor the precision required unless we study the hidden laws of psychic life whose interplay is revealed to us only inside our own consciousness. No one can achieve a profound knowledge of mankind unless he has studied man upon himself. This above-mentioned peculiarity of Tolstoy's talent proves that he has very carefully studied the mysteries of the life of human spirit in himself; this knowledge is precious not only because it has enabled him to paint pictures of the inner movements of human thought that we have brought to the reader's attention but, and perhaps even more important, because it provided him with a firm basis for the study of human life in general, for discerning character and the mainsprings of action, the struggle of passions and impressions. We shall not be wrong in asserting that self-observation had to sharpen extraordinarily his powers of observation, teach him to keep a penetrating eye upon people.

This quality is precious in a talent and is perhaps his most solid claim upon a reputation as a truly remarkable writer. Knowledge of the human heart, the ability to reveal before us its secrets, is this not the first word in the characteristic of every one of those writers whose works we re-read with amazement. And speaking of Tolstoy, a profound study of the human heart will invariably endow a very high quality to everything he may write, and in whatever spirit he may write it. He will probably write much of what will astound every reader with other, even more effective qualities, such as depth of ideas, interesting nature of his conceptions, powerful character outline, vivid scenery—and in those works of his that are already known to the public these virtues of his works have enhanced their value—but to the real connoisseur it will always be obvious—as it is obvious now—that the real strength of his talent lies in knowledge of the human heart. A writer may be carried away by other, more spectacular features; but his talent will be truly powerful and dependable only after he has acquired this skill.

Tolstoy's talent also has another quality that supplies his works with a very special value by their quite extraordinary freshness—the purity of their moral feeling. We are not preachers of puritanism; on the contrary, we are wary of it: the purest puritanism is bad because, first of all, it hardens the heart; the most sincere and truthful moralist is harmful because he is followed by dozens of hypocrites who hide behind his name. On the other hand we are not so blind as not to see the pure light of an exalted moral idea in all noteworthy works of literature in our age. Public morality has never before reached such high levels as in our noble age; that is noble and beautiful, despite all the residues of ancient dirt because it directs all its energies to wash off its inherited sins. And the literature of our times, in its noteworthy works, without exception, is a noble manifestation of the purest moral feeling. We do not wish to assert that in the works of Tolstoy this feeling is any stronger than in the works of some other remarkable writer of ours: in this respect they are all equally noble and exalted, but with him this feeling has a special hue. Some people acquire moral purity by growth and experience, a cruel and protracted process of self-denial and suffering that clarifies one's mind and conscience by reflection. They become pure as a result of many tests, after a long struggle with numerous temptations. This is hardly the case with Tolstoy. His moral fiber has not been restored to him through arduous effort in years of reflection and experience. It is the unsullied, pristine wholesomeness of youth, preserved intact in all its youthful spontaneity and freshness. We will not compare this or any other hue in terms of humanist values, will not say which has a higher absolute value—this is a subject for a philosophical or social tract and not a review—we are merely talking here about the correlation between the moral feeling and value of a literary work, and must admit that in this case such a pristine freshness of moral feeling, preserved in all its innocence since the pure age of youth, endows the text with a special, touching, and graceful charm. On this quality, in our opinion, depends much of the appeal of Tolstoy's stories. We shall not attempt to prove here that it was this freshness of the heart that enabled him to endow *Childhood* and *Boyhood* with that extraordinarily true coloring and tender grace that provide these novels with true vitality. Works such as *Childhood* and *Boyhood* could not have been conceived, let alone executed, without this element, as anyone can see. Let us point to another example — "The Notes of a Billiard Marker," the history of the fall of a soul created with noble aspirations, could only be conceived and executed with such astonishing truthfulness by a talent who has preserved his pristine purity. This feature of the talent extends its beneficial influence beyond those stories and episodes where it enters the foreground: it enlivens and refreshes the talent everywhere. What on earth is more poetic and charming than a pure young soul that responds with joyful love to everything that it perceives as exalted and noble, pure and beautiful as itself? Who hasn't felt his spirit rejuvenated, his thoughts clarified, and his entire being ennobled through the presence of a virginal being such as Cordelia, Ophelia, or Desdemona? Who could fail to note that the presence of such a being brings poetry to one's heart and fail to recite together with Turgenev's hero ("Faustus") [the following lines]:

> Cover me with your wing,
> Quiet my heart's agitation,
> Its shade will bring grace
> To the enchanted soul . . .

Such is the power of moral purity in poetry. A literary work that breathes its spirit, affects us with freshness, peace, like nature — and isn't it the innocence of nature that accounts for its ability to make us wax poetic? And the charm of Tolstoy's works depends to a large extent upon this atmosphere of moral purity.

These two features — a profound knowledge of the hidden activity within the psyche, and the pristine purity of moral feeling, which now endow Tolstoy's works with a special profile, will always remain essential features of his talent, whatever new aspects may be revealed in its future development.

It is self-evident that his artistry will also remain in his possession. In explaining the distinctive features of Tolstoy's works we have not yet mentioned this skill because it is inseparable from, or better still, constitutes the essence of, any poetic talent, and is, substantially, merely a general term to describe all the qualities that distinguish the works of gifted writers. But it is worthy of note that people who talk a lot about artistic qualities, understand least of all what their conditions are. We have actually read somewhere the nonplussed comment why there is not in the foreground of *Childhood* and *Boyhood* some beautiful maiden of eighteen or twenty who would be passionately in love with an equally beautiful youth . . . . This is an astonishing comment on the nature of artistic quality in a literary work! After all, the author wanted to depict childhood and boyhood years and not some volatile passion; so, is it not obvious that were he to introduce into his story such characters and such pathos, the children, upon whom he wanted to direct our attention, would have been overshadowed, their lovable feelings would cease to interest us once passionate love entered the story? In a word, don't you feel that the unity of the narrative would have been destroyed, the author's idea ruined, and conditions of art injured? Precisely because he wanted to preserve these conditions, the author could not depict in his stories about the life of a child anything of the sort that would make us forget the children, turn away from them. Moreover, we found a hint that Tolstoy erred by not presenting pictures of social life in *Childhood* and *Boyhood*; well, there are lots of other things that he did not present in these stories! For instance, there are no military scenes, no pictures of the Italian landscape, and no historical reminiscences; the stories lack lots of things that could be, but should not be told there, or would be inappropriate: after all, the author wants to transport us into the life of a child — and does a child understand social questions, does he know anything about the life of society? This entire element is as alien to the life of a child as life in a boot camp, and the conditions of art would have been injured just as much if social life would have been depicted in *Childhood* and *Boyhood*, as they would be if military or historical life would be depicted there. We are no less than anyone pleased to see the depiction of social life in stories; but one really ought to understand that not every artistic conception admits of the introduction of social questions; one ought not to forget that the first law of art is the unity of the work, and that therefore in depicting *Childhood* one must write about childhood and not something else, not social questions, not military scenes, not Peter the Great, and not Dr. Faustus, not Indiana and not Rudin, but a child with his feelings and ideas. And these people who make such restrictive demands, talk about artistic freedom! It is surprising that they are not looking in the *Iliad* for Macbeth, in Walter Scott for Dickens, and in Pushkin for Gogolianisms. One ought to understand that an artistic idea may be ruined if alien elements are introduced into a literary work, and if, for instance, Pushkin in *The Stone Guest* decided to depict Russian landowners, or express his sympathy for Peter the Great, *The Stone Guest* would have come out an artistically incongruous work. Everything has its place: pictures of sultry love belong in *The Stone Guest*, pictures of Russian life in *Eugene Onegin*, Peter the Great in *The Bronze Horseman*. Similarly, in *Childhood* or *Boyhood* only those elements are appropriate that fit the age being described, while patriotism, heroism, military life have their place in the

War Stories, a terrifying moral drama in the "Notes of a Billiard Marker," and the depiction of a woman in "Two Hussars." Do you remember the marvelous figure of a girl sitting by the window at night, remember how her heart beats, and her breast is filled with sweet anticipations of love? . . .

Tolstoy is gifted with true talent. This means that his works are artistic, that is to say that in every one of them exactly that idea is realized that he wanted to realize in this particular story. He never says anything extraneous because this would have been contrary to the conditions of art; he never disfigures his works by the addition of scenes and figures that are alien to the idea of the work. This is one of the central demands of art. One has to possess a good deal of taste to appreciate the beauty of Tolstoy's works; but a person who is able to appreciate true beauty, genuine poetry, is bound to see in Tolstoy a true artist, that is, a poet gifted with a remarkable talent. This talent belongs to a young man, with fresh vitality, who has a long road before him — he will meet on this road much that is new, many new feelings will stir his breast, many new issues will occupy his thought — what a splendid hope for our literature, what rich new sources life supplies him with to use in his art! We predict that everything produced by Tolstoy so far is only the beginning, only a preview of his future accomplishments; but how rich and beautiful are these beginnings!

Experiments in the Novel   Boris Eikhenbaum*

The young Tolstoy's basic inspiration was to negate Romantic cliches of style and genre. He does not think about the story (*Fabula*), and he does not worry about choosing a hero. The Romantic novella, with the hero as its central figure, with its peripeties of love creating a complex story, with its lyrical, conventional landscapes — all this is not to his taste. He reverts to the simplest elements — to the elaboration of details, to "minuteness," to the description and depiction of people and things. In this sense Tolstoy deviates from the line of "high" art, and from the very beginning brings into his creative work a simplifying tendency. Hence — an intense self-scrutiny and testing of himself, but also — a concern with the most direct rendering of his sensations, a striving to free himself from any kind of tradition. A passage in his diary is characteristic in this regard: "Things are presented in a false form to people who look at things with the purpose of noting them down; I experienced this for myself." Tolstoy intently examines himself and the world in order to give to us new forms for perceiving our psychological life and nature. It is natural, therefore, that

*From *Molodoy Tolstoy* (The young Tolstoy) (St. Petersberg and Berlin, 1922). Translated from the Russian for this volume by George Gutsche.

the first formal problems he sets for himself are problems of *description* and not of narration, problems of style and not of composition or genre.

The question of "generalization" also arises in connection with this general aim of his poetics. He is not a narrator, connecting himself in one way or another with his heroes, but an outsider, a sharp-sighted observer and even experimenter. His personal tone must be purged of any emotional intensity—he watches and reasons. Theoretical "digressions" are a necessary element of his poetics, which requires by its own basic preconditions a sharp rationality of tone. Generalization strengthens the position of the author observing from the side—it is to serve as a background against which the paradoxical details of psychological life can stand out in their sharp "minuteness."

The fundamentals of Tolstoy's artistic method were already determined in his early diaries. But the forms were not found right away—the entire period before *War and Peace* is not so much a period of achievements as of searches. In *Childhood* Tolstoy gives the impression of a prepared, accomplished writer, but only because here he is still very careful and even timid—he still needs to be convinced that he can write a "good" piece. It is therefore characteristic that right after *Childhood* comes a period of études and experiments, a period of tormenting doubts and struggle. Not without reason did Tolstoy's success begin to decline after *Childhood*, and by the sixties he is considered an almost forgotten writer.

The idea of an autobiographical "novel" consisting of the description of four periods of life (Childhood, Adolescence, Youth, and Young Manhood), is organically linked with Tolstoy's basic artistic tendencies. Tolstoy is not thinking about an adventure scheme in the spirit of Dickens's *David Copperfield*, for example—it should not be "a history of a life," but something quite different. Instead of joining together novellas or events, he joins together separate scenes and impressions. Tolstoy does not need a hero, in the old sense of the word, because he does not need to string events together. Not without reason was the planned novella supposed to stop with the period of "young manhood"—the question of the end was generally of little concern to Tolstoy; he needed only to have a certain perspective. The personality of the hero is drawn directly from self-observation and from the diaries—it is not a "type," not even a personality, but a bearer of generalization by whose perception Tolstoy motivates the "minuteness" of his descriptions. The material of the novel is not constructed by the personality of Nikolenka but, rather, the other way around: this personality is conditioned by the material. It is therefore characteristic that *after Childhood*, where Nikolenka is only a point defining lines of perception and where generalization and concern with details are in a state of equilibrium, Tolstoy begins to lose interest in his novella. The chronological movement of the novella is, in its essence, totally unnecessary to Tolstoy—he is not leading his hero anywhere and he does not want to do anything with him. The necessity of giving more and more attention to his personality leads to an accumulation of generalizations. It is not surprising that in 1852 Tolstoy wrote to Nekrasov: "The autobiographical form I have taken—with its compulsory link between the preceding part and succeeding ones—so constrains me that I often feel a desire to abandon the later ones and leave the first part without a continuation." This reference to the "compulsoriness" of the link between parts is especially characteristic. For Tolstoy the personality of Nikolenka by itself was evidently not a thread naturally linking the parts of the novella. The very form "autobiography" virtually lost its meaning after *Childhood*, because it entailed a centralization of material which was to be organized around the personality of the hero—and this did not at all correspond with Tolstoy's artistic intentions. The concentration of psychological material about one personality was generally alien to Tolstoy. *Childhood* turned out to be not a part of a novel, but a finished, self-enclosed piece.

Work on *Childhood* proceeds from the end of 1851 to the middle of 1852. At this time he is reading Sterne, Rousseau, Toepffer, and Dickens. The connection between his reading and his work is unquestionable: Sterne's *Tristram Shandy* and *Sentimental Journey*, Rousseau's *Confession*, Toepffer's *Library of My Uncle*, and Dickens's *David Copperfield*—these are the Western sources of *Childhood*. The selection is far from accidental—all these works are interconnected by a definite historico-literary thread. The line passes from Sterne to Toepffer by way of Xavier de Maistre—the French Sternian, author of the novella *Journey around My Room*. Many of the devices characteristic of Sterne are repeated here: the parodying of the plot scheme, the intentional retardation of the exposition with lyrical and philosophical digressions, the total miniaturism of the descriptions ("Kleinmalerei") and so forth, down to remarks to a certain Jenny and comparisons with Uncle Toby of *Tristram Shandy*. What is more, this is Sterne by way of the French tradition, without many of his specifically English features. Toepffer comes forward as a follower and pupil of de Maistre. At the request of a publisher to send something new, de Maistre answered in 1839: "I see such an enormous difference between those notions of literature which I formulated for myself in my youth and those leading our present-day authors, who enjoy public success, that I feel bewildered. . . . I hope that I have convinced you of my inability to add anything to my small collection; however the desire to respond to your good intention prompts me to send you some short pieces [by Toepffer] that I just received and that could serve as a continuation of my own. While I am not in a position to offer you works which I could not write, I recommend to you these which I would like to have written." Toepffer turns out to be a writer who continues a minor line of French literature linked with the 18th century, and who is perceived as a contrast to the

Romantics. The impression he made on French readers with his Swiss novellas was defined by Saint-Beuve in the following way: "We saw here a model which was actually supposed to be held up in opposition to our own works, so refined and so unhealthy." The whole literary filiation of Toepffer is characteristic of and very close to the young Tolstoy: Rousseau, from whom, by his own words, Toepffer did not part in the course of two or three years,[1] Bernardin de Saint-Pierre *(Paul et Virginie)*, Goldsmith *(The Vicar of Wakefield)* and, finally, Franklin again. Pointing to this return of Toepffer to old, seemingly outmoded literature, Saint-Beuve adds: "In a word, Toepffer began as we all did; he stepped back in order to jump better."

Uniting Toepffer on one side with Sterne and on the other with Rousseau turns out to be completely natural and significant for Tolstoy. Here we do not have a simple subordination to the individual influence of another writer, but a creative, active assimilation of a whole literary school which was close, in its artistic methods, to the intentions of the young Tolstoy. Characteristically, even Dickens is assimilated by Tolstoy only in that which historically links him with Sterne—that is, mainly, in the treatment of details, a total miniaturism in description. This whole circle of reading is determined by Tolstoy's basic tendency: to destroy Romantic poetics with all of its stylistic and plot structures. Hence Tolstoy does not directly imitate anything—there is only an assimilation of certain artistic devices necessary for the formation of his own system. For example, Tolstoy calls Sterne his favorite writer and translates him, but specifically English features of Sterne are alien to him—"the digressions are too heavy, even for him." He perceives Sterne against a particular background—the English tradition itself, and Sternianism as such is not necessary to him. What is important for him in Sterne is what was assimilated through de Maistre and Toepffer,—a general sincerity, a "domesticity" of style allowing copiously detailed description, the absence of complex plot schemes, and free composition. Besides, another Russian tradition proceeding from Karamzin apparently was working in Tolstoy—one which valued Sterne as the author not so much of *Tristram Shandy* as of *Sentimental Journey* (Tolstoy himself singled out just this work and translated it). Sterne the parodist, overturning the customary forms of English novel, was too alien to Russian literature, which was struggling to find safe ground for the development of prose. Hence—the specifically Russian Sterne, the "sensitive" narrator of touching histories. One can see traces of this Russian tradition in Tolstoy's *Childhood*—if only in the address to readers: "In order to be accepted as one of my select readers, I demand very little: that you be sensitive, i.e., that you be able sometimes to feel pity from your soul and even shed a few tears for someone whom you remembered and whom you loved from your heart, and that you be able to be glad for him without being ashamed; that you love your recollections, that you be a religious person, and that while reading my story you search for those places which touch your heart, and not those which make you laugh."

On the other hand, within the context of Russian literature Tolstoy's *Childhood* was not alone and not unexpected. The basis for such an autobiographical novel, and even the description of childhood, was laid by Karamzin (again we encounter this name) in his unfinished *A Knight of Our Time* (incidentally, neither *Tristram Shandy* nor Tolstoy's novel was finished). Karamzin's English source — *Tristram Shandy* most of all — is unquestionable here: the titles of chapters (especially the fourth, "which was written only for the fifth"), the verbal play, the style of unrestrained "chatter," the insertions ("An Excerpt from the Countess' History"), the unexpected break in a letter ("the last ten lines we could not make out: they have been almost completely effaced by time"), and finally, the mention of Sterne in the first chapter ("The Birth of My Hero"): "Leon's father was of the native Russian nobility, a retired captain who had been wounded, a man of about fifty, neither rich nor destitute, and — most important of all — an extremely good person; however, he was not in the least bit similar in character to the well-known *uncle* of Tristram Shandy — he was good in his own way and thoroughly Russian." What is interesting here is that Karamzin consciously sets his biographical novel in opposition to historical novels, as is evident from the introduction: "Recently *historical novels* have come into fashion. A restless race of people called *Authors* disturbs the sacred ashes of Numas, Aureliuses, Alfreds, and Karlomans, and exercising a right (which is hardly *right*) assumed since olden times, calls out ancient Heroes from their cramped little house (as Ossian says), so that once out on the stage they might entertain us with their stories. A beautiful Puppet Comedy! . . . I never was a zealous follower of clothing fashions; I do not want to follow author fashions either; I do not want to waken deceased giants of humanity; I do not want my readers to yawn — and for that reason, instead of an *historical novel*, I plan on telling a *romantic history* of my friend." Historical novels continue to be replaced by domestic or biographical novels up to the time of Tolstoy's appearance on the literary scene. After Karamzin Russian prose yields to verse which, by the thirties, reaches full bloom. Then — a new wave of prose and a new revival of the historical novel: Zagoskin, Lazhechnikov, Masal'skii, Kukol'nik, Polevoi and others. Pushkin's *The Captain's Daughter* and Gogol's *Taras Bul'ba* join the movement. Alongside all this appears Marlinskii's complex prose, stylistically refined and nurtured on poetic devices; by the forties it ripens into the prose of Lermontov. A sudden change occurs — devices are replaced, material is replaced. A whole period of biographical tales and novels begins, leading to Tolstoy's *Childhood*, Goncharov's *Oblomov's Dream*, and S. Aksakov's *Family Chronicle* and *Childhood Years of Bagrov's Grandson*. Even contemporary critics take note of this. B. N. Almazov wrote in *the*

Muscovite [Moskvitianin] of 1852: "One cannot help but be gladdened by the fact that recently many novels and tales have begun to appear which have as their subject the depiction of childhood." Tolstoy himself, after reading the issue of *The Contemporary* where his *Childhood* was printed, notes in his diary: "one good novella, similar to my Childhood, but not substantial." What is referred to is the novella by Nikolai M. (P. A. Kulish), *Iakov Iakovlich*, which is directly connected with his novella, *Story of Ul'iana Terent'evna*, published earlier. In genre both works are actually very close to *Childhood*; a connection is felt with English literature, especially with Dickens—if only in the chapter headings, which are entirely in the spirit of *David Copperfield*: "What Kind of a Person is Ul'iana Terent'eva," "My Dream is Realized, Though Not Right Away," "I Acquire Citizenship in the Household of Ul'iana Terent'eva," "On the Bright Horizon Appears a Storm Cloud," "The Surprising Discoveries Made by Me in Iakov Iakovlich," "I Make Discoveries Even More Surprising," and so forth. Traditional motifs of this genre are repeated—the tedious arithmetic studies, the favorite book, and departure for the city to study. The novella also presents itself as a contrast to plotted pieces, as something different: "My short story was composed such that it turned out like the beginning of a novella. I am afraid that the reader may forget what I promised him, and *may begin to expect from me the development of an intrigue which generally serves as the basis of novellas and novels.*"

He is writing a biography, and for this reason he will speak about the most ordinary circumstances of life, about the simplest actions, about all the details of everyday domestic life. "I would like," writes the author, "to be on the most sincere terms with my reader so that my speech for him will be akin to quiet conversations in a small circle of people who are close to each other, over evening tea, when the day's cares are over, when you feel secure from all distressing matters and when, with a trustful release of feelings, you reward yourself for the constraint you used that day in dealing with people foreign to our nature. Only with his soul so disposed could the image of Ul'iana Terent'eva present itself to the reader with that melancholy charm with which it presents itself to me."

As early as 1850 Tolstoy wanted to write a novella "from the window," one which evidently was to have consisted of a detailed description of different scenes mutually connected only by setting and manner of observation. His reading of Sterne and Toepffer probably had some connection with the origin of this idea. In Toepffer's novella the window is assigned a very significant role as an observation point. Jules spends whole hours at the window observing and reflecting; in this manner a series of separate descriptions, replacing one another in succession, is motivated: a hospital, a church, a fountain, cats, all kinds of street scenes—"and this is only a small sample of those wonders one can see from my window." It is precisely this concentration on details, this intensity of observation, making description valuable in itself, that Tolstoy likes in Sterne and

Toepffer. In his own words he, in *Childhood*, "was not original [*samos-toiatelen*] in my forms of expression." Actually, here we see not only a general tendency to depict details, but also a sentimental-melancholy tone Tolstoy derived from his reading of Sterne and Toepffer. Typical in this regard is Chapter XV—one of the lyrical digressions: "Will that freshness, that carefreeness, that need for love and strength of faith which you have in childhood ever return? What time could be better than when your two best virtues—innocent gaiety and boundless need for love—are the only impulses in life? Where are those fervent prayers? Where is the best gift—those pure tears of tender emotion? The consoling angel flew in and with a smile wiped away those tears, and induced sweet dreams in my untainted childish imagination. Has life really left such painful traces in my heart that these tears and delights have left me forever? Can it be that only memories remain?" This is almost the lexicon of Karamzin or Zhukovskii. Toepffer's digressions are also analogous: "A fresh May morning, an azure sky, a mirror-like surface on the lake, I see you even now, but . . . tell me, where has your brilliance gone, your purity, that charm of infinite gladness, of mystery, of hope, which you awakened in me? . . . How faithful, tender and sincere is the heart while it is pure and young!"

Childhood is held together not by the movement of events which form the story, but by the succession of different scenes. This succession is conditioned by time. Thus the entire first part of *Childhood* is a description of a number of scenes replacing one another during the course of one day—from morning to evening, by the movement of the clock hand: awakening, the morning hour, in Father's study, lesson, dinner, the hunt, games, and so forth. Time's only role here is in the external plan—its movement is therefore not felt. Parallel with the movement of time is the shifting from room to room—events of the first part barely go beyond the bounds of this limited space. Such a concentration of material appeared natural, a result of Tolstoy's striving for "minuteness" and the elaboration of descriptions. But in view of this tendency a question inevitably arises about the choice and disposition of the details. The more Tolstoy freed himself from the plot scheme, the more difficult it was to solve the problem of composition. In connection with this, the text of *Childhood* was subjected to significant modifications. The first part was finished at the end of 1851, but Tolstoy returned to it several additional times—he shortens it and he introduces something new. On March 22, 1852, he writes in his diary: "I did not continue the novella partly because I am beginning to have serious doubts about the worth of the first part. It seems too detailed to me, prolix, and not enough of life in it."

It is interesting that the question of the "second day" particularly vexed Tolstoy. The scale of the first part, with its small particles of one day, set a pattern for what followed; but to describe a second day, filling it with new details laid out in the same temporal order, would be too boring. Some drafts of this second day were apparently made—this is what Tolstoy writes on March 27: "Tomorrow I'll be rewriting . . . and I'll think over the second day; *can I correct it or should I throw it out completely?* One should be merciless in destroying all those passages that are unclear, prolix, irrelevant, or, in a word, unsatisfying, *even if they might be good in themselves.*" The first day, too, was subjected to considerable cutting, as one can see by comparing the journal text (*Contemporary* 25 [1852]) with one of the first versions published by S. A. Tolstaya in her edition; it is characteristic that Tolstoy at this time tries especially to shorten and eliminate the digressions—in the final text there is no description of the three means by which a landowner frees himself from the annoyances of neighbors (chapter 10), there is no lengthy discourse on music (chapter 9), and so forth.

In connection with the problem of the second day, there is one interesting note in the diary (from April 10), very unclear in form, but all the same comprehensible against the background of the general course of Tolstoy's reflections: "I planned to write a novel; but having written two pages—I stopped, because the thought came to me that the second day cannot be good without an interest, that a whole novel is like a drama. I'm not sorry, I'll throw out what's superfluous tomorrow." This apparently means: the composition of a novel, in order to be interesting, must be dramatic—hence the second day can not be descriptive like the first, but must serve only as a transition to what follows: hence the conclusion—to throw out all that is superfluous. In the end Tolstoy evidently decided to eliminate completely the second day—only one chapter remains (14), describing the departure to Moscow and forming, together with the chapter that followed, the tailpiece [*kontsovka*] for the first part. What results is something like a self-contained act built on the temporal sequence of the first day. The original scale of the first day set the pattern for the construction of the second part (chapters 16–24)—which also consists of the description of one day (the grandmother's nameday). The last chapters (25–28) form the finale, while chapter 28—recollections of Natalia Savishna's death—lyrically closes the second part with a melancholy question; in this sense the chapter is analogous to chapter 15: "Sometimes I quietly stop between the chapel and the black railing. Suddenly sad memories are awakened in my soul. The thought comes to me: did Providence really only unite me with these two beings in order to make me feel pity for them eternally? . . ."[2]

All this indicates Tolstoy's tendency to impart to the composition of the novella the best proportion possible. What disturbed him was the absence of dramatic "interest," that is, the absence of inner movement connecting all the separate scenes. Instead of a plot scheme determining the devices which would develop the material, we find something else. The theme of the mother, which runs through the whole novella (beginning with the fictitious dream about his mother's death and ending with her real death), serves as a leitmotif, lyrically drawing the story together into a unit. Its main features, in the sense of a construction, are determined by the tension and development of this leitmotif—the end of the first part (chapter 14–15) and the finale. The correspondence of chapter 15 with the last chapter was already pointed out above—actually, they correspond to each other as lyrical repetitions in emphasized places of a narrative poem or as refrains in short poems. They are the principal lyrical emphases of the whole novella, with the second (as the finale) stronger than the first. The chapter describing the parting (14) concentrates within it the lyrical tension of the first part and uses a melancholy digression as a cadence for it. Chapters describing the mother's death play exactly the same compositional role in relation to the second part and, in fact, to the whole novella; moreover, even here the novella does not simply break off, but uses as a cadence the chapter about the death of Natalia Savishna, a chapter written in a sentimental-melancholy tone that virtually destroys the tragic dissonance of the preceding chapter. The construction did not turn out to be dramatic, but lyrical, which is characteristic of Tolstoy at this time, who is reviving the traditions of Rousseau and Sterne and following in the footsteps of Toepffer. It is especially characteristic that the mother's death (generally speaking, this is the traditional motif of the "first sorrow") does not serve as a knot in the plot [*siuzhetnyi uzel*], as the death of the father does in *David Copperfield*, but forms a finale motivating the closure of the novella. Thus the fluidity of the autobiographical form is overcome; it unfolds not as a "*history* of childhood," but as a number of separate scenes laid out along small divisions of the temporal scale. An exhaustive description of two days with their respective tailpieces—that is all there is to *Childhood*.

For Tolstoy it was pointless, and even impossible, to develop his material over a large interval of time, as was done in *David Copperfield*. There is no adventure plan in the novel as planned, and Nikolenka is not a "hero." Nikolenka is not even a personality. The idea of a "novel" in four parts came to Tolstoy not from a desire to portray the psychological development of a definite personality with its typical-individual peculiarities, but from his need for "generalization," for an abstract program. In general Tolstoy requires a dual scale: one is micrographic, its divisions determined by details of psychological and physical life, and the other is macrographic, measuring the full expanse of the work. The composition of its elements is determined by the placement of the one scale on the other. Hence—there is a need for large forms, and hence—at the very outset, the question of combining generalization and "minuteness" arises. This combination displayed itself in its full strength and originality in *War and Peace*, but it was already conceived in his first novel. In *Childhood*, Nikolenka is only a "window" through which we look at the changing series of scenes and characters. Tolstoy's attention is focused here on "descriptiveness," on "minuteness"—the concreteness and sharpness of details are motivated by the perception of a child. The linking of scenes is completely external: each scene is played out to the end and mechanically yields its place to the next. The "unoriginality" of Tolstoy lies primarily in the fact that his basic artistic tendency is cloaked here in a sentimental-melancholy tone from which he escapes after *Childhood*.

Before us is a world examined through a microscope. In the tradition of Sterne, poses and gestures are described in detail, but here the device is motivated by the childish perception of Nikolenka. Karl Ivanovich sits by the little table: "in one hand he holds a book, the other hand rests on the arm of the chair"; Mamma "sat in the living room and was pouring tea; with one hand she held the teapot and with the other the tap of the samovar, from which the water flowed over the top of the teapot onto the tray." Father twitches his shoulder, the steward Iakov twiddles his fingers. Sometimes the gestures and movements are broken down into separate moments parallel to the conversation, and they form a whole system. This is the way the conversation between the father and the mother at the dinner table is rendered: " 'Pass me a pie please,' she said. 'Well, are they good today?' — 'No, it makes me angry,' Papa continued, after taking a pie in his hand, but holding it at such a distance that Mama could not reach it, — 'no, it makes me angry when I see intelligent and educated people deceived.' *And he struck the table with his fork.* — 'I asked you to pass me a pie,' she repeated, *extending her hand.* 'And they do well,' continued Papa, moving his hand away, 'who turn such people over to the police. The only thing they can do is disturb those whose nerves are weak enough already,' he added with a smile, having noticed that Mama was not liking this conversation very much, *and he gave her the pie*" (chapter 5). A device analogous to this is in *Adolescence*, in the description of the lesson. " 'Be so kind as to tell me something about the crusade of Saint Louis,' he said, rocking on his chair and pensively looking down at his feet. 'First you will tell me about the reasons inducing the King of France to take the cross,' he said, *raising his brows and pointing with his finger at the ink-bottle*, 'then explain to me the general characteristics of this crusade,' he added, *making a movement with his entire hand as if he wanted to catch something*, 'and finally the influence of this crusade on the European states in general,' he said, *striking the notebooks against the left edge of the table*, 'on the French monarchy in particular,' he concluded, *striking the right side of the table and bending his head to the right*." (chapter 11) Animals and insects (compare the ants Nikolenka observes with Toepffer's May beetle) are described in the same detail.

In addition to this — there are details of psychological life which appear not as a single current, but in several layers. Paradoxical combinations result, incongruencies (oxymora), which destroy the canon of the typical, generalized representation of psychological life. Attention passes from personality to psychological states, to their composition. This is not of course a matter of "realism," or psychological "verity" (both presuppose as common knowledge the objective content of psychological life, which is incorrect), but of providing a new hindrance to artistic perception, of renewing material which has become banal and for that reason artistically imperceptible. In *Childhood* Tolstoy is constrained by the motivation of self-observation (not without reason did he complain that the "autobiographical" form restricted him), but a method prepared by the diaries was already available to him: "After we came out on the big road, we saw a white handkerchief which someone was waving from a balcony. I began to wave with my own, and this movement calmed me a little. *I continued to cry, and the thought that my tears proved my sensitivity afforded me pleasure and consolation*" (chapter 14). Here there are two layers of feelings paradoxically united in one. Another passage is still more characteristic: "Remembering now my impressions, I find that only this one moment of self-oblivion was real misery. Before and after the burial I did not cease crying and felt sad, but I am ashamed to recall that sadness because some kind of selfish feeling was always mixed up with it: at the same time there was a desire to show that I grieved more than anyone else, there were concerns about the effect which I was producing on others, and there was a pointless curiosity which made me observe Mimi's cap and the faces of those present. *I hated myself for not experiencing exclusively the feeling of grief alone*, and I tried to hide all else: because of this my sadness was insincere and unnatural. In addition, *I experienced a kind of delight, knowing that I was unhappy*, and I tried to awaken the consciousness of unhappiness; this egotistical feeling, more than any other, stifled real sadness in me" (chapter 27). This is the very device by which Tolstoy stratified his own psychological life in his diary. There is a certain kinship here with Dickens: in *David Copperfield* there is an analogous passage — what makes it even more analogous is that it is also about a mother's death (chapter 9):

> When Mr. Creakle left me alone, I stood up on a chair and began to look in the mirror in order to determine to what degree my eyes had reddened from tears, how strongly sadness was expressed on my face. I reasoned, had all my tears been exhausted by this time, wasn't there one more drop? This would be very regrettable because at home, where they summoned me for the funeral, I all the same was supposed to cry over the coffin of my mother. Later it seemed to me that through all my physiognomy spread some kind of dignity which was a consequence of my grief, and I was convinced that my comrades should now feel a special respect for me. Nothing, of course, could be more sincere than my childish grief; *but I remember very well that this importance which spread through my physiognomy filled me with a feeling of satisfaction* when, toward evening, I entered the playground while my comrades were in school.

> [I stood upon a chair when I was left alone, and looked into the glass to see how red my eyes were, and how sorrowful my face. I considered, after some hours were gone, if my tears were really hard to flow now, as

they seemed to be, what, in connection with my loss, it would affect me most to think of when I drew near home — for I was going home to the funeral. I am sensible of having felt that a dignity attached to me among the rest of the boys, and that I was important in my affliction.

If ever a child were stricken with sincere grief, I was. But I remembered that this importance was a kind of satisfaction to me, when I walked in the playground that afternoon while the boys were in school.(*David Copperfield*, volume 15 of *The Works of Charles Dickens*[New York and London: Co-operative Publication Society, 1919], p. 137)]

Sometimes Tolstoy himself apparently found such analysis excessive — especially in the form it manifested itself in *Childhood*: "It came to mind (he writes in his diary May 11, 1852), that that year I was very similar, in my literary tendency, to certain people (in particular young ladies) who want to see a special subtlety and ingenuity in everything." Almost all of the critics contemporary to Tolstoy were critical of his "excessiveness" in analysis and the "minuteness" of his descriptions. Especially characteristic in this regard are the comments of K. S. Aksakov. He finds that in Tolstoy's autobiographical novel "the description of surrounding life sometimes reaches an unendurable, excessive minuteness and detailedness," and that his analysis "often notices details that do not deserve attention, that race through the soul like a light cloud, without a trace; when noted and fixed by analysis, they receive more significance than they have in fact, and for this reason they become false. Analysis in this case becomes a microscope. Microscopic phenomena exists in the soul, but if you enlarge them in the microscope and leave them that way, then their relative size with respect to everything around them will be destroyed, and, while they are truthfully enlarged, they become decidedly false; for to them is imparted an incorrect size, for the common measure of life is destroyed, its proportion, and it is this measure that constitutes real truth. . . . And so, here is the danger of analysis; having enlarged with a microscope and with all truthfulness details of the psychological world, it presents them for that very reason in a false form, in a *disproportionate* magnitude. . . . Finally, analysis can find something in a person which is not at all there; an uneasily fixed gaze into oneself often sees apparitions and distorts its own soul." The critical Aksakov is certainly much more in the right than unprincipled admirers of Tolstoy who keep talking about his "realism." Regardless of his appraisal, Aksakov with perfect accuracy caught the "dominant" of Tolstoy's method — the destruction of psychological proportions, the orientation toward "minuteness."

Deviating from generalized characterization and the representation of static types, Tolstoy unfolds details of movements, gestures, intonations, and so forth. Accordingly, the characters do not come forward immediately, but pass through a number of scenes: Karl Ivanovich in the nursery, in the living room, in the father's study, the father and Iakov, the father and mother, and so forth. Images are as if split, extended through the whole novella and passed through the perception of Nikolenka. But the need to motivate each description by Nikolenka's perception ("the form of the autobiography") restricts Tolstoy. Sometimes he deviates from it and makes a description from an adult's point of view, as if by recollections (the characterization of Iakov, Natalia Savishna, the father, Prince Ivan Ivanovich); sometimes, however, and this is especially interesting, a *lapse in motivation* occurs, once again showing that the personality of Nikolenka itself plays an auxiliary role. In chapter 11 a fact is described which remains outside the perception of Nikolenka (Karl Ivanovich is in the father's study), but the description is made as if he hears and sees—and what is more, there are details which could not have been motivated by Nikolenka's perception. Nikolenka sits in the living room and dozes, Karl Ivanovich passes by him into the father's study: "He was admitted and the door again closed. 'If only nothing bad happens,'—I thought:—'Karl Ivanovich is angry: he is ready for anything . . ." I again dozed off. . . . Having entered the study with notes in his hand and *with a prepared speech in his head, he intended*[3] eloquently to lay out before Papa all the injustices he endured in our house; but when he began to speak in that same touching voice and with those same sensitive intonations with which he usually dictated to us, his eloquence affected himself most of all: 'However sad it will be for me to leave the children,' he then completely lost control, his voice trembled, and he had to get the checkered handkerchief from his pocket, — 'Yes, Peter Aleksandrich,'—he said through tears *(this part was not at all in the prepared speech)*—'I am so used to the children that I do not know what I shall do without them. Better that I should serve you without pay,'—he added, with one hand wiping the tears, and with the other handing over the bill."

The general characteristics to which Tolstoy sometimes resorts in *Childhood* are very original: they communicate a number of features essential to the described personage, as if without any special plan or inner tie: "A large, stately stature, a peculiar gait with small short steps, a habit of jerking his shoulder, small ever-smiling eyes, a large aquiline nose, uneven lips which were awkwardly, somehow unpleasantly, set together, a speech defect—a lisp, a large bald spot extending over his entire head—that's the external appearance of my father as I remembered him then—an appearance which enabled him not only to pass for and be a man *à bonnes fortunes*, but to be liked without exception by all people of all classes, in particular by those whom he wished to please. *He* knew how to take the upper hand in relationships with any one. Never having been a man of *very high society*, he always kept company with people of this circle, and in such a way that he was respected. *He* knew that precise measure of pride and self-reliance which, without offending others, elevated him in the opinion of society. *He* was original, but not always, and he used his originality as a resource which replaced in some cases social standing or wealth . . . *He* could so well conceal from others and drive away from himself that dark side of life filled with petty vexations and griefs known to everyone, that it was impossible not to envy him. *He* was an expert in all things which afforded comfort and delight, and knew how to use them . . . *He*, like all former military people, did not know how to dress fashionably: but on the other hand he dressed originally and elegantly: always very broad and light outer garments, beautiful linen, large turned-down cuffs and collars . . . *He* was sensitive and even tearful . . . *He* loved music. . . ." One and the same form is repeated an infinite number of times — "he was," and an impression is given of some kind of accidental accumulation of facts — minor and major, important and immaterial. It seems that the main thing uniting all of these features is not expressed. Tolstoy examines a person from all sides, almost touching and feeling him. Not without reason had he pondered the problem of the portrait in his diary: "*to describe* a person is actually impossible . . . To say of a person: he is an original man, good, kind, stupid, consistent, and so forth — these are words which do not give any understanding of the person, but make a pretense of depicting the person, while they often only confuse." This thought is repeated in passing in the address to readers preceding *Childhood*: "It is difficult and even impossible, it seems to me, to divide people into intelligent and stupid, good and evil." And Tolstoy actually avoids generalizations of this type. In a late diary (1898) Tolstoy speaks very definitely: "How nice it would be to write an artistic work in which one could express clearly the fluidity of a person: that he is one and the same, a villain, and angel, a wise man, an idiot, a strongman, and the most powerless of beings." In *Resurrection* this is partially accomplished — Nekhliudov is motivated like this: "One of the most common and widespread superstitions is that each person has his own definite attributes, that there is a good man, an evil one, a stupid one, an energetic one, an apathetic one, and so forth. People are not like that . . . People are like rivers: the water in all is identical and everywhere the same, but individual rivers can sometimes be narrow, fast, wide, quiet, pure, cold, murky, and warm. So it is with people. Each person carries in himself the rudiments of human attributes, and sometimes he manifests some, and sometimes others, and he is often not like himself while remaining at the same time one and the same self" (chapter 59). This is evidently one of Tolstoy's favorite assertions — one of the "generalizations" by which the artistic device is motivated: its cutting edge is directed against the typifying canon. In this sense there are no personalities for Tolstoy. He always operates with a great number of characters, from which each emerges not in itself, but against the background of the others, and often combines in itself opposite attributes. Not without reason was it pointed out even in the old criticism that "his works differed from purely psychological conceptions in very many respects and very sharply" and that "in his creations we shall not find fully complete characters, we shall not find pure psychological types." Tolstoy's personalities are always paradoxical, always changeable and dynamic. Indeed this is necessary for Tolstoy because his works are built not on characters, not on "heroes" who bear constant attributes which determine their actions, but on sharp depictions of psychological states, on the "dialectic of the soul," as one critic expressed it: "Psychological analysis can take different directions: for one poet the features of personalities occupy the most attention; for another, it is the influence of social relationships and life's conflicts on human character; for a third—the connection between feelings and actions, for a fourth—the analysis of passions: for Count Tolstoy more than anything it is the psychic process itself, its forms, its laws, the dialectic of the soul, to express it with a definite term . . . The distinctiveness of Tolstoy's talent consists in the fact that he is not limited by his depictions of the results of the psychic process: what interests him is the very process,—and Count Tolstoy masterfuly depicts the barely perceptible phenomena of this inner life as they replace each other with unusual speed and inexhaustible variety."

Notes

1. Tolstoy's words: "I read all of Rousseau, all twenty volumes, including *Dictionnaire de Musique*. I was more than enraptured by him—I idolized him. At fifteen I wore on my neck a medallion with his portrait instead of a cross. Many of his pages are so close to me that it seems to me I wrote them myself." P. Biriukov, *Biography*, 1:279.

2. The last sentence of chapter 15 is: "Has life really left such painful traces in my heart that these tears and delights have left me forever? Can it be that only memories remain?"

3. I designate with italics those places that stand beyond any motivation and reveal Tolstoy's striving to free himself from it.

WAR AND PEACE

Reviews

[On *War and Peace*]   I. S. Turgenev*

[From a letter to P. P. Borisov, 16 March 1865]

. . . Since receiving your letter, I've succeeded in reading Ostrovsky's drama *Voevod* and the beginning of Tolstoy's novel. I am sincerely disappointed to admit that the novel strikes me as positively bad, boring, and unsuccessful. Tolstoy took a wrong turn and all his failings have become more obvious. All those little tricks, cunningly marked, and pretentiously put forth, those petty little psychological remarks, which he plucks out from the armpits and other dark places of his heroes and presents under the pretext of truth—how meager all that is on the broad canvas of a historical novel! And he puts this unfortunate product higher than *The Cossacks*! All the worse for him if he really means it. And how cold and dry everything is—how one feels the lack of imagination and the naïveté of the author, and how wearisome is the effect of a memory of so much that is petty, incidental, and useless. And what young ladies! All scrofulous and all putting on airs. No, one mustn't do it that way. That's going downhill, even with his talent. It pains me very much and I would enjoy being mistaken.

[From a letter to I. I. Borisov, 10 March 1868]

. . . I read Tolstoy's novel with pleasure, although I remain dissatisfied with a lot. The whole picture of military and daily life is done astonishingly well: There are things that will not die as long as the Russian language lives. But the whole *historical* side—forgive the expression—is a puppet show. Not to mention that there is no real reproduction of the times. What we learn about Alexander, Speransky, and others is only trifles, capriciously chosen by the author and put forth as characteristic traits. That's a form of charlantanism. . . .

[From a letter to P. V. Annenkov, 13 April 1868]

I was sent Tolstoy's fourth volume. There is much that is fine, but you

*From *Sobranie sochinenii* (Collected works), vol. 12 (Moscow, 1956). Translated from the Russian for this volume by Edward Wasiolek.

cannot overlook the deformities. It is a pity when an amateur, especially like Tolstoy, takes to philosophizing. He inevitably gets on some hobby horse, thinks up some system that settles everything right away, as for example, historical fatalism and starts to write. There where he touches the earth, like Antaeus, he gets back all his strength: the death of the old prince, Alpatych, the uprising in the village—all that is astonishingly well done. Natasha, though, comes out badly. . . .

[From a letter to Tolstoy in which Turgenev is quoting from a letter to him from Flaubert, 12 January 1880]
    Thanks for having me read Tolstoy's novel. It is first rate! What a painter and psychologist! The first two volumes are *sublime*, but the third goes downhill terribly. He repeats himself and he philosophizes. One sees finally the author and the Russian, and up to then one saw only *Nature* and *Humanity*. At times, it seemed to me there were things like Shakespeare's. I cried out in admiration while reading—but it is long!

[Review of *Peace and War*]   Anonymous*

    Peace and War, as it now appears in the French translation, forms three volumes very closely printed. It is called an historical novel, but it hardly deserves that name. It is not an historical novel; history is merely a thread which binds together the heroes and heroines of a complex human drama. It is not even a novel, as in a novel there are always favorite heroes or heroines, surrounded with accessory personages, and the novel is chiefly consecrated to the delineation of a few central figures. Here we have nothing of the sort. This single work might better be compared to the series of novels by our great Balzac, in which the same figures always reappear, sometimes more in the light, but sometimes more in the shade. The personages of Balzac, men and women, virtuous or criminal, weak or heroic, form a sort of human medium, an atmosphere of passions, sometimes almost nebulous, and sometimes condensed in brilliant constellations. Balzac himself gave to his huge work, which fills so many volumes, the graphic name of *La Comédie Humaine*. The world in which all his actors move, suffer, and die seems as real as the true world. Such is the power of this writer that he gives life, he creates; our memory preserves all his types as easily as the men or women who have been thrown in our path and in the vortex of our own destiny.
    This book of Tolstoi's might be called with justice "The Russian Comedy," in the sense in which Balzac employed the word. It gave me exactly the same impression: I felt that I was thrown among new men and

*From the *Nation* 40–41 (22 January 1885):70–71.

women, that I lived with them, that I knew them, that none of them could be indifferent to me, that I could never forget them. I entered into their souls, and it seemed almost as if they could enter into mine. Such a power in a writer is almost a miracle. How many novels have I not read, and, after having read them, and admired many qualities—the beauty of the style, the invention, the dialogues, the dramatic situations—have still felt that my knowledge of life had not increased, that I had gained no new experience. It was not so with *Peace and War*. The work begins in 1805, before Tilsit; it carried me through the great battles fought between Napoleon, Austria, and Russia, to the invasion of Russia, to Borodino, to the burning of Moscow; and all along I felt as if I was on the great stream of life—sometimes with the Emperors in the midst of their staff, in the councils of war, or on the battlefield; sometimes amidst the common soldiers, under the tent, on the high roads; sometimes in the great drawing-rooms of St. Petersburg with the diplomats, the fine ladies; sometimes in the great country houses of Russia—abodes of peace, of petty tyranny, of lazy, monotonous, and almost animal life, suddenly thrown into commotion by the news of the invasion.

History, in this extraordinary work, merely plays the part of a huge disturbing element: it acts on a host of actors, high or low, as a foreign body would act if a powerful hand threw it into the midst of our planetary system. It does not change men, but it gives them new and unforeseen opportunities. It changes the cold, heartless profligate, the man of prey, who lives but for his material pleasures, into a brave man, and sometimes into a hero. It brings out the dormant capacities and virtualities. It reveals all sorts of secrets to man. It brings men constantly before a formidable unknown. It exasperates some; it calms and soothes others. It gives to all the tender relations of life a new intensity, by depriving them of security. It is a powerful motor, but it is only a motor; the masses which it puts in motion are already formed of determined units, and each of these units is a human soul, a world in itself, shrouded in mystery. Conceived in this sense, Tolstoi's work has all the variety of human experience; it is less a novel than a succession of pictures, of small scenes, in which we often see the same actors. The book, in order to be well understood, must be read twice. The first time, you have to make the acquaintance of a number of people, and to become familiar with their barbarous Russian names. It is rather fatiguing at first, especially as there is no *story*, in the English sense of the word, as applied to a novel. You are constantly shifted from one place to another, from one set of people to another set of people. By degrees, all becomes clear, the action is fairly engaged, the drama—or, rather, the dramas, for there are several in one—develop themselves, and you soon feel the keenest interest in all the actors. I ran, so to speak, through the book the first time, in order to form a conception of the aim of the author, and then I read it a second time, *con amore*, interrupting myself so as to prolong the pleasure, finding infinite joy in some of its tableaux, in the descriptions of nature, in the conversations, in the accessory details.

It would be difficult to give a proper definition of the talent of Tolstoi. First of all, he is an *homme du monde*. He makes great people, emperors, generals, diplomats, fine ladies, princes, talk and act as they do act and talk. He is a perfect gentleman, and as such he is thoroughly humane. He takes as much interest in the most humble of his actors as he does in the highest. He has lived in courts: the Sainte-Andrés, the Saint-Vladimirs have no prestige for him — nor the gilded uniforms; he is not deceived by appearances. His aim is so high that whatever he sees is, in one sense, unsatisfactory. He looks for moral perfection, and there is nothing perfect. He is always disappointed in the end. The final impression of his work is a sort of despair. The cherished figures of his "Russian Comedy" are all fatally condemned to an untimely end, to continual mental and moral misery, to undeserved misfortune. It seems as if suffering was the mark of goodness, and as if a certain amount of virtue was incompatible with happiness. Then, by a sort of physical and natural necessity, the element of evil is always mixed up with the element of good. Natacha, one of the heroines of the book, who is represented as so charming, so good, so fascinating, has suddenly bad impulses. She does things or wishes to do things almost horrible. The women are all painted as somewhat irrational and unconscious; but it is not the privilege of their sex — the men are irrational also, led by instinct much more than by reason. Their courage, their honorable resolutions, their heroic actions, do not seem to belong to them. This fundamental idea of fatalism pervades the book. Fate governs empires as well as men: it plays with a Napoleon and an Alexander as it does with a private in the ranks; it hangs over all the world like a dark cloud, rent at times by lightning. We live in the night, like shadows; we are lost on the shore of an eternal Styx; we do not know whence we came or whither we go. Millions of men, led by a senseless man, go from west to east, killing, murdering, and burning, and it is called the invasion of Russia. Two thousand years before, millions of other men came from east to west, plundering, killing, and burning, and it was called the invasion of the barbarians. What becomes of the human will, of the proud *I*, in these dreadful events? We see the folly and the vanity of self-will in these great historical events; but it is just the same in all times, and the will gets lost in peace as well as in war, for there is no real peace, and the human wills are constantly devouring each other. The mother is devoured by the child, the husband by the wife, the slave by the master, the weak by the strong, the affectionate by the heartless, the rational by the irrational. We are made to enjoy a little, to suffer much, and, when the end is approaching, we are all like one of Tolstoi's heroes, on the day of Borodino.

Recent Fiction

Anonymous*

The most remarkable work of fiction recently presented to the English public is undoubtedly the translation of Tolstoï's *War and Peace*. This most important of living Russian authors has already been naturalized in French literature for a number of years. One of his minor works, "The Cossacks," appeared in an English translation ten or twelve years ago. His work entitled "My Religion," which has been called a Russian "Ecce Homo," has been translated quite recently, and was noticed in the January number of *The Dial*. The work to which we now call attention is of much more importance than either of these others, and for the first time enables English readers to form an estimate of one of the most extraordinary of living writers.

The author of this work is so little known to English readers that a brief sketch of his life may be given as a preliminary. Leo Nikolaievitch, Count Tolstoï, was born in the year 1828. He was educated, first at home, and then at the university of Kasan, where he applied himself to the study of oriental languages. Temperament marked him out for a recluse, and he soon returned to his country home. With the exception of ten years of active life, he has resided upon his estates ever since. These ten years, 1851–61, however, were marked by that active intercourse with men which is needful, even to the recluse, if his reflections are to have substantial worth, and to influence the life and thought of practical men. His plunge into the world of affairs was abruptly made and abruptly ended. In 1851 he entered the military service, was engaged in the Turkish war of 1853–56, left the service at its close, lived for five years alternately in St. Petersburg and Moscow, and then, enriched by his varied experiences, retired to his birthplace, where he still lives. During his years of military service he occupied himself with literature, "The Cossacks," among other works, dating from this period. His literary fame rests chiefly upon two great romances: *War and Peace*, published in 1860, and *Anna Karenine*, published in 1875–77. It is the former of these that our attention is now called. It is to be added that the author should not be confused with the dramatic poet, Alexis Tolstoï, nor with the present reactionary minister of public instruction, Dimitri Tolstoï.

War and Peace has been called a Russian "Human Comedy." It is not often that a single book presents so comprehensive a picture of an epoch in national history as this book presents of Russian society during the Napoleonic period. It begins in the year 1805, and the first part (which is all that is thus far translated) reaches to the Peace of Tilsit in 1807. The second part carries on the national history, and the fortunes of the fictitious characters of the romance as well, through the period of French invasion and retreat. The writer's military experience enables him to treat

*From the *Dial* 6 (March 1886):299–300.

with great vividness and precision the campaign of Austerlitz and the scenes preceding and following the French occupation of Moscow. At the same time his penetrative insight coupled with his keen observant faculties enable him to depict with rare sincerity the manifold aspects of Russian private life in the early years of the century. The writer of historical romance, and especially the one who narrates the course of battles, has the choice of two methods, both well approved. He can write from the standpoint of the philosophic observer, who has studied the facts and reduced them to a system, or he can write from the standpoint of the participant, who decries but dimly the issues concerned in the struggle, and sees only what is going on in his immediate vicinity. These diverse methods are well illustrated by two famous descriptions of the battle of Waterloo — that of Victor Hugo in *Les Misérables*, and that of Stendhal in *La Chartreuse de Parme*. Count Tolstoï's method is the latter of these. He takes us to the field of Austerlitz, and we see the battle with the eyes of those who are contesting it. Of the struggle as a whole, we receive only the confused ideas of a few individuals who are engaged in it, but the loss of perspective is compensated for by the vividness of those scenes at which we thus play the part of actual spectators. After all, it is peace rather than war to which our attention is chiefly called. In this rich and complex symphony of interwoven human relations, the great national stir of resistance appears as the bass, always present, but only at intervals giving to the movement its dominant character. So various are the types of character which appear, and so shifting are the scenes, that we do not feel at home among them until we are well along in the story. Having reached the point at which they seem familiar, it would not be a bad idea to begin over again. The work is certainly open to criticism upon this point. It attempts to do more than any single work ought to attempt, and a certain confusion is inevitable. Our state of mind is that of a visitor in a strange country, who is introduced to all sorts of people and hurried from place to place with hardly time to look around and get his bearings. After a while the surroundings become intelligible, and he begins to understand the relations of these people to each other. But the novelist ought to do more than reproduce this common experience. He ought to smooth the way, and make the world of his creation more intelligible than the everyday world in which we actually live. All this, however, does not prevent the work of Count Tolstoï from being very remarkable, and, what with the reader of jaded appetites is more to the point, very stimulating in its fresh novelty.

Tolstoï and the Russian Invasion
of the Realm of Fiction

Joseph Kirkland*

In *The Dial* (March and May, 1886), parts one and two of *War and Peace* are briefly noticed, and a short sketch is given of their author. Now have appeared (in English translation) part three of the same wonderful work, and also three of the earlier works of Tolstoï: "Childhood," "Boyhood," and "Youth," the three bound together and forming a connected series. Of them the translator says:

"That these memoirs reflect the man in his mental and moral youth, there can be no doubt; but they do not strictly conform to facts in other respects, and therefore merit the title which he gives them, novels."

Novels they are not. They lack a love-story or other plot, and a heroine; and they are without even a hero, unless we accept a thoughtless child, a bad boy, and an absurdly egotistical youth, as the hero. Pictures of Russian real life, they are — perfect pictures. The only open question is, are the subjects worth the canvas?

If there existed in this 19th century such a portrayal of English life in the 9th or any earlier century, its value would be simply inestimable. Hence we may conclude that such photographic views as these given to the world by the new school of "realism" will live through the ages, growing in value as they grow in years. As long as a copy of Tolstoï shall survive, the world need never be ignorant of what life meant in Russia when the nobles owned the serfs body and soul, and the Czar owned all. Meanwhile the question of current value must be settled by each reader largely according to his personal bias.

The boy's life begins in the country and is early transferred to Moscow. He finally, before the narrative closes, enters the university, where, through folly and bad guidance, he becomes dissipated, and fails in his examination for the second year's course. Everything, in the country and in the city, is detailed with the minuteness of a mosaic.

As a specimen of life-like detail, take these from among the earliest recollections of the Narrator:

"On the other side of the door . . . was the corner where we were put on our knees." (As a punishment.) "How well I remember that corner! I remember the stove-door, and the slide in it, and the noise this made when it was turned. You would kneel and kneel in that corner until your knees and back ached, and you would think, 'Karl Ivanitch has forgotten me. . . .' And then you would begin to hint of your existence, to softly open and shut the damper, or pick the plaster from the wall; but if too big a piece suddenly fell noisily to the floor the fright was worse than the

*Review of *Childhood, Boyhood, and Youth*, trans. Isabel Hapgood, and part 3 of *War and Peace*, trans. Clara Bell. From the *Dial* 6 (August 1886):79–81.

whole punishment. You would peep round at Karl Ivanitch; and there he sat, book in hand, as though he had not noticed anything."

Here is another typical bit:

"I knew, myself, not only that I could not kill a bird with my stick, but that it was impossible to fire it off. That was what the game consisted in. If you judge things in that fashion, then it is impossible to ride on chairs; but, thought I, Volodya himself must remember how, on long winter evenings, we covered an armchair with a cloth, and made a calash out of it, while one mounted as coachman, the other as footman, and the girls sat in the middle, with three chairs for a troika of horses, and we set out on a journey. And how many adventures happened on the way! And how merrily and swiftly the winter evenings passed! Judging by the present standard, there would be no games. And if there were no games, what is left?"

To show the boldness of the writer in treating of a boy's development, and also (by a side-light) the relation borne by female serfs to their masters, we will venture on one more excerpt from "Youth." (Volodya is the elder brother of the autobiographer.)

> But not one of the changes which took place in my views of things was so surprising to me myself as that in consequence of which I ceased to regard one of our maids as a female servant, and began to regard her as a woman. . . . . Mascha was twenty-five when I was fourteen; she was very pretty, . . . remarkably white, luxuriantly developed. . . . Some one in slippers was ascending the next turn of the stairs . . . the sound of the footsteps suddenly ceased and I heard Mascha's voice: 'Now, what are you playing pranks for? Will it be well when Marya Ivanovna comes?' "She won't come," said Volodya's voice in a whisper, and then there was some movement as if he had attempted to detain her. "Now what are you doing with your hands, you shameless fellow!" And Mascha ran past me with her neckerchief pushed one side, so that her plump white neck was visible beneath it.

The tiresomeness of an egotistical youth is graphically conveyed by the simple process of making the record of his mean thoughts and lying words tiresome to the reader. He talks—and talks—and talks—about himself and others, through 380 pages, and even then only reaches his seventeenth year. It is realistic—photographic—almost microscopic. But on the whole it reminds the reader of the Preraphaelite who wanted to paint the Rocky mountains life-size.

The translator has left some rugged spots which suggest the difficulties he has overcome in other places.

Now, turning to the closing part of *War and Peace*, we encounter the same minuteness; but being here applied to huge historical events, and personages whose very names make the blood boil, it is almost beyond criticism. Napoleon, Koutousow, Borodino, Moscow, the practical annihilation of 400,000 invaders: this is the theme; and dullness is not possible to it in the hands of Tolstoï.

Where graphic detail is the pride and glory of the work, it becomes extremely difficult even to indicate its quality, as a whole, by quotation. One might get a fair idea of it by reading, entire, the chapters devoted to the awful day of Borodino — the day when Napoleon's star left the zenith, on its way toward its setting. You pass the night preceeding the battle in the very tent with Napoleon: you hear him complain of his cold — blow his nose — rail at all doctors and all medicine — moralize on the art of war. You see him rubbed down, like a horse, by his valets. You see him drink his rum punch; and you go forth with him before dawn to peer into the darkness and listen to the firing of the first gun.

Thenceforth, all day long, you watch the hideous struggle; not with the free, roving glance of the historian, but with the shuddering eyes of a participant. Here and there, first on one side and then on the other, among the cavalry, the infantry, the artillery, the staff, you ride, you run, you walk: and when darkness has fallen, you spend the night in a hospital, with its sobs and groans and stenches. If you are a civilian it is all, probably, only the spectacle of a fine panorama: and you hail it as "glorious!" If you have ever seen the actuality, you are more likely, as you read this, to say to yourself once more, "Accursed be battles, and those who cause them to be fought!"

Here is a hospital scene which illustrates Tolstoï's fine boldness. (In the book it fills many pages. Want of space compels its injury by omissions.)

> Prince André was laid on an operating table that had just been cleared; a surgeon was sponging it down. The cries and moans, on one hand, and the agonizing pain he felt in his back, paralyzed his faculties. Everything was mixed up into one single impression of naked, blood-stained flesh filling the low tent. . . The further table was surrounded with people. A tall, strongly built man was stretched upon it, his head thrown back; there was something familiar to Prince André in the color of his curling hair, and the shape of his head. Several hospital attendants were leaning on him with all their weight to keep him from stirring. One leg, fat and white, was constantly twitching with a convulsive movement, and his whole body shook with violent and choking sobs. . . . Prince André felt himself in the hands of the attendant. . . . The surgeon bent down and examined his wound and sighed deeply; then he called another to help him, and the next instant Prince André lost consciousness from the intense agony he suddenly felt. When he came to himself, the pieces of his broken ribs, with the torn flesh still clinging to them, had been extracted from his wound, and it had been dressed. He opened his eyes, the doctor bent over him, kissed him silently and went away, without looking back. After that fearful torture, a feeling of indescribable comfort came over him. His fancy reverted to

the happy days of infancy, especially those hours when, after he had been undressed and put into his little bed, his old nurse had sung him to sleep. . . . The surgeons were still busy over the man he fancied he had recognized; they were supporting him in their arms and trying to soothe him. "Show it to me—show it to me," he said; fairly crying with pain. . . . . They showed him his amputated leg, with the blood-stained boot still on it. "Oh!" he exclaimed and wept as bitterly as a woman.

André recognizes him as a man who had grievously wronged him— had stolen his lady-love.

Prince André remembered everything; and tender pitifulness rose up in his heart, which was full of peace. He could not restrain tears of compassion and charity, which flowed for all humanity, for himself, for his own weakness, and for that of this hapless creature.

A fine smile is made by Tolstoï, when, in moralizing on the Moscow campaign, he compares the combatants to two swordsmen, of whom the attacked and defeated one, sorely wounded, kills his assailant with a club. Perhaps the greatest literary triumph of the whole work is the picture of Napoleon, at Moscow, publishing conciliatory addresses to the people whom he has defeated; and sinking into helpless despair as they repay his smiles with frowns and his futile blessings with curses.

The difficulty in realistic novel-writing (more even than in the other kind) is in knowing what to omit. Much detail is good. Too much detail is intolerable. Tolstoï seems sometimes to lose the sense of perspective. If it is in the painting of nature, he begins the description of a day with such minuteness that the reader expects a great event to make it memorable—a battle, a crime, a betrothal or marriage or death of a hero or heroine;— and when he finds that the appearance of that day is all there is of it, he feels himself fooled, and regrets that he broke the good general rule which is, to skip all scenery. So if it is a person, the words given to his characterization should be in proportion to the part he has to play.

In such places the author's fancy runs away with him. Also when he mounts a hobby; as, for instance, when he writes whole chapters on Free Masonry: chapters which no man except a Free Mason will dream of reading. The general result tends toward the overloading of the book with characters—the picture with elaborated accessories. Except the historic personages, and the heroes, heroines and villains of the chief plot, one confuses the characters together—hypocrites, buffoons, fools, statesmen, grannies, faithless wives, serfs;—one needs a "cast of the play" always in hand to identify them as their names appear, especially under the Russian system of multiplicity of titles and nicknames.

As to "perspective," it should be observed (when we criticise dialogues apparently superfluous and tiresome) that this is a translation—perhaps a double translation. Scenes of social life which in the original were doubtless droll, gay, scintillating with light and color, come to us shorn of grace and flavor—the fragments of a foreign feast. It is only solids which bear handling and transportation unharmed. Bones can survive mummification, while features perish. Austerlitz is as interesting in one language as another: the fun of a Russian soirée becomes a bore in an English translation.

War and Peace, here concluded, consists of three two-volume novels—some 2,000 duodecimo pages altogether—and is a work few men or women can willingly lay down after they have fairly begun to read. No one who loves either romance or history can afford to pass it by. It is the turning of a splendid two-sided tapestry, and the studying of its picture with action and colors reversed. Consciously, it is a fearful arraignment of Napoleonism. Unconsciously, it is a more terrible arraignment of all despotism; especially military despotism.

These Russian novels mark an era in literature. The romantic and the realistic are engaged in a life-and-death struggle. It is their Waterloo, and lo, in the eastern horizon appears a Blücher, with a force which must decide the battle in favor of realism. The Old Guard hurls itself on the foe—it is taken in flank and must perish if it cannot surrender. It seems that for the present literary generation the victory is won and the war virtually over. Photographic exactitude in scene-painting—phonographic literalness in dialogue—telegraphic realism in narration—these are the new canons for the art of fiction. Whether this is a novelty or only a restoration, it were bootless to inquire. Kismet—it is fate. Perhaps the height of art is shown by a return to nature. Certainly some of Tolstoï's "local color" (as he portrays the Patriarchs and bondsmen of wild Russia,) is *naïf* enough to remind the reader of the simplicity of the oldest of narratives: "And Abraham sat in his tent-door in the heat of the day."

Such books as Tolstoï's make the careful observer suspect that unless English fiction can shake off some of the iron trammels that bind it, it must yield all hope of maintaining its long-held supremacy.

Tolstoï's *War and Peace*   Anonymous*

With the appearance of the two compact volumes of the third part, Tolstoï's stupendous *War and Peace* at last is complete for English readers. The work is not new, it having been published first in Russian in 1860, and in French in 1884. Considered simply as an addition to recent English literature it is assuredly one of the most considerable events of the year—as important in its department as was the introduction to us of *Les Misérables*.

*Review of *War and Peace*, trans. Clara Bell. From *Literary World*, 16 October 1886, 348-49.

To those who are not freely conversant with literatures other than their own, it is often a misfortune that they are obliged to work backward, as it were, in the gradual acquaintance with the works of genius. In the case of Tolstoï, Mr. Huntington Smith's translation of *My Religion* no doubt gave the impulse in this country to the interest in him which has been excited within a few months, and which now seems likely to bring within reach what is really best in later Russian literature. Already the efforts of so able a scholar as Miss Hapgood have been turned in this direction, and we may expect that American letters will not now have cause to be ashamed of inadequate translation work. *My Religion* represents the latest development of the religious and philosophical system of Tolstoï — a man clearly stamped with the genius of his century, and without that suspicion of "charlatanism" which even those who admire him most have not been wholly able to deny in Hugo's make up. It is, furthermore, by no means certain that Tolstoï has come finally to his earthly Nirvana, beyond which there is no progress possible for him, as some would maintain since the appearance of *My Religion*. He is not an old man, being as yet only fifty-eight years of age, and for such minds as his, advance ends only with life itself. He has accepted the teachings of Christ implicitly, but rejects immorality; possibly, nay, probably, he will before long drop in this keystone of his arch!

Be all this as it may, *War and Peace* and the *Cossacks* (which we have not yet in English) do represent earlier phases of Tolstoï's existence; but all that *My Religion* has so far revealed may easily be prefigured in several characters of these earlier works. Much has already been said and more will continue to be said, in the heat of present enthusiasm, of Tolstoï the man, the moralist, the philosophical historian, the Christian communist. Before he has been thoroughly anatomized for the delectation of aesthetic criticism, there is yet a little space in which simple and healthy minds may rejoice over this fresh, strong vitality, which comes to us from that fascinating, because unknown, borderland of eastern and western civilization. Any translation is so welcome that we forbear to speak in particular of the failings of the present effort — though one has only to take the French version and find that in English *War and Peace* has been at times foully dealt with. Nevertheless, the worst second hand paraphrasing from Russian to French and from French to English cannot efface the brilliant effects of the original. And what pictures some of them are! The brutal bully Dologhow balanced on the lofty window-sill drinking off a bottle of rum for a trivial wager, the fascinating, weak, but really noble Pierre Besonkhow in his father's death room, the only honest soul there, the elopement of Natacha, the gleaming shoulders of Pierre's vile wife, those few awful seconds when Prince André speculated on the fateful shell which was to shatter him, the eternal calm of the peasant Platon, the most nearly perfect ideal of what Tolstoï now holds to! These and many more can never be forgotten, cannot even become dimmed in memory. Tolstoï's is no patent process in photography — it is rather the mirror of a river which suggests depths under its surface; the mirror truthfully reflects the objectivity of nature, but the reflection is subjective. It is much more than realism, for Tolstoï never could have come down so far as merely that. There are passages which to intelligences still unused to the savageries of an almost unintelligible semi-civilization must seem barbarous, but how different in all their sincerity from the horrors of such a book as *Salammbô*!

The chaos, the turbulence, the seeming incoherence of *War and Peace*, especially in the battle scenes, are felt to be like the unrest of life itself, even as the affairs of men and society appear to those who are in the mental condition in which Tolstoï found himself when he wrote. There are undoubtedly grave obstacles to those who decide to journey through this apparently fatalistic scheme of human existence; there are fair valleys and towering heights, but there are also *mauvaises terres*, wearisome perhaps beyond description, as there are in the course of daily life. This, then, is Tolstoï's accomplishment, the revivification, as it were, of humanity as it existed in Russia before and during the invasion of Napoleon.

The publisher has wisely put the work in the convenient form which is growing to be as pleasantly familiar as the volumes of the old Tauchnitz collection.

Articles and Essays

War and Peace

The present investigation is triggered by a fact of such enormous significance that one doubts one's ability to deal with it adequately. The details of this fact are as follows: In 1868 *War and Peace*, one of the best works of our literature, made its appearance. It was extraordinarily successful. It has been a long time since a book would be read with comparable eagerness. Moreover, this was a success of the highest order. *War and Peace* would be read attentively not only by ordinary lovers of the written word who still admire Dumas and Feval but by the most demanding readers, all those who, justifiably or not, can claim to be learned and educated; the book was read even by those who generally have nothing but contempt for Russian literature and never read anything in Russian. And because our readership grows every year, it came about that none of the classics of Russian literature, whether already successful or deserving of success, have sold so fast in such quantities as *War and Peace*. And let us add that none of the outstanding works of our literature can compare in size to the new work of Count L. N. Tolstoy.

Let us therefore attempt to analyze the fact that has come to pass. The success of *War and Peace* is an event of extraordinary simplicity and clarity, free of any complexity and confusion. This success cannot be attributed to any extraneous, irrelevant causes. Count Tolstoy did not try to lure his readers with any complex and mysterious adventures or descriptions of sordid and horrifying scenes, nor by depicting dreadful psychological torment or, lastly, some brash new tendencies; in a word, he used none of the tricks that provoke the readers' thought and imagination, morbidly stir curiosity with pictures of unknown, untried experience. Nothing could be simpler than the multitude of events depicted in *War and Peace*. All events of ordinary family life, conversations between brother and sister, mother and daughter, separation and reunion of kinfolk, the hunt, the celebration of Christmas and New Years, the mazurka, the card game, and so forth; all of this is made into a pearl of

*From *Kriticheskie stat'i ob I. S. Turgeneve i L. N. Tolstom, 1862-1885* [Critical articles about I. S. Turgenev and L. N. Tolstoy, 1862-1885], 3d ed. (St. Petersberg, 1895), 234-70. Translated from the Russian for this volume by Boris Sorokin.

creation with the same love that went into the description of the Borodino battle. Ordinary objects occupy in *War and Peace* as much space as did the immortal descriptions of the life of the Larins, winter, spring, and the trip to Moscow, in *Eugene Onegin*.

True, besides this Tolstoy also depicts great events and persons of great historical significance. But under no circumstances can it be said that it was these events and persons who have aroused the general interest of the readers. Even if there were some readers who were attracted by the depiction of historical events, or even the feeling of patriotism, there can be no doubt that there were many of those who do not in the least like to look for history in works of literature, or are prejudiced against any attempt to engage their patriotic feeling, yet who, nevertheless read *War and Peace* with the liveliest of interest. Let us remark, besides, that *War and Peace* is by no means a historical novel, that is, does not in the least intend to make historical persons into heroes of the novel and, by telling their exploits, to combine the interest of a novel with history.

The matter, then, is clean and clear. Whatever goals and intentions the author may have had, whatever lofty and important subjects he may have touched, the success of his work does not depend on these intentions and subjects but on what he did, guided by such goals and touching upon these subjects, that is, on the *high level of artistic execution*.

If Tolstoy achieved his goals, if he compelled everyone to direct their eyes upon that which occupied his soul, he did so only because he was in complete command of his tool, art. In this connection the case of *War and Peace* is most instructive. There were hardly many who realized what the thinking was all about that guided and inspired the author, but everyone is equally impressed by his creative work. People who approached this book with preconceived notions, with the idea to find a contradiction of their own tendency or its confirmation, often were puzzled, did not have the time to decide what to do, to be indignant or elated, but everyone equally acknowledged the extraordinary skill of the mysterious work. It has been a long time since art has revealed its triumphant, irresistible potential to such a degree.

But artistic ability does not come free. Let no one think that it can exist apart from profound thoughts and profound feelings, that it can be a phenomenon less than serious, devoid of important meaning. In this instance one must separate true artistry from its false and distorted forms. Let us try to analyze the artistry that we have found in Tolstoy's book and we shall see what depth lies at its foundation.

What was it that astounded everyone in *War and Peace*? Of course it was the objectivity, vividness. One would be hard pressed to visualize images more sharp, colors more vivid. It is as if one were to see with one's own eyes all that is being described, to hear the sounds of all that is going on. The author tells nothing from his own point of view: he directly brings out persons and makes them speak, feel, and act, whereby every word and every movement rings true to an amazingly accurate degree, that is, it fully bears the character of the person to whom it belongs. It is as if one were to deal with living people and see them much more clearly than one is able to see in real life. One can discern not only the modes of expression and feelings that distinguish every protagonist, but even his mannerisms, favorite gestures, his gait. The dignified Prince Vasily once, under difficult and unusual circumstances, had to walk on tiptoe; the author knows to perfection how every one of his protagonists walks. "Prince Vasily," he says, "did not know how to walk on tiptoe and awkwardly moved his entire body in little jerks." The author is aware with the same degree of precision and clarity of all movements, all feelings and thoughts of his heroes. Once he has made them appear on the scene, he no longer interferes in their affairs, does not help them, letting each one of them behave in accord with his nature.

The very same desire to maintain objectivity is responsible for the fact that Tolstoy has no images or descriptions made from his own point of view. Nature appears only in the way it is reflected in the actions of the protagonists; he does not describe the oak that stands in the middle of the path, or the moonlit night during which Natasha and Prince Andrei were unable to sleep but describes the impression this oak and this night made upon Prince Andrei. Just so, battles and happenings of all kinds are told not according to the conceptions formed about them by the author but according to the impressions of people who participated in them. The Schoengraben action is described mostly on the basis of Prince Andrei's impressions; the battle of Austerlitz on the basis of Nikolai Rostov's impressions; the arrival of Emperor Alexander in Moscow is reflected in Petja's excitement, and the effect of the prayer to save Russia from the invasion is depicted in Natasha's feelings. In this way, the author nowhere appears from behind his protagonists, and depicts events not in abstractions but with the flesh and blood of those people who contributed materially to the events.

In this respect *War and Peace* represents veritable marvels of artistry. It captures not just individual features but the entire atmosphere that varies around different persons and in different layers of society. The author himself speaks of the *loving and familial atmosphere* in the house of Rostov; but remember other depictions of the same kind: the atmosphere surrounding Speransky; the atmosphere surrounding the Rostov *uncle*; the atmosphere of the opera in which Natasha found herself; the atmosphere of the military hospital which Rostov entered. Persons who enter one of these atmospheres or move from one to another, invariably feel its effect, and we experience it with them. . . .

What is the outstanding feature of Tolstoy's talent? It must be his ability to depict the movements within the psyche with extraordinary accuracy and precision. One might call Tolstoy primarily a *psychological realist*. He has made a reputation for himself in his previous works as an amazing master in the skill of analyzing all kinds of psychological changes and conditions. This analysis, which was at times pursued with a certain impassioned bias, sometimes became picayune, acquired a tense, incorrect slant. In the new work all these excesses have been eliminated, while leaving intact all of his previous precision and discernment; The artist's powers found their limits and settled within their shores. His whole attention is now focused on the human soul. He has few brief and incomplete descriptions of the surroundings, costumes, in a word, the entire outer side of life; on the other hand, he never misses the opportunity to describe the impression and the effect of this outer side on the soul of people; but the center of attention is on their inner life, for which the outer one serves only as a stimulus or its imperfect expression. The smallest shadings of psychic life, as well as its most staggering disturbances are expressed with equal clarity and truthfulness. The feeling of boredom after the holidays in the Otradnoe house of the Rostovs, and the feelings of the entire Russian army in the midst of the Borodino battle, the youthful excitement of Natasha, and the senile agitation of old Bolkonsky who is losing his memory and is about to have a stroke, all this is bright, vivid, and accurate in Tolstoy's narrative.

So, this is where the author's entire interest is concentrated and, because of that, the entire interest of the reader as well. No matter what huge and important events take place, be it the Kremlin, overflowing with people because of the sovereign's visit, or the meeting of the emperors, or a terrible battle with the roar of cannons and thousands dying, nothing distracts the author, and with him the reader, from peering intently into the inner world of individual characters. It is as if the artist is not at all concerned with the event, but only with how the human psyche reacts to it, what it feels and contributes to the event.

Ask yourself, what then is the author looking for? What kind of stubborn curiosity forces him to follow the slightest sensations of all those people, beginning with Napoleon and Kutuzov and on to those little girls whom Prince Andrei encountered in his own devastated garden?

There is only one answer: the artist is looking for traces of beauty in the human soul, he looks in every person he depicts for that divine spark which represents his human dignity, in a word, the author tries to find and define with utmost accuracy in what way and to what extent the ideal aspirations of man are realized in daily life.

II

It is very difficult to explain, even in broad outline, the main idea of a profound work of art; the idea is embodied in the work in so full and many faceted a fashion that an abstract description of it will always be something inadequate, less than accurate, it will not, as they say, exhaust the subject.

One could formulate the idea of *War and Peace* in a number of ways.

One could say, for example, that the leading thought of the novel is *the idea of heroic life*. The author himself hints at this when, in the midst of the Borodino battle he makes the following remark: "The ancients have left us models of heroic poems wherein the entire *interest of history* is contained in *the heroes*, and we still cannot get used to the fact that for our times such a history makes no sense."

In this way the artist directly asserts that he wants to depict for us a life that we would describe as heroic, but to depict it as it is, and not in those incorrect images that have been bequeathed to us by the antiquity; he wants to wean us away from these false images and presents us therefore with correct ones. Instead of the ideal we are getting the real.

So, where is one to look for the heroic life? In history, of course. We are used to thinking that people upon whom history depends, who make history, are heroes. Therefore the artist's thought is focusing on the year 1812 and the preceding wars, as on a primarily heroic epoch. If Napoleon, Kutuzov, Bagration, are not heroes, who is, after all? Tolstoy chose to depict a sequence of vast historical events, an awesome national struggle, in order to catch the superior manifestations of that which we call heroism.

But nowadays, as Tolstoy writes, heroes alone do not exhaust the interest of history. No matter how we understand heroic life, it is necessary to define the ways in which ordinary life is related to it, and this is even the main problem. What is an ordinary person compared to a hero? What is a private person in relation to history? In a general sense, this is the same question that has been dealt with for a long time by our realism: what is the relation of everyday life to the ideal, beautiful life?

Tolstoy has attempted to answer this question as completely as possible. He has depicted for us, for example, Bagration and Kutuzov in amazing, incomparable glory. It is as if they were able to rise above anything human. This is especially obvious in the case of Kutuzov, who is depicted as weak with age, a lazy old man of deplorable moral habits who has kept, in the words of the author, "only the old habits of lust but was devoid of any of the lustful passions themselves." Bagration and Kutuzov, whenever they begin to function as national heroes, lose everything personal about them: expressions such as bravery, restraint, or calm are hardly applicable to them — they are not really being brave, restrained, tense, or calm. Simply and naturally they do their job as though they were disembodied spirits, lucid and dispassionate, able only to know and be guided unerringly by the purest motives of duty and honor. They look straight in the face of destiny and the very thought of fear is denied them, they cannot have any hesitation in action, because they do *all they can*, otherwise submitting to the course of events and their own human frailty.

But beyond these lofty spheres of valor that reach their upper limits, the artist depicts for us that entire world where the demands of duty struggle with all the turmoil of the human passions. He has depicted for us *all kinds of bravery, and all kinds of cowardice.* What a distance there is between the initial panic of junker Rostov and the brilliant bravery of Denisov, the firm valor of Prince Andrei, or the unconscious bravery of Captain Tushin! All the sensations and forms of battle, from panic, fear, and running during the Austerlitz battle to the invincible fortitude and bright burning of *the hidden inner fire* at Borodino, are depicted for us by the artist. These people appear before us now as *scoundrels,* as Kutuzov called the running soldiers, now as fearless, selfless warriors. In substance, though, they are simple people, and the artist has shown with an astonishing skill how, in varying degrees and measure, in the heart of each one of them is kindled, dims, then brightens again, the spark of bravery that is innate in every man.

And the main thing is, we are shown what all these souls mean in the course of history, what they contribute to the great events, what is their contribution to the heroic life. We are shown that emperors and military leaders are truly great only if and when they can learn to function as such quasi nuclei in which a heroism that lives in simple and unenlightened souls, tends to concentrate. To understand this heroism, to be able to empathize with it and believe in it, this is what makes men such as Bagration and Kutuzov great. Inability to understand it, disregard of, or even contempt for it constitute the wretchedness and the smallness of men like Barclay-de-Tolly and Speransky.

War, affairs, and calamities of state constitute the field of history, a field that is heroic in the main. After having depicted with faultless veracity how people behave, what they feel and do in that field, the artist, to complete his thought, also wanted to depict for us the same people in their private sphere, where they appear simply as people. "Meanwhile life," he writes in one passage, "*the real life* of people with its substantial interests of health, sickness, work, leisure, with its intellectual, scientific, poetic, musical interests, its concerns of love, friendship, hate, passions, went on, as always, independent and outside of political proximity or enmity with Napoleon Bonaparte, and outside all possible reforms."

What constitutes human dignity? How is one to understand the meaning of the life of all those men, from the strongest and the most brilliant, down to the weakest and most insignificant ones, so that one does not overlook its most salient ingredient, the human soul?

To this formulation we have found a hint of an answer in the words of the author himself. In his discussion of the insignificant role played by Napoleon in the battle of Borodino, and the participation of every soldier in it with all his heart, the author remarks: "*human dignity informs me* that every one of us is, if not more, in any *case no less of a man than the great Napoleon* himself."

So, the artist's broadest goal is to depict that which makes every man no less of a person than the next one, that which makes the simple soldier

Napoleon's equal, a stupid blockhead the equal of a most brilliant man, in a word, that which we must respect in every man, in which his value resides. To achieve this goal, he depicted great men, great events, and next to them the adventures of Junker Rostov, the salons of the *beau monde* as well as the country life of the Rostov uncle, Napoleon, and the janitor Ferapontov. For the same reason he told us about the family quarrels of simple, weak people and the strong passions of brilliant, richly endowed natures, he depicted expressions of nobility and generosity as well as pictures of greatest human frailties.

The dignity of human beings is hidden from us by their various shortcomings, or because we overvalue other characteristics, and therefore, value people according to the presence in them of wit, beauty, strength, and so forth. The poet teaches us to break through these superficialities. What can be simpler, more common, more humble than the characters of Nikolai Rostov and Princess Mary? They excel in nothing, can do nothing well, in no way are they distinct from the most basic level of the most ordinary people; and yet these ordinary creatures who, without a struggle, follow the simplest path in life, are obviously beautiful creatures. The irresistible charm, with which the artist has endowed these two persons who appear to be so insignificant, but in substance are not inferior to anyone in inner beauty, this charm points to one of the outstanding accomplishments of *War and Peace*. Nikolai Rostov is obviously a man of a very limited mental capacity; but, as the author remarks in one place, "he had the common sense of a mediocrity that showed him *what had to be done.*"

And indeed, Nikolai does many stupid things, does not understand people or circumstances, but he always understands *what has to be done*; and this priceless wisdom in all cases preserves the purity of his simple and hotheaded nature.

Shall we speak of Princess Mary? Despite all her shortcomings, this image reaches an almost angelic purity and meekness; and occasionally one imagines that it is surrounded by a halo.

At this moment we are mortified by the dreadful picture of the relationship between the elder Bolkonsky and his daughter. If Nikolai Rostov and Princess Mary are obviously engaging characters, it seems impossible to forgive the old man for the suffering his daughter has to endure from him. Of all the personages depicted by the artist, no one, apparently, deserves greater condemnation. But then, what is the situation? With consummate skill, the author has depicted for us one of the worst and most pathetic human frailties — one that is impervious to assault by either mind or will — and one that deserves our most sincere pity. Actually the old man is dissolved in boundless devotion to his daughter — he literally *cannot live without her*; but this love has become perverted in his heart into a desire to inflict pain upon himself and his love object. He is constantly tugging at this inseparable bond that links him to his daughter, and in so doing, finds morbid pleasure in *such* feeling of being bound to her. All shadings of this strange relationship are caught by Tolstoy with incredible accuracy and the denouement — when the old man, broken by illness and near death, expresses at last all his tenderness for his daughter — makes a profoundly moving impression.

The strongest, purest feeling can be perverted to such a degree! People can inflict upon themselves such suffering through their own fault! One can hardly imagine a picture that would prove more conclusively that man is sometimes totally unable to control himself. The relations between the dignified old man Bolkonsky and his son and daughter, based in a jealous and perverted sense of love represent that evil, which often is found in intimate family relationships, and proves to us that the holiest and most natural feelings can acquire an insane and savage character.

Nevertheless, these feelings are at the root of the matter, and their perversion must not hide from us their pure source. And during a shattering experience, their true nature often comes fully to the fore: in dying, old Bolkonsky is overwhelmed by love for his daughter.

To see what is hidden in the soul of man under the play of passions, under all forms of selfishness, greed, animal desires — this is what Tolstoy knows how to do brilliantly. Pathetic, unwise, and disgraceful are the things that transport people like Pierre Bezukhov and Natasha Rostov; but the reader sees that behind all that, these are people *with a golden heart*, and will not doubt for a moment that whenever self-sacrifice is needed, and a response to that which is beautiful and good, they will both respond wholeheartedly and readily. Pierre is a child in an adult's frame, huge of body, and terrible in his sensuality, impractical and unreasonable like a child, with a childlike purity and tenderness of heart joined to a soaring intellect. His is a character for whom all meanness is not only alien but incomprehensible. This is a man who, like a child, is afraid of nothing, and knows of no evil in himself. Natasha is a girl gifted with such a full inner life that (as Pierre puts it) *she does not deign to be clever*, that is, has neither the time nor the inclination to translate this life into abstractions. This immense fullness of life (which leads her sometimes into a *state of intoxication* as the author puts it), leads her into a terrible mistake, a mad passion for Kuragin, a mistake that is later atoned for by great suffering. Pierre and Natasha are people who, due to their very nature, must suffer mistakes and disappointments in life. As if to provide a contrast to them, the author has also depicted the happy couple: Vera Rostov and Adolf Berg, people who are strangers to any mistakes and disappointments, and know how to arrange their lives quite comfortably. One cannot help being bemused by the degree of pettiness with which the author endows these heartless creatures who are depicted mercilessly, yet without a hint of derision or anger. This is true realism, true authenticity. The same authenticity is found in the depiction of the Kuragins, Hélène and

Anatôle; these heartless creatures, too, are depicted mercilessly, yet without a hint of a desire to castigate them.

What kind of an effect has this pure even daylight, which the author shines upon his picture? We see neither classical villains, nor classical heroes; the human psyche appears before us in an extraordinarily wide variety of types: it appears weak, subject to passions and circumstances, but, in essence, motivated by pure and good aspirations. Among all this variety of persons and events we feel the presence of certain firm and unshakable foundations upon which life stands: family, social, and conjugal obligations as well as concepts of good and evil. Having depicted with the greatest authenticity the false life of the uppermost layers of society and various headquarters that surround highly placed persons, the author has juxtaposed them to two firm and truly alive spheres: family life and the real military life, that is, army life. Two families, the Bolkonskys and the Rostovs, represent for us a life that is guided by clear, positive values to comply with which, members of these families consider themselves duty and honor bound, and from which they derive their dignity and satisfaction. In the same way, army life (which in one place Tolstoy compares with paradise) presents us with a firm code of duties and human dignity; so that the simpleminded Nikolai Rostov at one time even preferred to remain with his regiment, and not to go home to his family where he could not clearly see his way to behaving himself.

In this way Russia in 1812 is depicted for us in clear, bold strokes, as a mass of people who know what their human dignity demands of them, what they must do with regard to themselves and others as well as their country. Tolstoy's entire narrative depicts merely all kinds of struggles which this sense of duty must endure against the passions and contingencies of life, as well as the struggle which this strong, most populous layer of Russian society must sustain against the upper, false, and insubstantial layer. The year 1812 was a moment when the lower layer got the upper hand and, because of its strength, withstood Napoleon's assault. All this is very clearly reflected, for example, in the actions and thoughts of Prince Andrei, who left the headquarters for regimental duty and, talking to Pierre on the eve of the Borodino battle, keeps being reminded of his father who was killed by the news of the invasion. It is feelings like those of Prince Andrei that saved Russia at the time. "The French have desecrated *my home*," he says, "and are going to desecrate Moscow. They have insulted me, and are continuing to insult me every second. They are my enemies, they are all criminals in my view."

After this and similar talks, Pierre, as the author says, "began to understand the entire meaning and significance of this war and the forthcoming battle."

This war was, on the Russian side, a defensive war and, therefore, had a holy and national character; whereas on the French side it was offensive, aggressive, and unjust. At Borodino all other considerations and relations were erased and nonexistent; two nations were facing each other, an aggressor and a defender. The relative strength of the two ideas that at this time moved the two nations and put them into the given situation emerged with the greatest clarity. The French appeared as the representatives of a cosmopolitan idea, capable in the name of general principles of resorting to violence, genocide; the Russians appeared as the representatives of the national idea, which defends lovingly the spirit and character of a spontaneously, organically formed way of life. Thus the question of national integrity was put forward at the Borodino field, and the Russians decided it here for the first time in favor of nationalism.

It is obvious why Napoleon did not, and never could understand what happened at the Borodino field; it is obvious that he should have been confounded by apprehension and fear in the face of an unexpected and unknown force that rose against him. Since the matter was, after all, apparently quite simple and clear, it is understandable, in the last analysis, why the author found himself entitled to say about Napoleon the following things:

> And it was not only in this hour and day that *the mind and conscience of this man were benighted*, a man who, more than anyone else among the participants in this affair, bore the responsibility for what happened here, for never, in the rest of his life *could he understand neither the good, nor beauty, or justice* or significance of his actions, which were too opposed to goodness and justice, too far removed from all that is human, for him to comprehend their meaning. He could not repudiate his actions, praised by half the world, and therefore had to *repudiate justice and goodness, and with them all* of mankind.

So, this is one of the final conclusions: in Napoleon, this superhero, the author sees merely a man who has sunk so low morally that he has lost all true human dignity—a man afflicted with a benighted mind and conscience. The proof is there for all to see. As Barclay-de-Tolly was denigrated, once and for all, by his inability to understand the meaning of the Borodino battle; as Kutuzov rises above praise by the fact that he completely understood what was happening during that battle; so Napoleon is forever condemned by the fact that he could not understand the meaning of that simple, holy work that we did at Borodino and which every one of our soldiers understood. In an affair that so loudly proclaimed its meaning, Napoleon did not understand that justice was on our side. Europe wanted to strangle Russia and in its pride deluded itself that it acted beautifully and justly.

And so, it seems that the artist wanted to present us in the person of Napoleon with a human soul that has gone blind, wanted to show that a heroic life can sometimes contradict true human dignity, that goodness, truth, and beauty can be much more accessible to simple and little people than to some great heroes. The simple man, simple life, are placed by the poet above heroism, both in virtue and power.

[Body Imagery in Tolstoy]   Dmitri Merezhkovsky*

The Princess Volkonski, wife of Prince Andreï, as we learn from the first pages of Tolstoï's great novel *Peace and War*, was rather pretty, with a slight dark down on her upper lip, which was short to the teeth, but opened all the more sweetly, and still more sweetly lengthened at times and met the lower lip. For twenty chapters this lip keeps reappearing. Some months have passed since the opening of the story: "The little princess, who was *enceinte*, had meanwhile grown stout, but her eyes and the short downy lip and its smile, were curled up just as gaily and sweetly." And two pages later, "The princess talked incessantly: her short upper lip with its down constantly descended for a moment, touched at the right point the red lower one, and then again parted in a dazzling smile of eyes and teeth." The princess tells her sister-in-law, Prince Andreï's sister, Princess Maria, of the departure of her husband for the war. Princess Maria turns to her, with caressing eyes on her person; "Really?" The princess's face changed, and she sighed. "Yes, really!" she replied, "Ah, it is all very terrible!" and the lip of the little princess descended. In the course of one hundred and fifty pages we have already four times seen that upper lip with its distinguishing qualifications. Two hundred pages later we have again, "There was a general and brisk conversation, thanks to the voice and the smiling downy lip that rose above the white teeth of the little princess." In the second part of the novel she dies in a confinement. Prince Andreï entered his wife's room: she lay dead in the very attitude in which he had seen her five minutes before, and the same expression, in spite of the still eyes and the paleness of the cheeks, was on this charming child-like face with the lips covered with dark down. "I love you all, have harmed nobody. What have you done with me?" This takes place in the year 1805.

The war had broken out, and the scene of it was drawing near the Russian frontiers. In the midst of its dangers the author does not forget to tell us that over the grave of the little princess there had been placed a marble monument: an angel that had a slightly raised *upper lip*, and the expression which Prince Andreï had read on the face of his dead wife, "Why have you done this to me?"

Years pass. Napoleon has completed his conquests of Europe. He is already crossing the frontier of Russia. In the retirement of the Bare Hills, the son of the dead princess "grew up, changed, grew rosy, grew a crop of

*From *Tolstoi as Man and Artist with an Essay on Dostoievsky* (London, 1902), 165–78.

curly dark hair, and without knowing, smiling and gay, raised the *upper lip* of his well-shaped mouth just like the little dead princess." Thanks to these underlinings of one physical feature first in the living, then in the dead, and then again on the face of her statue and in her son the upper lip of the little princess is engraved on our memory with ineffaceable distinctness. We cannot remember her without also recalling that feature.

Princess Maria Volkonski, Prince Andreï's sister, has a heavy footstep which can be heard from afar. "They were the heavy steps of the Princess Maria." She came into the room "with her heavy walk, going on her heels." Her face "grows red in patches." During a delicate conversation with her brother about his wife, she "turned red in patches." When they are preparing to dress her up upon the occasion of the coming betrothed, she feels herself insulted: "she flashed out, and her face became flushed in patches."

In the following volume, in a talk with Pierre about his old men and beggars, about his "bedesmen," she becomes confused and "grew red in patches." Between these two last reminders of the patches of the princess, is the description of the battle of Austerlitz, the victory of Napoleon, the gigantic struggle of nations, events that decided the destiny of the world, yet the artist does not forget, and will not to the end, the physical trait he finds so interesting. We are forced to remember the glaring eyes, heavy footsteps, and red patches of the Princess Maria. True, these traits, unimportant as they may seem, are really bound up with deep-seated spiritual characteristics of the *dramatis personae*. The upper lip, now gaily tilted, now piteously dropped, expresses the childlike carelessness and helplessness of the little princess. The clumsy gait of the Princess Maria expresses an absence of external feminine charm; both the glaring eyes and the fact that she blushes in patches are connected with her inward womanly charm and spiritual modesty. Sometimes these stray characteristics light up a vast and complex picture, and give it startling clearness and relief.

At the time of the popular rising in deserted Moscow, before Napoleon's entry, when Count Rostopchin, wishing to allay the bestial fury of the crowd, points to the political criminal Verestchagain (who happened to be at hand and was totally innocent) as a spy, and the scoundrel who had ruined Moscow, the thin long neck and the general thinness, weakness and fragility of his frame of course express the defencelessness of the victim in face of the coarse mass of the crowd.

"Where is he?" said the Count, and instantly saw round the corner of a house a young man with a long thin neck coming out between two dragoons. He had "dirty, down at heel, thin boots. On his lean, weak legs the fetters clanked heavily. 'Bring him here,' said Rostopchin, pointing to the lower step of the *perron*. The young man, walking heavily to the step indicated, sighed with a humble gesture, crossed his thin hands, unused to work, before his body. 'Children,' said Rostopchin, in a metallic ringing voice, 'this man is Verestchagin, the very scoundrel that ruined Moscow.' Verestchagin raised his face and endeavoured to meet the Count's eyes, but he was not looking at him. On *the long thin neck* of the young man a vein behind the ear stood out like a blue cord. The people were silent, only pressed more closely together. 'Kill him! Let the traitor perish, and save from slur the Russian name,' cried Rostopchin. 'Count!' was heard saying amid the renewed stillness the timid yet theatrical voice of Verestchagin, 'Count, one God is above us.' And again the large vein in his *thin neck* was swollen with blood. One of the soldiers struck him with the flat of the sword on the head. Verestchagin, with a cry of terror, with outstretched hands plunged forward towards the people. A tall youth against whom he struck clung with his hands to his *thin neck* and with a wild cry, fell with him under the feet of the onrushing roaring populace." After the crime, the very people who committed it with hang-dog and piteous looks gazed on the dead body with the purple blood-stained and dusty face and the mangled *long thin neck*. Scarce a word of the inward state of the victim, but in five pages the word *thin* eight times repeated in various connexions — and this outward sign fully depicts the inward condition of Verestchagin in relation to the crowd. Such is the ordinary artistic resource of Tolstoi, from the seen to the unseen, from the external to the internal, from the bodily to the spiritual, or at any rate to the emotional.

Sometimes in these recurrent traits are implicated deeper fundamental ideas, main motives of the book. For instance, the weight of the corpulent general Kutuzov, his leisurely old man's slowness and want of mobility, express the apathetic, meditative stolidity of his mind, his Christian or more truly Buddhistic renunciation of his own will, the submission to the will of Fate or the God of this primitive hero; in the eyes of Tolstoi, a hero pre-eminently Russian and national, the hero of inaction or inertia. He is in contrast with the fruitlessly energetic, light, active, and self-confident hero of Western culture, Napoleon.

Prince Andreï watches the commander in chief at the time of the review of the troops at Tsarevoe Jaimishche: "Since Andreï had last seen him Kutuzov had grown still stouter and unwieldy with fat." An air of weariness was on his face and in his figure. "*Snorting and tossing heavily* he sat his charger." When after finishing the inspection he entered the court, on his face sat "the joy of a man set free, purposing to take his ease after acting a part. He drew his left leg out of the stirrup, rolling his whole body and, frowning from the effort, with difficulty raised it over the horse's back. Then he gasped and sank into the arms of supporting Cossacks and aides-de-camp; stepped out with a plunging gait and heavily ascended the staircase creaking under his weight." When he learns from Prince Andreï of the death of his father, he sighs "profoundly, heaving his whole chest, and is silent for a time." Then he "embraced Prince Andreï, pressed him to his stout chest, and for long would not let him go. When he did so, the prince saw that the swollen lips of Kutuzov quivered, and tears were in his eyes." He sighs, and grasping the bench with both hands to rise, rises heavily and *the folds of his swollen neck disappear*.

Even more profound is the significance of *rotundity* in the frame of another Russian hero, Platon Karataev. This rotundity typifies the eternal completeness of all that is simple, natural and artificial, a self-sufficing-ness, which seems to the artist the primary element of the Russian national genius. "Platon Karataev always remained in Pierre's mind as the strongest and dearest memory and personification of all that is Russian, good, and *rounded off*. When next day, at dawn, Pierre saw his neighbour, the first impression of something round was fully confirmed; the whole figure of Platon in his French cloak, with a cord girdle, a forage-cap and bast shoes, was *round*, the head was completely *round*, the back, the chest, the shoulders, even the arms, which he carried as if he was always going to lift something, all were *round*: the pleasant smile, and the great brown tender eyes were *round*. Pierre felt something "*round*, if one might strain language, *in the whole savour of the man*." Here, by one physical trait, carried to the last degree of geometrical simplicity and obviousness, is expressed a huge abstract generalization. Tolstoi's religion and metaphysics enter into the delineation by this single trait.

Similar deep expressiveness is given by him to the hands of Napoleon and Speranski, the hands of men that wield power. At the time of the meeting of the Emperors in face of the assembled armies, the former gives a Russian soldier the Legion of Honour, he "draws off the glove from his *white small hand*, and tearing it, throws it away." A few lines later, "Napoleon reaches back *his small plump hand*." Nicolai Rostov remembers "that self-satisfied Bonaparte with *his little white hand*." And in the next volume, when talking with the Russian diplomat Balashiev, Napoleon makes "an energetic gesture of inquiry with *his little white, plump hand*."

He sketches, too, the whole body of the Emperor, stripping the studious demi-god, till he stands, like other men, food for cannon.

In the morning, just before the battle of Borodino, the Emperor, in his tent, is finishing his toilette. "Snorting and panting, he turned, now his plump back, now his overgrown fatty chest to the brush with which the valet was rubbing him down. Another valet, holding the mouth of the bottle with his finger, was sprinkling the pampered little body with eau-de-cologne, with an air that said he alone could know how much and where to sprinkle. Napoleon's short hair was damp and hanging over his forehead. But his face, though bloated and yellow, expressed physical well-being. 'More now, harder now!' he cried, stretching and puffing, to the valet who was rubbing him, then bending and presenting his fat shoulders."

This white hand denotes the upstart hero who exploits the masses.

Speranski too, has white fat hands, in the description of which Tolstoi plainly somewhat abuses his favourite device of repetition and emphasis. "Prince Andreï watched all Speranski's movements; but lately he was an insignificant seminarist, and now in his hands, those white plump hands, he held the fate of Russia, as Volkonski reflected." "In no one had the Prince seen such delicate whiteness of the face, and still more the hands, which were rather large, but unusually plump, delicate and white. Such whiteness and delicacy of complexion he had only seen in soldiers who had been long in hospital." A littler later he again "looks involuntarily at the white delicate hands of Speranski, as men look generally at the hands of people in power. The mirror-like glance and the delicate hand somehow irritated prince Andreï."

The detail is repeated with unwearying insistence till in the long run this white hand begins to haunt one like a spectral being.

In comparing himself with Pushkin as an artist, Tolstoi said to Bers that the difference between them, amongst other things, was this, that Pushkin in depicting a characteristic detail does it lightly, not troubling whether it will be noticed or understood by the reader, while he himself, as it were, stood over the reader with this artistic detail, until he had set it forth distinctly." The comparison is acute. He *does* "stand over the reader," not afraid of sickening him, and flogs in the trait, repeats, lays on colours, layer after layer, thickening them more and more, where Pushkin, barely touching, slides his brush over in light and careless, but invariably sure and faithful strokes. It seems as if Pushkin, especially in prose harsh, and even niggardly, gave little, that we might want the more. But Tolstoi gives so much that there is nothing more for us to want; we are sated, if not glutted.

The descriptions or Pushkin remind one of the light watery tempera of the old Florentine masters of Pompeian frescoes, dim, airily translucent colours, like the veil of morning mist. Tolstoi paints in the more powerful oil colours of the great Northern Masters. And side by side with the dense black and living shadows we have sudden rays of the blinding all-penetrating light, drawing out of the dark some distinct feature, the nakedness of the body, a fold of drapery, a keen, quick movement, part of a face stamped with passion or suffering. We get a startling, almost repulsive and alarming vividness. The artist seeks through the natural, strongly emphasized, the supernatural; through the physical exaggerated the hyperphysical.

In all literature there is no writer equal to Tolstoi in depicting the human body. Though he misuses repetitions, he usually attains what he needs by them, and he never suffers from the *longueurs* so common to other vigorous masters. He is accurate, simple, and as short as possible, selecting only the few, small, unnoticed facial or personal features and producing them, not all at once, but gradually and one by one, distributing them over the whole course of the story, weaving them into the living web of the action. Thus at the first appearance of old Prince Volkonski we get only a fleeting sketch, in four or five lines, "the short figure of the old man with the powdered wig, small *dry hands* and grey, overhanging brows that sometimes, when he was roused, dimmed the flash of the clever youthful eyes." When he sits down to the lathe "by the movement of his small foot, the firm pressure of his thin veined hand" (we already know his hands are dry, but Tolstoi loves to go back to the hands of his heroes), "you could still see in the Prince the obstinate and long-enduring force of hale old age." When he talks to his daughter, Princess Maria, "he shows in a cold smile, his strong but yellowish teeth." When he sits at the table and bends over her, beginning the usual lesson in geometry, she "feels herself surrounded with the snuffy, old-age, acrid savour of her father," which had long been a sign to her. There he is all before us as if alive, height, build, hands, feet, eyes, gestures, brows, even the peculiar savour belonging to each man.

Or take the effect on Vronski when he first sees Anna Karénina. You could see at a glance she belonged to the well-born; that she was very beautiful, that she had red lips, flashing grey eyes, which looked dark from the thickness of the lashes, and that "an excess of life had so filled her being that in spite of herself it showed, now in the flash of her eyes, now in her smile." And again as the story progresses, gradually, imperceptibly, trait is added to trait, feature to feature: when she gives her hand to Vronski he is delighted "as by something exceptional with the vigorous clasp with which she boldly shook his own." When she is talking to her sister-in-law Dolly, Anna takes her hand in "her own vigorous little one." The wrist of this hand is "thin and tiny," we see the "slender tapering fingers," off which the rings slip easily.

In the hands of Karénina, as in those of other characters (it may be because the hands are the only part of the human body always bare and near elemental nature, and unconscious as the animal), there is yet greater expressiveness than in the face. In the hands of Anna lies the whole charm of her person, the union of strength and delicacy. We learn when she is standing in the crowd at the ball "that she always held herself exceptionally erect"; when she leaves the railway carriage or walks through the room she has "a quick, decisive gait, carrying with strange ease her full and perfectly proportioned body." When she dances she has "a distinguishing grace, sureness and lightness of movement"; when, having gone on a visit to Dolly, she takes off her hat, her black hair, that catches in everything, "ripples into waves all over," and on another occasion "the unruly short waves of her curly hair keep fluttering at the nape and on the temples."

In these unruly curls, so easily becoming unkempt, there is the same tension, "the excess of something" ever ready for passion, as in the too bright flash of the eyes, or the smile, breaking out involuntarily and "fluctuating between the eyes and the lips." And lastly, when she goes to the ball, we see her skin. "The black, low-cut velvet bodice showed her full shoulders and breast polished like old ivory, and *rounded* arms." This polishedness, firmness, and *roundness* of the body, as with Platon Karataev, is to Tolstoi very important and subtle, a mysterious trait. All these scattered, single features complete and tally with one another, as in beautiful statues the shape of one limb always corresponds to the shape of another. The traits are so harmonized that they naturally and involuntarily unite, in the fancy of the reader, into one living, personal whole: so that when we finish the book we cannot but recognize Anna Karénina.

This gift of *insight into the body* at times, though seldom, leads Tolstoi into excess. It is easy and pleasant to him to describe living bodies and their movements. He depicts exactly how a horse beings to start when touched by the spur: "Jarkov touched his horse with the spurs and it thrice in irritation shifted its legs, not knowing with which to begin, reared and leaped." In the first lines of *Anna Karénina* Tolstoi is in a hurry to tell us how Stepan Arcadievich Oblonski, of whom we as yet know nothing, "draws plenty of air into his broad pectoral structure," and how he walks with "his usual brisk step, turning out the feet which so lightly carry his full frame." This last feature is significant, because it records the family likeness of the brother Stepan with his sister Anna. Even if all this seems extravagant, yet extravagance in art is not excess, it is even in many cases the most needful of all things. But here is a character of third-rate importance, one of those which vanish almost as soon as they appear, some paltry regimental commander in *Peace and War*, who has no sooner flitted before us than we have already seen he "is broader from the chest to the back than from one shoulder to the other," and he stalks before the front "with a gait that shakes at every step and his back slightly bent." This shaky walk is repeated four times in five pages. Perhaps the observation is both true and picturesque, but it is here an inappropriate touch and in excess. Anna Karénina's fingers, "taper at the ends," are important; but we should not have lost much if he had not told us that the Tartar footmen who hand dinner to Levin and Oblonski were broad-hipped. Sometimes the distinguishing quality of an artist is shown, not so much by what he has in due proportion as by the gift which he as to excess.

The language of gesture, if less varied than words, is more direct, expressive and suggestive. It is easier to lie in words than by gesture or facial expression. One glance, one wrinkle, one quiver of a muscle in the face, may express the unutterable. Succeeding series of these unconscious, involuntary movements, impressing and stratifying themselves on the face and physique, form the expression of the face and the countenance of the body. Certain feelings impel us to corresponding movements, and, on the other hand, certain habitual movements impel to the corresponding *internal* states. The man who prays, folds his hands and bends his knees, and the man too who folds his hands and bends his knees is near to the praying frame of mind. Thus there exists an uninterrupted current, not only from the internal to the external, but from the external to the internal.

[Craft in *War and Peace*]   Percy Lubbock*

A great and brilliant novel, a well-known novel, and at the same time a large and crowded and unmanageable novel — such will be the book to consider first. It must be one that is universally admitted to be a work of genius, signal and conspicuous; I wish to examine its form, I do not wish to argue its merit; it must be a book which it is superfluous to praise, but which it will never seem too late to praise again. It must also be well known, and this narrows the category; the novel of whose surpassing value every one is convinced may easily fall outside it; our novel must be one that is not only commended, but habitually read. And since we are concerned with the difficulty of controlling the form of a novel, let it be an evident case of the difficulty, an extreme case on a large scale, where the question cannot be disguised — a novel of ample scope, covering wide spaces and many years, long and populous and eventful. The category is reduced indeed; perhaps it contains one novel only, *War and Peace*.

Of *War and Peace* it has never been suggested, I suppose, that Tolstoy here produced a model of perfect form. It is a panoramic vision of people and places, a huge expanse in which armies are marshalled; can one expect of such a book that it should be neatly composed? It is crowded with life, at whatever point we face it; intensely vivid, inexhaustibly stirring, the broad impression is made by the big prodigality of Tolstoy's invention. If a novel could really be as large as life, Tolstoy could easily fill it; his great masterful reach never seems near its limit; he is always ready to annex another and yet another tract of life, he is only restrained by the mere necessity of bringing a novel somewhere to an end. And then, too, this mighty command of spaces and masses is only half his power. He spreads further than any one else, but he also touches the detail of the scene, the single episode, the fine shade of character, with exquisite lightness and precision. Nobody surpasses, in some ways nobody approaches, the easy authority with which he handles the matter immediately before him at the moment, a roomful of people, the brilliance of youth, spring sunshine in a forest, a boy on a horse; whatever his shifting panorama brings into view, he makes of it an image of beauty and truth that is final, complete, unqualified. Before the profusion of *War and Peace* the question of its general form is scarcely raised. It is enough that such a world should have been pictured; it is idle to look for proportion and design in a book that contains a world.

But for this very reason, that there is so much in the book to distract attention from its form, it is particularly interesting to ask how it is made. The doubt, the obvious perplexity, is a challenge to the exploring eye. It may well be that effective composition on such a scale is impossible, but it

*From *The Craft of Fiction* (New York: Viking, 1964). pp. 26-42. First published in 1921. Reprinted by permission of the author's estate.

is not so easy to say exactly where Tolstoy fails. If the total effect of his book is inconclusive, it is all lucidity and shapeliness in its parts. There is no faltering in his hold upon character; he never loses his way among the scores of men and women in the book; and in all the endless series of scenes and events there is not one which betrays a hesitating intention. The story rolls on and on, and it is long before the reader can begin to question its direction. Tolstoy *seems* to know precisely where he is going, and why; there is nothing at any moment to suggest that he is not in perfect and serene control of his idea. Only at last, perhaps, we turn back and wonder what it was. What is the subject of *War and Peace*, what is the novel *about*? There is no very ready answer; but if we are to discover what is wrong with the form, this is the question to press.

What is the story? There is first of all a succession of phases in the lives of certain generations; youth that passes out into maturity, fortunes that meet and clash and re-form, hopes that flourish and wane and reappear in other lives, age that sinks and hands on the torch to youth again — such is the substance of the drama. The book, I take it, begins to grow out of the thought of the processional march of the generations, always changing, always renewed; its figures are sought and chosen for the clarity with which the drama is embodied in them. Young people of different looks and talents, moods and tempers, but young with the youth of all times and places — the story is alive with them at once. The Rostov household resounds with them — the Rostovs are of the easy, light-spirited, quick-tongued sort. Then there is the dreary old Bolkonsky mansion, with Andrew, generous and sceptical, and with poor plain Marya, ardent and repressed. And for quite another kind of youth, there is Peter Besukhov, master of millions, fat and good-natured and indolent, his brain a fever of faiths and aspirations which not he, but Andrew, so much more sparing in high hopes, has the tenacity to follow. These are in the foreground, and between and behind them are more and more, young men and women at every turn, crowding forward to take their places as the new generation.

It does not matter, it does not affect the drama, that they are men and women of a certain race and century, soldiers, politicians, princes, Russians in an age of crisis; such they are, with all the circumstances of their time and place about them, but such they are in secondary fashion, it is what they happen to be. Essentially they are not princes, not Russians, but figures in the great procession; they are here in the book because they are young, not because they are the rising hope of Russia in the years of Austerlitz and Borodino. It is laid upon them primarily to enact the cycle of birth and growth, death and birth again. They illustrate the story that is the same always and everywhere, and the tumult of the dawning century to which they are born is an accident. Peter and Andrew and Natasha and the rest of them are the children of yesterday and to-day and to-morrow; there is nothing in any of them that is not of all time. Tolstoy has no thought of showing them as the children of their particular conditions, as the generation that was formed by a certain historic struggle; he sees them simply as the embodiment of youth. To an English reader of to-day it is curious — and more, it is strangely moving — to note how faithfully the creations of Tolstoy, the nineteenth-century Russian, copy the young people of the twentieth century and of England; it is all one, life in Moscow then, life in London now, provided only that it is young enough. Old age is rather more ephemeral; its period is written on it (not very deeply, after all), and here and there it "dates." Nicholas and Natasha are always of the newest modernity.

Such is the master-motive that at first sight appears to underlie the book, in spite of its name; such is the most evident aspect of the story, as our thought brushes freely and rapidly around it. In this drama the war and the peace are episodic, not of the centre; the historic scene is used as a foil and a background. It appears from time to time, for the sake of its value in throwing the nearer movement of life into strong relief; it very powerfully and strikingly shows what the young people *are*. The drama of the rise of a generation is nowhere more sharply visible and appreciable than it is in such a time of convulsion. Tolstoy's moment is well chosen; his story has a setting that is fiercely effective, the kind of setting which in our Europe this story has indeed found very regularly, century by century. But it is not by the war, from this point of view, that the multifarious scenes are linked together; it is by another idea, a more general, as we may still dare to hope, than the idea of war. Youth and age, the flow and ebb of the recurrent tide — this is the theme of Tolstoy's book.

So it seems for a while. But Tolstoy called his novel *War and Peace*, and presently there arises a doubt; did he believe himself to be writing *that* story, and not the story of Youth and Age? I have been supposing that he named his book carelessly (he would not be alone among great novelists for that), and thereby emphasized the wrong side of his intention; but there are things in the drama which suggest that his title really represented the book he projected. Cutting across the big human motive I have indicated, there falls a second line of thought, and sometimes it is this, most clearly, that the author is following. Not the cycle of life everlasting, in which the rage of nations is an incident, a noise and an incursion from without — but the strife itself, the irrelevant uproar, becomes the motive of the fable. *War and Peace*, the drama of that ancient alternation, is now the subject out of which the form of the book is to grow. Not seldom, and more frequently as the book advances, the story takes this new and contradictory alignment. The centre shifts from the general play of life, neither national nor historic, and plants itself in the field of racial conflict, typified by that "sheep-worry of Europe" which followed the French Revolution. The young people immediately change their meaning. They are no longer there for their own sake, guardians of the torch for their hour. They are re-disposed, partially and fitfully, in another relation; they are made to figure as creatures of the Russian scene, at the impact of East and West in the Napoleonic clash.

It is a mighty antinomy indeed, on a scale adapted to Tolstoy's giant imagination. With one hand he takes up the largest subject in the world, the story to which all other human stories are subordinate; and not content with this, in the other hand he produces the drama of a great historic collision, for which a scene is set with no less prodigious a gesture. And there is not a sign in the book to show that he knew what he was doing; apparently he was quite unconscious that he was writing two novels at once. Such an oversight is not peculiar to men of genius, I dare say; the least of us is capable of the feat, many of us are seen to practise it. But two such novels as these, two such immemorial epics, caught up together and written out in a couple of thousand pages, inadvertently mixed and entangled, and all with an air of composure never ruffled or embarrassed, in a style of luminous simplicity — it was a feat that demanded, that betokened, the genius of Tolstoy. *War and Peace* is like an *Iliad*, the story of certain men, and an *Aeneid*, the story of a nation, compressed into one book by a man who never so much as noticed that he was Homer and Virgil by turns.

Or can it perhaps be argued that he was aware of the task he set himself, and that he intentionally coupled his two themes? He proposed, let us say, to set the unchanging story of life against the momentary tumult, which makes such a stir in the history-books, but which passes, leaving the other story still unrolling for ever. Perhaps he did; but I am looking only at his book, and I can see no hint of it in the length and breadth of the novel as it stands; I can discover no angle at which the two stories will appear to unite and merge in a single impression. Neither is subordinate to the other, and there is nothing above them (what more *could* there be?) to which they are both related. Nor are they placed together to illustrate a contrast; nothing *results* from their juxtaposition. Only from time to time, upon no apparent principle and without a word of warning, one of them is dropped and the other resumed. It would be possible, I think, to mark the exact places — not always even at the end of a chapter, but casually, in the middle of a page — where the change occurs. The reader begins to look out for them; in the second half of the novel they are liberally sprinkled.

The long, slow, steady sweep of the story — the *first* story, as I call it — setting through the personal lives of a few young people, bringing them together, separating them, dimming their freshness, carrying them away from hopeful adventure to their appointed condition, where their part is only to transmit the gift of youth to others and to drop back while the adventure is repeated — this motive, in with the book opens and closes and to which it constantly returns, is broken into by the famous scenes of battle (by some of them, to be accurate, not by all), with the reverberation of imperial destinies, out of which Tolstoy makes a saga of his country's tempestuous past. It is magnificent, this latter, but it has no bearing on the other, the universal story of no time or country, the legend of every age, which is told of Nicholas and Natasha, but which might have been told as well of the sons and daughters of the king of Troy. To Nicholas, the youth of all time, the strife of Emperor and Czar is the occasion, it may very well be, of the climax of his adventure; but it is no more than the occasion, not essential to it, since by some means or other he would have touched his climax in any age. War and peace are likely enough to shape his life for him, whether he belongs to ancient Troy or to modern Europe; but if it is *his* story, his and that of his companions, why do we see them suddenly swept into the background, among the figures that populate the story of a particular and memorable war? For that is what happens.

It is now the war, with the generals and the potentates in the forefront, that is the matter of the story. Alexander and Kutusov, Napoleon and Murat, become the chief actors, and between them the play is acted out. In this story the loves and ambitions of the young generation, which have hitherto been central, are relegated to the fringe; there are wide tracts in which they do not appear at all. Again and again Tolstoy forgets them entirely; he has discovered a fresh idea for the unification of this second book, a theory drummed into the reader with merciless iteration, desolating many a weary page. The meaning of the book — and it is extraordinary how Tolstoy's artistic sense deserts him in expounding it — lies in the relation between the man of destiny and the forces that he dreams he is directing; it is a high theme, but Tolstoy cannot leave it to make its own effect. He, whose power of making a story *tell itself* is unsurpassed, is capable of thrusting into his book interminable chapters of comment and explanation, chapters in the manner of a controversial pamphlet, lest the argument of his drama should be missed. But the reader at last takes an easy way with these maddening interruptions; wherever "the historians" are mentioned he knows that several pages can be turned at once; Tolstoy may be left to belabour the conventional theories of the Napoleonic legend and rejoined later on, when it has occurred to him once more that he is writing a novel.

When he is not pamphleteering Tolstoy's treatment of the second story, the national saga, is masterly at every point. If we could forget the original promise of the book as lightly as its author does, nothing could be more impressive than his pictures of the two hugely-blundering masses, Europe and Russia, ponderously colliding at the apparent dictation of a few limited brains — so few, so limited, that the irony of their claim to be the directors of fate is written over all the scene. Napoleon at the crossing of the Niemen, Napoleon before Moscow, the Russian council of war after Borodino (gravely watched by the small child Malasha, overlooked in her corner), Kutusov, wherever he appears — all these are impressions belonging wholly to the same cycle; they have no effect in relation to the story of

Peter and Nicholas, they do not extend or advance it, but on their own account they are supreme. There are not enough of them, and they are not properly grouped and composed, to *complete* the second book that has forced its way into the first; the cycle of the war and the peace, as distinguished from the cycle of youth and age, is broken and fragmentary. The size of the theme, and the scale upon which these scenes are drawn, imply a novel as long as our existing *War and Peace*; it would all be filled by Kutusov and Napoleon, if their drama were fully treated, leaving no room for another. But, mutilated as it is, each of the fragments is broadly handled, highly finished, and perfectly adjusted to a point of view that is not the point of view for the rest of the book.

And it is to be remarked that the lines of cleavage—which, as I suggested, can be traced with precision—by no means invariably divide the peaceful scenes of romance from the battles and intrigues of the historic struggle, leaving these on one side, those on the other. Sometimes the great public events are used as the earlier theme demands that they should be used—as the material in which the story of youth is embodied. Consider, for instance, one of the earlier battlepieces in the book, where Nicholas, very youthful indeed, is for the first time under fire; he comes and goes bewildered, laments like a lost child, is inspired with heroism and flees like a hare for his life. As Tolstoy presents, this battle, or a large part of it, is the affair of Nicholas; it belongs to him, it is a piece of experience that enters his life and enriches our sense of it. Many of the wonderful chapters, again, which deal with the abandonment and the conflagration of Moscow, are seen through the lives of the irrepressible Rostov household, or of Peter in his squalid imprisonment; the scene is framed in their consciousness. Prince Andrew, too—nobody can forget how much of the battle in which he is mortally wounded is transformed into an emotion of *his*; those pages are filched from Tolstoy's theory of the war and given to his fiction. In all these episodes, and in others of the same kind, the history of the time is in the background; in front of it, closely watched for their own sake, are the lives which that history so deeply affects.

But in the other series of pictures of the campaign, mingled with these, it is different. They are admirable, but they screen the thought of the particular lives in which the wider interest of the book (as I take it to be) is firmly lodged. From a huge emotion that reaches us through the youth exposed to it, the war is changed into an emotion of our own. It is rendered by the story-teller, on the whole, as a scene directly faced by himself, instead of being reflected in the experience of the rising generation. It is true that Tolstoy's good instinct guides him ever and again away from the mere telling of the story on his own authority; at high moments he knows better than to tell it himself. He approaches it through the mind of an onlooker, Napoleon or Kutusov or the little girl by the stove in the corner, borrowing the value of indirectness, the increased effect of a story that is seen as it is mirrored in the mind of another. But he chooses his onlooker at random and follows no consistent method. The predominant point of view is simply his own, that of the independent story-teller; so that the general effect of these pictures is made on a totally different principle from that which governs the story of the young people. In that story — though there, too, Tolstoy's method is far from being consistent — the effect is *mainly* based on our free sharing in the hopes and fears and meditations of the chosen few. In the one case Tolstoy is immediately beside us, narrating; in the other it is Peter and Andrew, Nicholas and Natasha, who are with us and about us, and Tolstoy is effaced.

Here, then, is the reason, or at any rate one of the reasons, why the general shape of *War and Peace* fails to satisfy the eye — as I suppose it admittedly to fail. It is a confusion of two designs, a confusion more or less masked by Tolstoy's imperturbable ease of manner, but revealed by the look of his novel when it is seen as a whole. It has no centre, and Tolstoy is so clearly unconcerned by the lack that one must conclude he never perceived it. If he had he would surely have betrayed that he had; he would have been found, at some point or other, trying to gather his two stories into one, devising a scheme that would include them both, establishing a centre somewhere. But no, he strides through his book without any such misgiving, and really it is his assurance that gives it such an air of lucidity. He would only have flawed its surface by attempting to force the material on his hands into some sort of unity; its incongruity is fundamental. And when we add, as we must, that *War and Peace*, with all this, is one of the great novels of the world, a picture of life that has never been surpassed for its grandeur and its beauty, there is a moment when all our criticism perhaps seems trifling. What does it matter? The business of the novelist is to create life, and here is life created indeed; the satisfaction of a clean, coherent form is wanting, and it would be well to have it, but that is all. We have a magnificent novel without it.

So we have, but we might have had a more magnificent still, and a novel that would not be *this* novel merely, this *War and Peace*, with the addition of another excellence, a comeliness of form. We might have had a novel that would be a finer, truer, mover vivid and more forcible picture of life. The best form is that which makes the most of its subject — there is no other definition of the meaning of form in fiction. The well-made book is the book in which the subject and the form coincide and are indistinguish-able — the book in which the matter is all used up in the form, in which the form expresses all the mater. Where there is disagreement and conflict between the two, there is stuff that is superfluous or there is stuff that is wanting; the form of the book, as it stands before us, has failed to do justice to the idea. In *War and Peace*, as it seems to me, the story suffers twice over for the imperfection of the form. It is damaged, in the first place, by the importation of another and an irrelevant story — damaged because it so loses the sharp and clear relief that it would have if it stood alone. Whether the story was to be the drama of youth and age, or the drama of war and peace, in either case it would have been incomparably more impressive if *all* the great wealth of the material had been used for its purpose, all brought into one design. And furthermore, in either case again, the story is incomplete; neither of them is finished, neither of them is given its full development, for all the size of the book. But to this point, at least in relation to one of the two, I shall return directly.

Tolstoy's novel is wasteful of its subject; that is the whole objection to its loose, unstructural form. Criticism bases its conclusion upon nothing whatever but the injury done to the story, the loss of its full potential value. Is there so much that is good in *War and Peace* that its inadequate grasp of a great theme is easily forgotten? It is not only easily forgotten, it is scarcely noticed—on a first reading of the book; I speak at least for one reader. But with every return to it the book that *might* have been is more insistent; it obtrudes more plainly, each time, interfering with the book that is. Each time, in fact, it becomes harder to make a book of it at all; instead of holding together more firmly, with every successive reconstruction, its prodigious members seem always more disparate and disorganized; they will not coalesce. A subject, one and whole and irreducible—a novel cannot begin to take shape till it has this for its support. It seems obvious; yet there is nothing more familiar to a novel-reader of to-day than the difficulty of discovering what the novel in his hand is about. What was the novelist's intention, in a phrase? If it cannot be put into a phrase it is no subject for a novel; and the size or the complexity of a subject is in no way limited by that assertion. It may be the simplest anecdote or the most elaborate concatenation of events, it may be a solitary figure or the widest network of relationships; it is anyhow expressible in ten words that reveal its unity. The form of the book depends on it, and until it is known there is nothing to be said of the form.

[Great Chords and *War and Peace*]

E. M. Forster*

What about *War and Peace*? That is certainly great, that likewise emphasizes the effects of time and the waxing and waning of a generation. Tolstoy, like Bennett, has the courage to show us people getting old—the partial decay of Nicolay and Natasha is really more sinister than the complete decay of Constance and Sophia: more of our own youth seems to have perished in it. Then why is *War and Peace* not depressing? Probably because it has extended over space as well as over time, and the sense of space until it terrifies us is exhilarating, and leaves behind it an effect like

*From E. M. Forster, *Aspects of the Novel*, 38-39. Copyright 1927 by Harcourt Brace Jovanovich, Inc.; renewed 1955 by E. M. Forster. Reprinted by permission of the publisher.

music. After one has read *War and Peace* for a bit, great chords begin to sound, and we cannot say exactly what struck them. They do not arise from the story, though Tolstoy is quite as interested in what comes next as Scott, and quite as sincere as Bennett. They do not come from the episodes nor yet from the characters. They come from the immense area of Russia, over which episodes and characters have been scattered, from the sum-total of bridges and frozen rivers, forests, roads, gardens, fields, which accumulate grandeur and sonority after we have passed them. Many novelists have the feeling for place — Five Towns, Auld Reekie, and so on. Very few have the sense of space, and the possession of it ranks high in Tolstoy's divine equipment. Space is the lord of *War and Peace*, not time.

The Chronicle   Edwin Muir*

Obviously a theory of the novel which does not find a place for *War and Peace* is untenable. Nor does it better things to call the story two or several novels, as Mr. Percy Lubbock has done, not without justice; for the problem would still remain to fit these into our scheme. In both or in all of them the story would still seem to be advancing in time and exploring space.

But though formidable, the problem is not unanswerable. Space and time seem equally real in *War and Peace*; but in fact its action takes place in time and time alone. The houses, the drawing-rooms, the streets, the country estates, are evoked, it is true, as definite and recognisable as those in *Vanity Fair*; but they have not the immutability of Russell Square and Queen's Crawley; they alter, like the characters, and altering become mere aspects of time. At the start they are simply places where people live, like the scenes in *Vanity Fair*; but presently they become places where people have lived, like the village which Rip Van Winkle returned to after his long sleep. Tolstoy's aim in *War and Peace* is not the same as Thackeray's, to show a static representation of society in which people behave in a uniform way and in a generalised present; it is, I quote Mr. Percy Lubbock, "to enact the cycle of birth and growth, death and birth again." The characters, he goes on, "illustrate the story that is the same always and everywhere"; but in that story time is everything; it is more even than it is in the dramatic novel. For in the dramatic novel the action is a single action, and it may appear therefore against a changeless background; but here, in the perpetual succession of actions following one another, even the background must be subject to change. The universal behind the particu-

*From *The Structure of the Novel* (New York: Harcourt, Brace and Company, 1929), 95-103. Reprinted by permission of the author's literary estate, Chatto & Windus Ltd., and the Hogarth Press Ltd.

lar in the dramatic novel is the earth, or, if one likes, the cosmos; it is a stage. The universal behind the particular in *War and Peace* is change itself; it is a process. In the first the particular is set sharply against the universal; in the second is is not even an image, but rather a part of it, and finally melts into it. "The cycle of birth and growth, death and birth again," can neither be called merely particular, nor simply universal. It is both, because it is human life.

In *War and Peace*, then, human life is not set against fate or society, but against human life in perpetual change. It is not a particular image of a general law; it is particular and general at the same time; it is typical rather than symbolical. We cannot think of the dramatic novel without thinking of the idea of Fate, an abstraction, or of the character novel without thinking of society, another abstraction. But the only abstraction, the only point of general reference in *War and Peace* is "life," or more comprehensively, change. It is the most inclusive, it is also the vaguest, of the three.

For the novelist, as we have seen, fate is an organising conception of the first power, and society an organising conception of secondary power. Life or change, however, is hardly an organising conception at all; as it is comprehensive it includes everything; and we shall find that the structure of the kind of novel of which *War and Peace* is the greatest example is the loosest of the three. This kind of novel I shall call the chronicle. Its action is almost accidental, but we shall find later that all the events happen within a perfectly rigid framework. A strict framework, an arbitrary and careless progression; both of these, we shall find, are necessary to the chronicle as an aesthetic form. Without the first it would be shapeless; without the second it would be lifeless. The one gives it its universal, the other its particular reality. As Time, however, is the main ground of the chronicle, so each of those two planes of the plot is a separate aspect of Time. They may be called Time as absolute process, and Time as accidental manifestation.

We have already pointed out the primacy of the sense of time in the dramatic novel. In it Time is incarnated and articulated in the characters; its speed therefore is psychological, determined by the slowness or rapidity of the action. Turning to *War and Peace* we shall find that there Time is not so much articulated as generalised and averaged. Its speed is not determined by the intensity of the action; it has, on the contrary, a cold and deadly regularity, which is external to the characters and unaffected by them. The characters grow, or grow old. The emphasis is on that; on the fact that they are twenty now, that they will be thirty, then forty, then fifty, and that in essential respects they will then be like everybody else at twenty, thirty, forty, and fifty. We watch the change taking place within Catherine and Heathcliff; it is as if in them Time were dramatised. They change in a particular direction and for specific causes, and it is the strict concatenation of those causes that makes the change inevitable. Change in

War and Peace, on the other hand, is primarily general, and its inevitability consists in its generality. It is not organic with the action, now rapid, now almost stationary, coinciding with the movement of the passions and the feelings; it follows the remote astronomical course which for mankind determines time's measurement; it is regular, arithmetical, and in a sense inhuman and featureless. It has one kind of necessity, that of increasing the ages of all the characters arithmetically, of continuing to change them at a uniform rate without paying attention to their desires or their plans. But everything except its own progression is indifferent to it. Natasha, Nicholas, and Prince Peter in *War and Peace* pass through sufferings which they feel at the time they cannot survive; nevertheless Tolstoyan time carries them indifferently on, as if experience did not matter, through a typical youth and maturity to a typical middle-age. Therefore—this is the other aspect of time seen in this way—everything may happen; and everything does happen. The action on the human plane does not unfold inevitably; we do not see a drama contained within itself and building itself up on its own consequences; we see life in all its variety of accidents and inventions, marked off here and there by certain very important milestones, inscribed with different figures which designate the march of an external and universal process. This process, which is the framework of the action, is empty seen in one way, and seen in another contains all that is possible; it is accident and law, confusion and meaning, everything and nothing.

In the dramatic novel, as we saw, the characters are revealed by time; in the chronicle too, they are revealed by time, but here the revelation follows a different path. To the chronicler describing a number of lives from birth to death, ten, twenty, thirty, forty, fifty, are critical stages, poignant categories of reality, and that because the single life is the unit, and each halting-place takes the character farther from its beginning or gives a nearer view of its end. A young man, an old man: when we are in the mood of the chronicler these simple classifications have all the pathos of life and change. But if we are thinking of a complex of relationships which must be resolved, they fall into a secondary place. So to the dramatic novelist time reckoned in this way has not the same significance. There is one point in *Wuthering Heights* where we are told, as if by chance, that Heathcliff is twenty-seven. Here, after a period of intense experience, in which time has been pure inward reality, the arithmetical, external aspect of time is suddenly and prosaically recognised, and it is as if the characters had awakened from a dream. So this almost reassuring ordinary fact has an unexpectedly pathetic effect, the mere recognition of it seeming to draw Heathcliff from the more profound tides in which the action was moving, and to set him down in his diurnal surroundings, a pitiable and ordinary human being. It has the effect for an instant—so great is the power of suggestion—of making us think of Heathcliff as a man who will soon be thirty, and may conceivably live to a ripe old age;

and we forget – in this pause – the destiny towards which we know, with another part of our mind, that he is moving. It is destiny, its foreknowledge and its approach, that measures time in the dramatic novel; and when destiny falls time ends – the problem has been resolved. But in the chronicle time is not measured by human happenings, no matter how important; it is; and it continues to exist unchanged after its story has been told, still as regular in its movement, still as rich in accident and in the multitudes of figures it will discover. So we find Mr. Lubbock saying of *War and Peace* that "there is no perceptible horizon, no hard line between the life in the book and the life beyond it. The communication between the men and women of the story and the rest of the world is unchecked. It is impossible to say of Peter and Andrew and Nicholas that they inhabit 'a world of their own,' as the people in a story-book so often appear to do; they inhabit *our* world, like everybody else." When we have closed *War and Peace*, in other words, we feel that time "goes on." The process, ten, twenty, thirty, forty, fifty, and all the people by means of whose lives we count it, remain in our minds and in the world. "The cycle of birth and growth, death and birth again"; this has been the pattern of the story; but this is the pattern of life too. So that, finished, the chronicle releases an echo which wanders in larger spaces than those in which it has just been confined, spaces, moreover, which repeat on an unimaginably vaster scale the proportions of their original, and respond to the same tones. Tolstoy describes only a few generations, but the emphasis of his imagination makes the endless cycle of generations unroll in our imagination; and we see human life as birth, growth, and decay, a process perpetually repeated. This then is the framework, ideal and actual, of the chronicle; its framework of universality.

But at the same time, within this process of birth, growth and decay, as its content, are all the diverse manifestations of life, everything that can happen; and it is these that make up the particular incidents in the chronicle; that fill and animate it. Here, too, as in the dramatic novel, variety is set against uniformity, freedom against necessity. If one is overstressed in the chronicle, the story will be untrue. If one is omitted, the story will not be a work of imagination at all.

To bring out as clearly as possible the difference between the sense of time in the dramatic novel and the chronicle, I shall restate it now in another way. Time in the dramatic novel is internal; its movement is the movement of the figures; change.

The Dilemma of History
Isaiah Berlin*

Tolstoy's central thesis — in some respects not unlike the theory of the inevitable "self-deception" of the *bourgeoisie* held by his contemporary Karl Marx, save that what Marx reserves for a class, Tolstoy sees in almost all mankind — is that there is a natural law whereby the lives of human beings no less than those of nature are determined; but that men, unable to face this inexorable process, seek to represent it as a succession of free choices, to fix responsibility for what occurs upon persons endowed by them with heroic virtues or heroic vices, and called by them "great men." What are great men? they are ordinary human beings, who are ignorant and vain enough to accept responsibility for the life of society, individuals who would rather take the blame for all the cruelties, injustices, disasters justified in their name, than recognize their own insignificance and impotence in the cosmic flow which pursues its course irrespective of their wills and ideals. This is the central point of those passages (in which Tolstoy excelled) in which the actual course of events is described, side by side with the absurd, egocentric explanations which persons blown up with the sense of their own importance necessarily give to them; as well as of the wonderful descriptions of moments of illumination in which the truth about the human condition dawns upon those who have the humility to recognize their own unimportance and irrelevance. And this is the purpose, too, of those philosophical passages where, in language more ferocious than Spinoza's, but with intentions similar to his, the errors of the pseudo-sciences are exposed. There is a particularly vivid simile[1] in which the great man is likened to the ram whom the shepherd is fattening for slaughter. Because the ram duly grows fatter, and perhaps is used as a bell-wether for the rest of the flock, he may easily imagine that he is the leader of the flock, and that the other sheep go where they go solely in obedience to his will. He thinks this and the flock may think it too. Nevertheless the purpose of his selection is not the role he believes himself to play, but slaughter — a purpose conceived by beings whose aims neither he nor the other sheep can fathom. For Tolstoy, Napoleon is just such a ram, and so to some degree is Alexander, and indeed all the great men of history. Indeed, as an acute literary historian has pointed out,[2] Tolstoy sometimes seems almost deliberately to ignore the historical evidence and more than once consciously distorts the facts in order to bolster up his favourite thesis. The character of Kutuzov is a case in point. Such heroes as Pierre Bezukhov or Karataev are at least imaginary, and Tolstoy had an undisputed right to endow them with all the attributes he admired — humility, freedom from bureaucratic or scientific or other rationalistic kinds of blindness. But Kutuzov was a real person, and it is all the more

*From *The Hedgehog and the Fox* (New York: Mentor, 1957), 28-51. Copyright 1953 by Isaiah Berlin. Reprinted by permission of Simon and Schuster, Inc.

instructive to observe the steps by which he transforms him from the sly, elderly, feeble voluptuary, the corrupt and somewhat sycophantic courtier of the early drafts of *War and Peace* which were based on authentic sources, into the unforgettable symbol of the Russian people in all its simplicity and intuitive wisdom. By the time we reach the celebrated passage — one of the most moving in literature — in which Tolstoy describes the moment when the old man is woken in his camp at Fili to be told that the French army is retreating, we have left the facts behind us, and are in an imaginary realm, a historical and emotional atmosphere for which the evidence is flimsy, but which is artistically indispensable to Tolstoy's design. The final apotheosis of Kutuzov is totally unhistorical for all Tolstoy's repeated professions of his undeviating devotion to the sacred cause of the truth. In *War and Peace* Tolstoy treats facts cavalierly when it suits him, because he is above all obsessed by his thesis — the contrast between the universal and all-important but delusive experience of free will, the feeling of responsibility, the values of private life generally, on the one hand; and on the other, the reality of inexorable historical determinism, not, indeed, experienced directly, but known to be true on irrefutable theoretical grounds. This corresponds in its turn to a tormenting inner conflict, one of many, in Tolstoy himself, between the two systems of value, the public and the private. On the one hand, if those feelings and immediate experiences, upon which the ordinary values of private individuals and historians alike ultimately rest, are nothing but a vast illusion, this must, in the name of the truth, be ruthlessly demonstrated, and the values and the explanations which derive from the illusion exposed and discredited. And in a sense Tolstoy does try to do this, particularly when he is philosophizing, as in the great public scenes of the novel itself, the battle pieces, the descriptions of the movements of peoples, the metaphysical disquisitions. But, on the other hand, he also does the exact opposite of this when he contrasts with this panorama of public life the superior value of personal experience, the "thoughts, knowledge, poetry, music, love, friendship, hates, passions" of which real life is compounded — when he contrasts the concrete and multi-coloured reality of individual lives with the pale abstractions of scientists or historians, particularly the latter, "from Gibbon to Buckle," whom he denounces so harshly for mistaking their own empty categories for real facts. And yet the primacy of these private experiences and relationships and virtues presupposes that vision of life, with its sense of personal responsibility, and belief in freedom and possibility of spontaneous action, to which the best pages of *War and Peace* are devoted, and which is the very illusion to be exorcized, if the truth is to be faced.

This terrible dilemma is never finally resolved. Sometimes, as in the explanation of his intentions which he published before the final part of *War and Peace* had appeared,[3] Tolstoy vacillates; the individual is "in some sense" free when he alone is involved: thus in raising his arm, he is free within physical limits. But once he is involved in relationships with others, he is no longer free, he is part of the inexorable stream. Freedom is real, but it is confined to trivial acts. At other times even this feeble ray of hope is extinguished: Tolstoy declares that he cannot admit even small exceptions to the universal law; causal determinism is either wholly pervasive or it is nothing, and chaos reigns. Men's acts may seem free of the social nexus, but they are not free, they cannot be free, they are part of it. Science cannot destroy the consciousness of freedom, without which there is no morality and no art, but it can refute it. "Power" and "accident" are but names for ignorance of the causal chains, but the chains exist whether we feel them or not; fortunately we do not; for if we felt their weight, we could scarcely act at all; the loss of illusion would paralyse the life which is lived on the basis of our happy ignorance. But all is well: for we never shall discover all the causal chains that operate: the number of such causes is infinitely great, the causes themselves infinitely small; historians select an absurdly small portion of them and attribute everything to this arbitrarily chosen tiny section. How would an ideal historical science operate? By using a kind of calculus whereby this "differential," the infinitesimals — the infinitely small human and non-human actions and events — would be integrated, and in this way the continuum of history would no longer be distorted by being broken up into arbitrary segments.[4] Tolstoy expresses this notion of calculation by infinitesimals with great lucidity, and with his habitual simple, vivid, precise use of words. The late M. Henri Bergson, who made his name with his theory of the flow of events which the artificial fragmentation, such as is made in the natural sciences, distorts, "kills," and so on, developed a very similar point at infinitely greater length, less clearly, less plausibly, and with an unnecessary parade of terminology.

It is not a mystical or an intuitionist view of life. Our ignorance of how things happen is not due to some inherent inaccessibility of the first causes, only to their multiplicity, the smallness of the ultimate units, and our own inability to see and hear and remember and record and co-ordinate enough of the available material. Omniscience is in principle possible even to empirical beings, but, of course, in practice unattainable. This alone, and nothing deeper or more interesting, is the source of human megalomania, of all our absurd delusions. Since we are not, in fact, free, but could not live without the conviction that we are, what are we to do? Tolstoy arrives at no clear conclusion, only at the view, in some respect like Burke's, that it is better to realize that we understand what goes on as we do in fact understand it — much as spontaneous, normal, simple people, uncorrupted by theories, not blinded by the dust raised by the scientific authorities, do, in fact, understand life — than to seek to subvert such common-sense beliefs, which at least have the merit of having been tested by long experience, in favour of pseudo-sciences, which, being founded on absurdly inadequate data, are only a snare and a delusion. That is his case against all forms of optimistic rationalism, the natural sciences, liberal theories of progress, German military *expertise*, French sociology, confident social engineering of all kinds. And that is his reason for inventing a Kutuzov who followed his simple, Russian, untutored instinct, and despised or ignored the German, French, and Italian experts; and for raising him to the status of a national hero which he has, partly as a result of Tolstoy's portrait, retained ever since.

Notes

1. *War and Peace*, Epilogue, pt. 1, ch. ii.

2. See V. Shklovsky, *Material i stil' v romane L'va Tolstogo, "Voyna i Mir"* (Matter and style in Leon Tolstoy's novel *War and Peace*), p. 6, note 3, chs. vii-ix and also K. Pokrovsky, "Istochniki romana *Voyna i Mir*" (Sources of the novel *War and Peace*), ed. Poner and Obninsky (Moscow, Zadruga, 1912), p. 8, note 1.

3. "Neskol'ko slov po povodu knigi *Voyna i Mir*" (Some words about the book *War and Peace*), in *Russki Arkhiv*, 1868, coll. 515-28.

4. *War and Peace*, vol. III, pt, iii, ch. i.

[Tolstoy and Homer]   George Steiner*

Hugo von Hofmannsthal once remarked that he could not read a page of Tolstoy's *Cossacks* without being reminded of Homer. His experience has been shared by readers not only of *The Cossacks* but of Tolstoy's works as a whole. According to Gorky, Tolstoy himself said of *War and Peace*: "Without false modesty, it is like the *Iliad*," and he made precisely the same observation with regard to *Childhood, Boyhood and Youth*. Moreover, Homer and the Homeric atmosphere appear to have played a fascinating role in Tolstoy's image of his own personality and creative stature. His brother-in-law, S. A. Bers, tells in his *Reminiscences* of a feast which took place on Tolstoy's estate in Samara:

> a steeplechase of fifty versts. Prizes were got ready, a bull, a horse, a rifle, a watch, a dressing-gown and the like. A level stretch was chosen, a huge course four miles long was made and marked out, and posts were put up on it. Roast sheep, and even a horse, were prepared for the entertainment. On the appointed day, some thousands of people assembled, Ural Cossacks, Russian peasants, Bashkirs and Khirgizes, with their dwellings, koumiss-kettles, and even their flocks. . . . On a cone-shaped rise, called in the local dialect, "Shiska" (the Wen), carpets and felt were spread, and on these the Bashkirs seated themselves in a ring,

*From *Tolstoy or Dostoevsky* (New York: Vintage, 1961), 71–81. © 1959 by George Steiner. Reprinted by permission.

with their legs tucked under them. . . . The feast lasted for two days
and was merry, but at the same time dignified and decorous. . . .[1]

It is a fantastic scene; the millennia dividing the plains of Troy from
nineteenth-century Russia are bridged and Book XXIII of the *Iliad* springs
to life. In Richmond Lattimore's version:

> But Achilleus
> held the people there, and made them sit down in a wide
>   assembly,
> and brought prizes for games out of his ships, cauldrons
>   and tripods,
> and horses and mules and the powerful high heads of
>   cattle
> and fair-girdled women and grey iron.

Like Agamemmon, Tolstoy thrones upon the hillock; the steppe is dotted
with tents and fires; Bashkirs and Khirgizes, like Achaeans, race the four-
mile course and take their prizes from the hands of the bearded king. But
there is nothing here of archaeology, of contrived reconstruction. The
Homeric element was native to Tolstoy; it was rooted in his own genius.
Read his polemics against Shakespeare and you will find that his sense of
kinship with the poet, or poets, of the *Iliad* and *Odyssey* was palpable and
immediate. Tolstoy spoke of Homer as equal of equal; between them the
ages had counted for little.

What was it that struck Tolstoy as peculiarly Homeric in his collection
of early memories? Both the setting, I think, and the kind of life he
recalled to mind. Take the account of "The Hunt" in the volume on
Childhood:

> Harvesting was in full swing. The limitless, brilliantly yellow field
> was bounded only on one side by the tall, bluish forest, which then
> seemed to me a most distant, mysterious place beyond which either the
> world came to an end or uninhabited countries began. The whole field
> was full of sheaves and peasants. . . . The little roan papa rode went
> with a light, playful step, sometimes bending his head to his chest,
> pulling at the reins, and brushing off with his thick tail the gadflies and
> gnats that settled greedily on him. Two borzois with tense tails raised
> sickle-wise, and lifting their feet high, leapt gracefully over the tall
> stubble, behind the horse's feet. Milka ran in front, and with head lifted
> awaited the quarry. The peasants' voices, the tramp of horses and
> creaking of carts, the merry whistle of quail, the hum of insects
> hovering in the air in steady swarms, the odour of wormwood, straw,
> and the horses' sweat, the thousands of different colours and shadows
> with which the burning sun flooded the light yellow stubble, the dark
> blue of the forest, the light lilac clouds, and the white cobwebs that
> floated in the air or stretched across the stubble—all this I saw, heard,
> and felt.

There is nothing here that would have been incongruous on the plains of
Argos. It is from our own modern setting that the scene is oddly remote. It

is a patriarchal world of huntsmen and peasants; the bond between master and hounds and the earth runs native and true. The description itself combines a sense of forward motion with an impression of repose; the total effect, as in the friezes of the Parthenon, is one of dynamic equilibrium. And beyond the familiar horizon, as beyond the Pillars of Hercules, lie the mysterious seas and the untrodden forests.

The world of Tolstoy's recollections, no less than that of Homer, is charged with sensuous energies. Touch and sight and smell fill it at every moment with rich intensity:

> In the passage a samovár, into which Mítka, the postilion, flushed red as a lobster, is blowing, is already on the boil. It is damp and misty outside, as if steam were rising from the odorous manure heap; the sun lights with its bright gay beams the eastern part of the sky and the thatched roofs, shiny with dew, of the roomy pent-houses that surround the yard. Under these one can see our horses tethered to the mangers and hear their steady chewing. A shaggy mongrel that had had a nap before dawn on a dry heap of manure, stretches itself lazily, and wagging its tail, starts at a jog-trot for the opposite side of the yard. An active peasant-woman opens some creaking gates and drives the dreamy cows into the street, where the tramping, the lowing and the bleating of the herd is already audible. . . .

So it was when "rosy-fingered Dawn" came to Ithaca twenty-seven hundred years ago. So it should be, proclaims Tolstoy, if man is to endure in communion with the earth. Even the storm, with its animate fury, belongs to the rhythm of things:

> The lightning flashes become wider and paler, and the rolling of the thunder is now less startling amid the regular patter of the rain. . . .

> . . . an aspen grove with hazel and wild cherry undergrowth stands motionless as if in an excess of joy, and slowly sheds bright raindrops from its clean-washed branches on to last year's leaves. On all sides crested skylarks circle with glad songs and swoop swiftly down. . . . The delicious scent of the wood after the spring storm, the odour of the birches, of the violets, the rotting leaves, the mushrooms, and the wild cherry, is so enthralling that I cannot stay in the brichka. . . .

Schiller wrote in his essay *Ueber naive und sentimentalische Dichtung* that certain poets "are Nature" while others only "seek her." In that sense, Tolstoy is Nature; between him and the natural world language stood not as a mirror or a magnifying glass, but as a window through which all light passes and yet is gathered and given permanence.

It is impossible to concentrate within a single formula or demonstration the affinities between the Homeric and the Tolstoyan points of view. So much is pertinent: the archaic and pastoral setting; the poetry of war and agriculture; the primacy of the senses and of physical gesture; the luminous, all-reconciling background of the cycle of the year; the recognition that energy and aliveness are, of themselves, holy; the acceptance of a chain of being extending from brute matter to the stars and along which men have their apportioned places; deepest of all, an essential sanity, a determination to follow what Coleridge called "the high road of life," rather than those dark obliquities in which the genius of a Dostoevsky was most thoroughly at home.

In both the Homeric epics and the novels of Tolstoy the relationship between author and characters is paradoxical. Maritain gives a Thomistic analogue for it in his study of *Creative Intuition in Art and Poetry*. He speaks "of the relationship between the transcendent creative eternity of God and the free creatures who are both acting in liberty and firmly embraced by his purpose." The creator is at once omniscient and everywhere present, but at the same time he is detached, impassive, and relentlessly objective in his vision. The Homeric Zeus presides over the battle from his mountain fastness, holding the scales of destiny but not intervening. Or, rather, intervening solely to restore equilibrium, to safeguard the mutability of man's life against miraculous aid or the excessive achievements of heroism. As in the detachment of the god, so there is in the clear-sightedness of Homer and Tolstoy both cruelty and compassion.

They saw with those blank, ardent, unswerving eyes which look upon us through the helmet-slits of archaic Greek statues. Their vision was terribly sober. Schiller marvelled at Homer's impassiveness, at his ability to communicate the utmost of grief and terror in perfect evenness of tone. He believed that this quality — this "naïveté" — belonged to an earlier age and would be unrecapturable in the sophisticated and analytic temper of modern literature. From it Homer derived his most poignant effects. Take, for example, Achilles' slaying of Lykaon in Book XXI of the *Iliad*:

> "So, friend, you die also. Why all this clamour about it? Patroklos also is dead, who was better by far than you are. Do you not see what a man I am, how huge, how splendid and born of a great father, and the mother who bore me immortal?
>
> Yet even I have also my death and my strong destiny, and there shall be a dawn on an afternoon on a noontime when some man in the fighting will take the life from me also either with a spearcast or an arrow flown from the bowstring."
>
> So he spoke, and in the other the knees and the inward heart went slack. He let go of the spear and sat back, spreading wide both hands; but Achilleus drawing his sharp sword struck him beside the neck at the collar-bone, and the double-edged sword plunged full length inside. He dropped to the ground, face downward, and lay at length, and the black blood flowed, and the ground was soaked with it.

The calm of the narrative is nearly inhuman; but in consequence the horror speaks naked and moves us unutterably. Moreover, Homer never sacrifices the steadiness of his vision to the needs of pathos. Priam and

Achilles have met and given vent to their great griefs. But then they bethink themselves of meat and wine. For, as Achilles says of Niobe: "She remembered to eat when she was worn out with weeping." Again, it is the dry fidelity to the facts, the poet's refusal to be outwardly moved, which communicate the bitterness of his soul.

In this respect, no one in the western tradition is more akin to Homer than is Tolstoy. As Romain Rolland noted in his journal for 1887, "in the art of Tolstoy a given scene is not perceived from two points of view, but from only one: things are as they are, not otherwise." In *Childhood*, Tolstoy tells of the death of his mother: "I was in great distress at that moment but involuntarily noticed every detail," including the fact that the nurse was "very fair, young, and remarkably handsome." When his mother dies, the boy experiences "a kind of enjoyment," at knowing himself to be unhappy. That night he sleeps "soundly and calmly," as is always the case after great distress. The following day he becomes aware of the smell of decomposition:

> It was only then that I understood what the strong oppressive smell was that mingling with the incense filled the whole room; and the thought that the face that but a few days before had been so full of beauty and tenderness, the face of her I loved more than anything on earth, could evoke horror, seemed to reveal the bitter truth to me for the first time, and filled my soul with despair.

"Keep your eyes steadfastly to the light," says Tolstoy, "this is how things are."

But in the unflinching clarity of the Homeric and Tolstoyan attitude there is far more than resignation. There is joy, the joy that burns in the "ancient glittering eyes" of the sages in Yeats's *Lapis Lazuli*. For they loved and revered the "humanness" of man; they delighted in the life of the body coolly perceived but ardently narrated. Moreover, it was their instinct to close the gap between spirit and gesture, to relate the hand to the sword, the keel to the brine, and the wheel-rim to the singing cobblestones. Both the Homer of the *Illiad* and Tolstoy saw action whole; the air vibrates around their personages and the force of their being electrifies insensate nature. Achilles' horses weep at his impending doom and the oak flowers to persuade Bolkonsky that his heart will live again. This consonance between man and the surrounding world extends even to the cups in which Nestor looks for wisdom when the sun is down and to the birch-leaves that glitter like a sudden riot of jewels after the storm has swept over Levin's estate. The barriers between mind and object, the ambiguities which metaphysicians discern in the very notion of reality and perception, impeded neither Homer nor Tolstoy. Life flooded in upon them like the sea.

And they rejoiced at it. When Simone Weil called the *Iliad* "The Poem of Force" and saw in it a commentary on the tragic futility of war, she was only partially right. The *Iliad* is far removed from the despairing nihilism of Euripides' *Trojan Women*. In the Homeric poem, war is valorous and ultimately ennobling. And even in the midst of carnage, life surges high. Around the burial mound of Patroklus the Greek chieftains wrestle, race, and throw the javelin in celebration of their strength and aliveness. Achilles knows that he is foredoomed, but "bright-cheeked Briseis" comes to him each night. War and mortality cry havoc in the Homeric and Tolstoyan worlds, but the centre holds: it is the affirmation that life is, of itself, a thing of beauty, that the works and days of men are worth recording, and that no catastrophe — not even the burning of Troy or of Moscow — is ultimate. For beyond the charred towers and beyond the battle rolls the wine-dark sea, and when Austerlitz is forgotten the harvest shall, in Pope's image, once again "embrown the slope."

This entire cosmology is gathered into Bosola's reminder to the Duchess of Malfi when she curses nature in agonized rebellion: "Look you, the stars shine still." These are terrible words, full of detachment and the harsh reckoning that the physical world contemplates our afflictions with impassiveness. But go beyond their cruel impact and they convey an assurance that life and star-light endure beyond the momentary chaos.

The Homer of the *Iliad* and Tolstoy are akin in yet another respect. Their image of reality is anthropomorphic; man is the measure and pivot of experience. Moreover, the atmosphere in which the personages of the *Iliad* and of Tolstoyan fiction are shown to us is profoundly humanistic and even secular. What matters is the kingdom of *this* world, here and now. In a sense, that is a paradox; on the plains of Troy mortal and divine affairs are incessantly confounded. But the very descent of the gods among men and their brazen involvement in all-too-human passions give the work its ironic overtones. Musset invoked this paradoxical attitude in his account of archaic Greece in the opening lines of *Rolla*:

> Où tout était divin, jusq' aux douleurs humaines;
> Où le monde adorait ce qu'il tue aujourd'hui;
> Où quatre mille dieux n'avaient pas un
> athee. . . .

Precisely; with four thousand deities warring in men's quarrels, dallying with mortal women, and behaving in a manner apt to scandalize even liberal codes of morality, there was no need for atheism. Atheism arises in contrariety to the conception of a living and credible God; it is not a response to a partially comic mythology. In the *Iliad* divinity is quintessentially human. The gods are mortals magnified, and often magnified in a satiric vein. When wounded they howl louder than men, when they are enamoured their lusts are more consuming, when they flee before human spears their speed exceeds that of earthly chariots. But morally and intellectually the deities of the *Iliad* resemble giant brutes or malevolent children endowed with an excess of power. The actions of gods and goddesses in the Trojan War enhance the stature of man, for when odds are equal mortal heroes more than hold their own and when the scales are against them a Hector and an Achilles demonstrate that mortality has its own splendours. In lowering the gods to human values, the "first" Homer achieved not only an effect of comedy, though such an effect obviously contributes to the freshness and "fairy-tale" quality of the poem. Rather, he emphasized the excellence and dignity of heroic man. And this, above all, was his theme.

The pantheon in the *Odyssey* plays a subtler and more awesome role, and the *Aeneid* is an epic penetrated with a feeling for religious values and religious practice. But the *Iliad*, while accepting the mythology of the supernatural, treats it ironically and humanizes its material. The true centre of belief lies not on Olympus but in the recognition of *Moira*, of unyielding destiny which maintains through its apparently blind decimations an ultimate principle of justice and equilibrium. The religiosity of Agamemnon and Hector consists in an acceptance of fate, in a belief that certain impulses towards hospitality are sacred, in reverence for sanctified hours or hallowed places, and in a vague but potent realization that there are daemonic forces in the motion of the stars or the obstinacies of the wind. But beyond that, reality is immanent in the world of man and of his senses. I know of no better word to express the non-transcendence and ultimate physicality of the *Iliad*. No poem runs more strongly counter to the belief that "we are such stuff as dreams are made on."

And this is where it touches significantly on the art of Tolstoy. His also is an immanent realism, a world rooted in the veracity of our senses. From it God is strangely absent. In Chapter IV, I shall attempt to show that this absence can not only be reconciled to the religious purpose of Tolstoy's novels but that it is a hidden axiom of Tolstoyan Christianity. All that needs saying here is that there lies behind the literary techniques of the *Iliad* and of Tolstoy a comparable belief in the centrality of the human personage and in the enduring beauty of the natural world. In the case of *War and Peace* the analogy is even more decisive; where the *Iliad* evokes the laws of *Moira*, Tolstoy expounds his philosophy of history. In both works the chaotic individuality of battle stands for the larger randomness in men's lives. And if we consider *War and Peace* as being, in a genuine sense, a heroic epic it is because in it, as in the *Iliad*, war is portrayed in its glitter and joyous ferocity as well as in its pathos. No measure of Tolstoyan pacifism can negate the ecstasy which young Rostov experiences as he charges down on the French stragglers. Finally, there is the fact that *War and Peace* tells of two nations, or rather of two worlds, engaged in mortal combat. This alone has led many of its readers, and led Tolstoy himself, to compare it with the *Iliad*.

But neither the martial theme nor the portrayal of national destinies should blind us to the fact that the philosophy of the novel is anti-heroic. There are moments in the book in which Tolstoy is emphatically preaching that war is wanton carnage and the result of vainglory and stupidity in high places. There are also times at which Tolstoy is concerned solely with seeking to discover "the real truth" in opposition to the alleged truths of official historians and mythographers. Neither the latent pacifism nor this concern with the evidence of history can be compared to the Homeric attitude.

War and Peace is most genuinely akin to the *Iliad* where its philosophy is least engaged, where, in Isaiah Berlin's terms, the fox is least busy trying to be a hedgehog. Actually, Tolstoy is closest to Homer in less manifold works, in *The Cossacks*, the *Tales from the Caucasus*, the sketches of the Crimean War and in the dread sobriety of *The Death of Ivan Ilych*.

But it cannot be emphasized too strongly that the affinity between the poet of the *Iliad* and the Russian novelist was one of temper and vision; there is no question here (or only in the minute instance) of a Tolstoyan imitation of Homer. Rather, it is that when Tolstoy turned to the Homeric epics in the original Greek in his early forties, he must have felt wondrously at home.

Note

1. D. S. Merezhkovsky: *Tolstoi as Man and Artist, with an Essay on Dostoievski* (London, 1902).

ANNA KARENINA

Reviews

Tolstoi's New Novel

Anonymous*

Paris, June 16.

The success of Tolstoi's *Guerre et Paix* has been very great among that class of the public which has not been totally depraved by the coarse vulgarity of some of our novel writers. The great book of the Russian novelist was almost a revelation: not only did it show us a new world, almost unknown—it was the type of a new literary method, which could not be compared to anything we knew. It is not to be wondered at if there was much curiosity felt when *Anna Karénine* came out in a French translation. Our Russian friends said to us: "You admire *Guerre et Paix*; wait till you read *Anna Karénine*." They consider this novel Tolstoi's masterpiece. I cannot, I may as well say at once, agree with this opinion. Is it because *Guerre et Paix* was the first I read, and because it gave me sensations and emotions which novelty alone can give? I do not think so. There is in *Guerre et Paix* a heroic part which is wanting in *Anna Karénine*. The element of war infuses color into the first of the two novels, and gives it an extraordinary originality. The invasion of Russia—Borodino—the burning of Moscow—the retreat and the destruction of the French army—the quietness of the steppe and of the old châteaux of the Russian nobility disturbed by the roar of cannon, by the tramping of huge armies—Napoleon, Alexander, Kutuzoff, appearing here and there in the midst of their armies—what a *cadre*, as the French say, for a picture of human passions! And the picture is as fine as the *cadre* itself. There is no discordance, no incongruity felt; a human heart, full of passion, is a world in itself, and its tempests are comparable to the greatest tempests of nature, or those other tempests which we call wars. History must always be summed up in the struggle of a few individual wills; and these wills are more often led by instinct, by blind forces, than by reason and fixed purpose. The element of fatality is found in history as it is in the development of a woman or of a child—the terrible curse, the weight of past ages, the law of heredity. Religion as well as science struggles

*From the *Nation* 41 (August 6, 1885):112–13.

incessantly with the awful problems which are hidden in the enigmatic phrase "original sin."

Anna Karénine is purely a novel, and a Russian novel. But it is not a novel in the ordinary sense of the word; there is, so to speak, no story. It is not the development of a certain plot, with a beginning, a middle, and an end; it is rather a succession of pictures, of scenes, some of which seem hardly to have any connection with the principal scenes. Such is Tolstoi's manner, so far as he has a manner. He paints life such as it is, sometimes solemn and sometimes dull; tragical and commonplace — light and shadow constantly intermingled. His actors are numerous, their name is legion. The heroes and heroines are not always alone on the stage; they are constantly drawn among people who care nothing or who care little for their passions, their preoccupations. They move in a real atmosphere of dullness, of banality, of vulgarity, of levity, of indifference. It would seem as if the interest we took in them would be diminished by this juxtaposition or interposition; it is not so. On the contrary, the contrast between the tragical elements of life and the comical or dull elements increases our interest. Tolstoi shows us life as it really is, with its complexities, its necessary tedium, its frivolities. He does not deceive us: his finest characters have their weak points; he knows that perfection is not human. It would be an impossible task to give a suitable account of *Anna Karénine*, considered as a novel. We must go a little beneath the surface, and try to find out if Tolstoi had an object in this extraordinary delineation of human life. He does not belong to the school of writers who let you know at once what their aim is, and where they are leading you; still, it seems as if he had been thinking of contrasting love, considered in its domestic aspects — legal love, if I may say so — observed in the family life, under common, ordinary, provincial circumstances; and love, as an uncontrollable passion — wild, lawless, destructive of the family affections and ties, of all social rules.

We have in *Anna Karénine* two couples. One is Lévine and his wife Kitty, who married for love, and the husband remains a lover. Kitty is very charming, very feminine, very pure; Lévine is very good, very ordinary, very weak, jealous when he has not the slightest occasion to be jealous. He is an honest gentleman-farmer, timid, awkward; he detests St. Petersburg and society; he is fond of his country-house, his peasants, his dogs, his horses. He writes a book on agriculture which he will never finish. He is a warm friend, a good neighbor, a capital shot. Tolstoi makes you positively see him, and you feel at the end of the book as if you had always known him, and gone with him after woodcock, and heard him and Kitty discuss small domestic matters. They are happy, and their troubles are only like the small clouds that float a moment in a summer's sky and are soon absorbed by the warm rays of the sun.

It is not so with Anna Karénine. She is married to a high functionary, a slave of official duties, respectable, hard-working, a rising statesman, a type of the class which is produced by the Russian *tchinn*. But Anna is lawless: she is one of the born rebels of the world. She admires, she even likes her husband—she cannot love him; and she loves another man, a handsome, spirited, fashionable young officer named Vronsky. Fatality draws her to him, and he belongs to that class of men who may be said to recognize no duties except to themselves, no obedience except to their own desires and passions. He is a man without a conscience. He has principles, or says that he has; but these principles are totally at variance with those of Lévine. They allow him, I would almost say they force him, to despise the laws of matrimony, the bonds of friendship. He only submits to the world; but *his* world allows much, and he is determined to profit largely by its indulgence. He is not exactly the bold villain, the bandit, the outlaw, who has long been made prominent in literature. He is the correct man of the world, who pays his gambling debts at the appointed time; he is a brave, even a brilliant soldier, an accomplished courtier; but his code of morals is not inspired by any higher law. He is eminently and essentially selfish, and knows no God but his own will.

Anna Karénine is above him: she has a soul; she can feel commiseration and pity. She was made for good, not for evil; but her fate has tied her to a husband who does not satisfy the cravings of her imagination and her heart. She falls into the hands of Vronsky, like a bird fascinated by a serpent. When she feels herself, to her surprise and almost to her horror, in love, she tries to escape. The description of her feelings in the train which takes her away is very admirable: the tortures of a diseased mind have never been painted with more truth. She feels so agitated that, at one of the stations on the road, she goes out on the platform, though the night is cold and tempestuous:

> The wind was blowing with rage through the wheels, round the axles, covering carriages and men with snow. People were running here and there, opening and shutting the great doors, talking gayly, while the snow cracked under their feet. . . . "Send the despatch," said an irritated voice from the other side of the railway. Two gentlemen, with cigarettes in their mouths, passed by Anna. She was on the point of remounting into the carriage after having breathed a vast supply of fresh air. She had already taken her hand out of her muff, when the vacillating light from the lamp-post was cut off from her by a man in a military coat who approached her. It was Vronsky; she knew him at once. . . .
>
> It was useless to ask why he was there; she knew as well as if he had said he was only there to see her.
>
> "I did not know that you were on the way to Petersburg. Why do you go there?" she asked, letting her hand fall, while an irrepressible joy lighted her visage.
>
> "Why do I go?" said he, looking fixedly at her. "You know I go only in order to be where you are; I cannot do otherwise."
>
> At this moment the wind, as if it had conquered all obstacles, blew

the snow off the roof of the carriages and shook triumphantly a piece of sheet-iron which it had detached; the engine uttered a plaintive sound. Never had the horror of the tempest seemed so fine to Anna. She had just heard the words which her reason had feared and her heart desired.

This passage is not a bad specimen of Tolstoi's manner. Anna is drawn by degrees into the vortex of passion. She is not a hypocrite; she has not the quiet assurance of a Parisienne, who can go through life leading with the same hand and by the same string husband and lovers. She is a creature of impulse; and when, one fine day, after a steeple-chase in which Vronsky falls with his horse and is thought for a moment to be dead, Anna is reproved by her husband for having shown too violent an interest in him in the presence of too many people, she throws off the mask. "No, you are not mistaken," said she to him slowly, casting at the same time a look of despair on the impassive face of her husband. "You are not mistaken. I have been in despair, and I am still. I hear you, and I think only of him. I love him: I am his mistress. I cannot bear you: I fear you, I hate you. Do with me what you will."

As soon as Anna has sinned, the expiation begins. She begins almost at once to hate the cause of her sin. She hates him first unconsciously, and by degrees she is brought to hate him consciously. Vronsky, in his turn, first loves his victim, and then becomes tired of her. They try everything—a palace at Venice, country life on one of Vronsky's estates; they try St. Petersburg again. Alas! nothing will do. The world makes them feel that they must remain everything to each other, and they are no longer everything to each other. What was to be a paradise becomes an inferno. Anna was too bold when she left husband and child and defied society. She is not bold enough to make herself an "æs triplex circum pectus," and to impose herself again on society. She has the Slavic impetuosity and the Slavic weakness. She is bad, but she is not bad enough. She tortures herself; she bears her fatal love like a cross; and when she finally can fathom the selfishness of Vronsky, when she see through the man who has destroyed the whole equilibrium of her existence, she feels like a child who must escape from some cruel, brutal tyrant. She runs away, hardly knowing where she goes. She met Vronsky on the railway on a fatal night; he is not there now. The dark, brutal engine, more insensible than even the heart of a villain, is there. She throws herself at the feet of the iron monster: she cannot suffer any more; the monster touches her, and she dies.

[Review of *Anna Karenina*]   Anonymous*

Count Tolstoi's *Anna Karénina* is a long, intricate, and crowded novel of Russian life. It is really two novels, we might almost say three novels, in one. It sets out with an unhappy domestic experience, in which Prince Stepan Oblonsky is detected by his wife, Darya, in a *liaison* with the French governess of their children, the husband barely escaping an irretrievable rupture with her whom he has wronged. But this is only an introduction — a dish of soup before meat. From this beginning the story branches in two lines: one following the innocent but tearful experiences of Konstantin Levin and Kitty Shcherbatskaïa, together with the fortunes of Levin as a large landed proprietor in connection with agrarian problems of a socialistic kind; the other the guilty love of Count Alekséi Vronsky for Anna Karénina, the wife of Alekséi Karénin, their defiant and illicit union, and the tragic fate which concludes their history. This variety of interests and motives, the multiplicity of characters, and a confusion as to names which the translater might have saved his readers by a stern independence of Russian nomenclature, make the opening chapters perplexing and toilsome; until the stream of the story gets fairly under way and falls clearly into its several channels. Then it becomes interesting, at times absorbing, and will retain the attention of those who have leisure, throughout the entire 769 capacious pages, to the end.

The two leading themes act as if one were set as a foil to the other; Vronsky's and Anna's lawless passion and its fruits over against Levin's agrarian experiments on his country estate of Pokrovsky. The great mass of materials employed gives cumbersomeness and complexity to the product, molded though it be by a powerful and steady hand. The reader does not ever feel that the guide is losing the way, but rather that he is being led through a mountainous and rugged country, with an immense range of ground to cover, and ground of a difficult character. The story oscillates, swings, sways from side to side like an express train at forty miles an hour over the twistings and climbings of the Baltimore & Ohio Railway; one chapter, for example, ends in a most dramatic passage between Anna and her wronged husband, the next begins in the hay-loft at Pokrovsky.

As a socialistic novel *Anna Karénina* is wholesome, and for a novel on the transgression of the Seventh Commandment it is inoffensive. Yet on its latter side, on these relations of the sexes, on the facts of parentage and motherhood, the book speaks with a plainness of meaning, sometimes with a plainness of words, which is at least new. We do not know that we have ever before read a novel in which the details of an *accouchement*, for example, were made to do service for one chapter. A very effective chapter it is of its kind, but — !

*Review of *Anna Karenina*, trans. Nathan Haskell Dole. From *Literary World* 17 (17 April 1886):127–28.

With the moral intent of the work no fault can be found. The sinfulness of sin, the wretchedness of sin, the bitter fruits of sin, are all in the sad story of Vronsky and Anna. The stern virtuousness of Alekeséi Karénin when he suspects the error of his wife, and as suspicion settles into discovery; the first severity of his anger, his later compassion, his final magnanimity; these are some lines only in a noble and majestic figure, a lay figure, in whose person and purpose the author would incarnate the Sermon on the Mount. If there are few scenes in fiction, which for pure vividness of portraiture equal the snowy journey by night from Moscow to St. Petersburg, upon which Vronsky, dominated by his passion, follows Anna, so are there few which for dramatic intensity and tender pitifulness equal that in which Karénin and Vronsky meet by Anna's bedside, as she lies hovering between life and death over the birth of a daughter, of whom her husband is not the father.

The book has many striking portraits among its subordinate characters; and there are graphic descriptions of Russian scenery and incident — the farm-yard at Pokrovsky; the brilliant wedding of Levin and Kitty, at which Levin is late for a ludicrous reason; the exciting races at which Vronsky has his fall; the *salon* receptions in which nobles and statesmen figure; the officers' mess in the barracks; the sojourn in Italy and the two tragedies of the railway station. Impressions the book certainly makes, makes and leaves; and impressions on the moral sensibilities as well as on the imagination.

The great lesson of Anna Karénina's melancholy history is that for a woman to marry a man twenty years her senior when she does not love him, is to place her under conditions of terrible temptation when afterwards she comes to be thrown with a man whom she can love, and who is not unselfish enough to save her from herself when she has put herself in his power; and that, surrendering to that temptation, the wages of her sin is — death.

It must have taken some resolution to translate this book, and some courage to publish it; and the reading of it some persons will find a work which requires perseverance and application. But it is large and strong; we remember nothing with which exactly to compare it since Elizabeth De Ville's *Johannes Olaf* of 1873.

[Review of *Anna Karenina*]   Anonymous*

Anna Karénina (1875-1977) was first published in a Russian review. It is the most mature and probably the greatest of the products of its author's imagination. Unlike *War and Peace* it is purely domestic in its subject

*From the *Dial* 7 (May 1886): 13-14.

matter, but there is no lack of variety in its scenes and characters. It is, indeed, a world in itself, so comprehensive is its grasp, and so intimately does it bring us into relations with the manifold aspects of country and city life in Russia. Were this work the sole available document, it would be possible to construct from its pages a great deal of Russian contemporary civilization. It is, of course, realistic to the last degree. But its realism is not confined to minute descriptions of material objects, and is no less made use of in the treatment of emotion. There are few works of art in which the art is so well concealed; few works of fiction which give so strong a sense of reality as this. We seem to look upon life itself and forget the medium of the novelist's imagination through which we really view it. And right here we are brought to compare the methods of Tolstoï with those of his better known and unquestionably greater countryman, Tourguénieff. In the marvellous novels of Tourguénieff we have this same feeling of immediate contact with the facts of material existence and of emotional life, and the effect is produced with much less machinery than Tolstoï is compelled to use. The work of Tourguénieff surpasses the work of Tolstoï, in revealing that final sublimation of thought and imagination which give to it an artistic value beyond that of almost any other imaginative prose. Tolstoï lacks this power of concentration and this unerring judgment in the choice of word or phrase. He cannot sum up a situation in a single pregnant sentence, but he can present it with great force in a chapter. Now that this story of *Anna Karénina* has been brought to the cognizance of the western world, it is not likely to be soon forgotten. It will be remembered for its minute and unstrained descriptions, for its deep tragedy, unfolded act after act as by the hand of fate, and for its undercurrent of gentle religious feeling, never falling to the offensive level of dogmatism, yet giving a marked character to the book, and revealing unmistakably the spiritual lineaments of the Russian apostle of quietism.

Not Fiction but Life   Anonymous*

Mrs. Garnett has already displayed her skill in the translation of Turgenev; but her version of Tolstoi, of which *Anna Karenin* (London: Heinemann & Co.), the first instalment, has been published, is a far more difficult project. Whether the style of Tolstoi be more complicated than that of Turgenev we know not, but surely Mrs. Garnett's later work is far more closely involved than her former. None the less we are exceedingly grateful to her, since she has given us for the first time the complete and workmanlike version of a masterpiece, and has afforded us a chance to

*Review of *Anna Karenina*, trans. Constance Garnett. From *Edinburgh Folio* 194 (1901): 713–15.

renew our acquaintance with the greatest novelist of the age. It is a
commonplace that the most of men have a dual nature, but no one ever
lived two lives so distantly separate as those which have made Count
Tolstoi famous. On the one hand he is an artist, on the other he is a
fanatic. The present generation knows him best as a preacher of impossible dogmas, as a pietist who deems renunciation the first and last duty of
man, and who looks with a kind of guilty regret upon the brilliant works
of earlier years. It is unlikely that his gospel will ever be more than the
sport of cranks and interviewers. The excellence of manual labour, a
favourite article of his faith, is disputed by no one, while his communism
has been tried and has failed too often to be of interest or importance. But
the very simplicity of his fanaticism would be engaging, if it had not been
made common by the newspapers; for Count Tolstoi is that rarest of
creatures — a fanatic who has lived. If he believes to-day that a primitive
life is best for us all, he has arrived at that belief by proving to his own
satisfaction that most other lives are unsatisfying. He is a noble, he has
great estates, he has served in a distinguished regiment; yet he now sees no
beauty save in the life of the peasants who till the soil, who sow the grain,
and who reap the harvest. But his fanaticism will pass and be forgotten
with other systems of the same kind; his masterpieces of fiction will guard
their niche in the temple of fame for all time.

To attach him to this school or that would be an impertinence, since,
indeed, he seems to have fashioned his own method. For such mechanical
contrivances as the novelists call plot or construction you will look in vain
in his pages. He is not a professed psychologist, though he pierces deeper
than most into human character. He makes no claim to realism, though he
is always closer to the truth than the rhapsodical M. Zola. But he exhibits
the characters of his personages as much in deed as in thought; he does not
analyse their motives as does Turgenev; he prefers that their qualities,
either good or evil, should be displayed in action. For this reason he packs
his canvas full of figures. He attains his effects by a mass of details
introduced into a vast space. Some of them, at a first reading, may seem
superfluous; but there are few which do not add a new touch to the
portrait, or show a character in a new light before his friends or foes. And
it is this method which creates the impression of realism. In reading such
works as *Anna Karenin* or *Peace and War* you seem to be confronted not
by fiction but by life. There are no jerky "curtains" to disturb the illusion;
the chapters do not end upon a note of interrogation, designed to force the
interest on to another page. The plot develops itself as does life, simply,
inevitably, and without accent; and in accord with this simplicity the
characters are rarely either above or below the stature of men. That is to
say, he deals neither with giants nor pigmies. His characters are not
grotesquely sombre, like Dostoievsky's; nor grotesquely humorous, like the
characters of Dickens. They are, indeed, merely the men and women that

he has encountered in his career—nobles and peasants, statesmen, sports-men, and soldiers. And here we may note the result of an aristocratic prejudice: for him the great middle class does not exist. Even the lawyer in *Anna Karenin* is not treated quite seriously; when he is not enunciating foolish platitudes in a pompous style, he is catching moths to save his rep curtains.

But with this limitation Tolstoi knows the world of Russia intimately, and he pictures it with a philosophic calm and impartiality which should belong to the perfect realist. But his books have no construction, the critic may object. Nor has Life; and though you might leave out half of *Peace and War* or *Anna Karenin* without destroying its meaning, there is still more in Life, at whose significance we cannot guess. Again objects the critic, the artist should select no more than is useful to his purpose. But Tolstoi only differs from other novelists in that he selects with a more generous hand. He is no symbolist attempting to represent the world in a blade of grass; rather he sets Life impartially before you, and leaves you to draw your own conclusions.

But there is one limit even to Tolstoi's impartiality. Though he holds the scales of justice with an even hand, though he looks with hatred upon none of his personages, though even Karenin in his eyes (and in ours) is redeemed from contempt, he is still partial where he himself is concerned. In other words, he cannot keep himself out of his books, and in some subtle fashion lets you know when fiction turns to autobiography. There is little doubt that in the vacillant, magnanimous, simple-hearted Levin he is drawing his own character, not with any slavish accuracy in fact, but with a perfect fidelity to thought. The actions of Levin may not have been Tolstoi's; the opinions of the two men (one is sure) are always identical. So, too, we detect the author in the valiant Peter, a hero in the heroic *Peace and War*. But while these resemblances are intuitive, as it were, the student may judge how much Tolstoi borrowed from his own experience, if he will study his *Memoirs*, and compare their incidents with the incidents of his two great romances. To give an impression of his gallery would be impossible, but surely no artist ever boasted so noble an array of portraits. Prince Andry is the noblest gentleman known to fiction, and though only the greatest hand can draw a gentleman, it is not only by this supreme test that Tolstoi excels: he has depicted gamblers and men about town with a clairvoyant sympathy which can come of experience alone. His Cossacks are living heroes; and Turgenev, with all his sympathy with young Russia, never saw so deep into the peasant's mind as Tolstoi. He has unfolded war with all its accessories of splendour, courage, and passion in a grandiose panorama. In *Ivan Iliitch* he has softened by his art the common, hopeless horror of death; and he has done all this with so deep a knowledge of human nature, with so fine a sympathy with human weakness, that he can rank only with the great ones of the earth. Such is Tolstoi the artist, and as for Tolstoi the fanatic, we may leave him to other fanatics who, not having his genius, are proud to ape his folly. But all the fanaticism in the world cannot recall or abolish a published masterpiece, and not even the indecent folly of the *Kreutzer Sonata* can dim the brilliancy of *Peace and War*.

Articles and Essays

Anna Karenina   F. M. Dostoevsky*

Anna Karenina is perfection as a work of art, and a work that turned
up just at the right time, and also one with which none of the European
literatures of the present epoch can compare. Moreover, according to its
main idea it is a peculiarly Russian, indigenous piece, representing that
which constitutes the difference between us, Russians, and the European
world, representing that which is already our own, national, "new word"
or, at least, the beginning of it, a word that one would never hear in
Europe, and which, nevertheless, Europe needs [to hear] very badly,
despite its pride. I cannot get involved here in literary criticism and will
say only a few words. In *Anna Karenina* a certain view of human guilt and
criminality is expressed. Human beings are depicted in abnormal circumstances. Evil existed before them. Caught in a whirlpool of falsehoods,
they transgress and perish inevitably: obviously an idea that has been near
and dear to European thinkers for a long time. How, then, is this problem
solved in Europe? All over Europe it is handled in a twofold manner. One
solution is as follows: the law has been laid down, framed, formulated,
developed and refined for thousands of years. Evil and good are defined,
weighed, their measurements are taken and degrees defined historically by
the sages of mankind in tireless efforts to fathom the human soul as well as
by precise scientific research into the extent of the unifying power of
communal living. This elaborate code must be obeyed blindly. Those who
do not—those who violate it—are made to pay for their transgressions
with their liberty, property, life, pay for it dearly, by the letter of the law,
and without mercy. "I know," says their civilization, "that this is all very
blind and inhuman and really impossible, because one cannot work out
the final formula for the human problem while mankind is still only
halfway down the road of its evolution; nevertheless since there is no other
way, one must stick to that which is written and stick to it verbatim and
without humanitarian considerations. Or else the consequences may be
even worse. At the same time, regardless of the fact that what we call our

*From *The Diary of a Writer*, July–August 1877. (Paris: YMCA Press, n.d.) 278–286.
Translated from the Russian for this volume by Boris Sorokin.

great European civilization is organized in an abnormal and incongruous way, nevertheless, let the powers of the human spirit remain healthy and unimpaired, let society remain firm in its belief that it is progressing toward perfection, let no one dare think that the ideal of the beautiful and exalted has become dimmed, that the concepts of good and evil are becoming corrupted and distorted, that what is normal is continuously being supplanted by convention, that simplicity and naturalness perish, overwhelmed by endlessly accumulating lies!" The other solution is the opposite: "Since society is still organized abnormally, individuals cannot be called to account for its abuses and consequences. Therefore a criminal is not responsible for his actions, and for the time being there can be no such thing as a crime. In order to do away with crimes and human guilt, the abnormal nature of society and its structure must first be dealt with. Since to cure the existing order of things would take a long time and would be hopeless anyway, and besides there are no cures, one must destroy the entire society and sweep away the old order as if with a broom. After that one should begin everything anew, based in different premises yet unknown, but those that cannot possibly be any worse than the present order of things and, on the contrary, have an excellent chance of success. One hopes that science will provide all the necessary answers." So this, then, is the second solution: one expects the coming of the future anthill; in the meantime, the world is being flooded with blood. Other than these two, the Western European world does not seem to have any solutions to the problem of human guilt and culpability.

In the Russian author's approach to human delinquency and culpability one can clearly see that no anthill, and no success of the "fourth estate," no elimination of poverty, and no organization of fair labor practices will save mankind from abnormality and, consequently, from guilt and criminality. This vastly complex idea is executed with formidable psychological analysis of the human soul, reaching enormous depth and power of artistic portrayal and unparalleled realism. What is made clear and plausible to the point of obviousness is that evil is rooted in mankind deeper than any socialists, clumsy healers of social ills, will concede; that no form of social organization can dispose of evil; that the human soul is what it is, that abnormality and sin issue from its own fiber, and, finally, that the laws of human consciousness are as yet so utterly unknown, so totally unexplored by science, so undefined, and so mysterious that, for the time being at least, there are not, and cannot be, any healers or *final* judges of human problems other than He who says "Vengeance is mine; I shall repay." He alone knows the *whole* enigma of the world and the final destiny of man. Meanwhile man cannot undertake to pass final judgment on anything, in his arrogant belief in his infallibility; the time and the season have not yet come for that. The human judge must realize of his own accord that he can scarcely think of himself as the final judge, that he is a sinner himself, that the measure and the scales in his hands are an absurdity, *unless* he himself, holding in his hands the measure and the scales, bows down before the law of the as yet impenetrable mystery and resorts to the only feasible solution — compassion and love. And that man should not perish in despair because he cannot understand his paths and destinies and is so easily swayed to acquiesce in the mysterious inevitability and fatal ubiquity of evil, he is indeed shown a way out. This way out is brilliantly suggested by the author in the brilliant scene in the penultimate part of the novel, in the scene where the heroine lies mortally ill, when culprits suddenly are transfigured into superior beings, brothers who have forgiven one another everything, beings who by mutual exculpation have cleansed themselves of all falsehood, guilt, and culpability, and thereby immediately acquitted themselves, with full awareness that they deserve now to be free of guilt. But later, at the end of the novel, in the gloomy and dreadful picture of growing despair that is traced step by step, in the depiction of that irresistible state when evil takes possession of one's innermost being, puts fetters on every move, paralyzes all strength to resist, every thought, every urge to fight the darkness that is descending upon the soul, until the soul suddenly, knowingly, lovingly, and with lustful vengeance reverses itself and accepts this darkness as light — in that picture there is such a profound lesson for human judges, for those who are accustomed to hold in their hands the measure and the scales, that they are bound to exclaim in fear and confusion: "No, I see now that vengeance is not always mine, and it is not always I who shall repay!" and will not condemn the culprit who succumbed to this darkness for having neglected the light of an eternally indicated solution and consciously rejected it. At the very least, the human judge will hesitate to apply the letter of the law. . . .

If we have works of literature of such power of thought and execution, then why can we not have *in the future our own* science, and our own solutions for economic, social problems; why does Europe deny us the right to independence, *our own word*, one cannot help asking oneself. Besides, how can anyone entertain the ridiculous idea that nature has endowed us only with literary gifts. All the rest is a matter of history, circumstances, a question of time. This is what at least our own Europeans might be expected to realize, until Europe's Europeans eventually render their judgment. . . .

Now that I have expressed my feelings, people will, perhaps, realize how I was affected by the falling away of such an author, his decision to segregate himself from the Russian common and great cause, and the paradoxical untruth that he slanderously slings at the Russian people in that wretched eighth part of his novel published by him separately. He simply robs the Russian people of their most precious possession, takes away from them the main meaning of their life. He would have liked it much better if our people would not rise everywhere in their hearts in support of their brethren suffering for their faith. It is only in this sense that he denies the existence of this phenomenon, despite its obviousness. Of course, all this is expressed merely in fictional characters of the novel but, I repeat, the author himself is more than obviously going along with them. It is true, this [separately published] booklet is quite sincere, the author speaks from his heart. Even most embarrassing things (and there are *embarrassing* things there) have found their way into the context, as it were, inadvertently so that, despite their embarrassing nature, one accepts them merely as a straightforward statement, without any twists. Nevertheless, I do not consider this booklet all that innocent. Of course, now it does not, and cannot have any influence, other than as a confirmation of the opinions of a certain exclusive group. But the fact that such an author writes in such a way is very sad. It is sad for our future. However, let me get down to business, I want to rebut, to point out what it is that has startled me more than anything else.

First, though, let me talk about Levin, obviously the main protagonist of the novel; in him is expressed all that positive matter, as if in contrast to those aberrations that have caused the destruction or suffering of the other protagonists, and he, apparently, was expressly designed by the author in order to project all this stuff through him. And yet, lo and behold, Levin is still imperfect, is still lacking in something or other, and this is what the author should have busied himself with and solved, so that there would be no more doubts and questions left for Levin to represent. The reader will realize later the reason why I am dwelling on this, without touching upon my main point.

Levin is happy, the novel ends for his greater glory, but he still lacks inner, spiritual peace. He is plagued by the eternal questions of mankind: about God, about eternal life, about good and evil. He is plagued by the fact that he is an unbeliever, and that he cannot acquiesce to that which most people acquiesce to, namely, self-interest, adoration of his own person or his own ideals, and vanity. A sign of a generous nature, isn't it? Well, no less could be expected of Levin. Moreover, it turns out that Levin has read a lot: he is familiar with the philosophers, the positivists, as well as ordinary naturalists. But nothing satisfies him and, on the contrary, confuses him even more, so that he, whenever he can spare a moment from his household duties, runs off to the copses and groves, gets all upset, even failing to appreciate his Kitty as much as she ought to be appreciated. And then suddenly he meets a peasant who, on telling him of the moral difference between two peasants, Mitiukha and Fokanych, expresses himself thusly:

> . . . Mitiukha never fails to strike a bargain! He puts on pressure until he gets what he wants. He does not care for the peasant, whereas uncle Fokanych will never attempt to skin the peasant alive. Sometimes he lets one have a loan, at other times he may even forget the debt. So, he does not always get what he wants, the good man.
> "But why should he forget the debt?"

"Well, I suppose, people are different; one man merely lives for his own advantage like, for example, Mitiukha, merely fills his belly. But Fokanych is not like that. He is a righteous old man. He lives for his soul, remembers the Lord."

"How's that—'remembers the Lord?' What do you mean 'lives for his soul'?"—Levin almost shouted.

"Well, I mean, its obvious: leads a righteous life, according to the Lord's teachings. People are different. Let's take you, sir, for instance, you won't hurt a man either."

"Yes, yes, good-bye!" said Levin, choking with excitement and, turning around, grabbed his stick and walked rapidly toward the house. . . .

Actually, he again runs off to the grove, throws himself down on the ground under the dogwood trees and begins to think in a kind of ecstasy. The [magic] word was found, all the everlasting mysteries solved with just this one simple statement from the peasant: "live for the soul, remember the Lord." Plainly, the peasant did not tell him anything new, he knew all this himself for a long time; still, the peasant nudged him toward the idea, and suggested the solution at the trickiest moment. After this we get a series of Levin's reasonings, very true and expressed to the point. Levin's idea is as follows: why search with your brain for that which is already given by life itself, that which every man is born with and which he (even willy-nilly) has to follow and does. Every man is born with a conscience, a knowledge of good and evil and, therefore, he is born even with a purpose in life: to live for good and to dislike evil. Born with it is the peasant, the master, the Frenchman and the Russian and the Turk—every one respects good even though some do that in awfully peculiar ways of their own. But I, says Levin, wanted to comprehend all this with the help of mathematics, science, reason, or waited for a miracle, and yet all this is given to me for free, I was born with it. And there is direct proof available that this is given to us for free: everyone in the world understands, or can understand, that one must *love one's neighbor like oneself*. In this knowledge, essentially, is contained all the law of mankind, just as it was announced to us by Christ himself. Besides, this meaning is inborn, and thus given for free, because reason could have never arrived at such a knowledge, and why?—Because to "love one's neighbor" is not a reasonable thing to do, if you think about it.

"Where did I take this from (asks Levin). Did I arrive at it logically that one must love one's neighbor, and not strangle him? I was told this as a child, *and I gladly believed it*, because I was told that which was in my heart. And who discovered it? Not reason. Reason discovered the struggle for existence and the law that says strangle all those who interfere with the satisfaction of my desires. This is the conclusion of reason. And to love another could not be discovered by reason because it is unreasonable.

Later on Levin imagines a recent incident with the children. The children began to fry raspberries in cups over candles and squirt milk into their mouths. The mother, who caught them doing it, began to persuade them that if they ruin the cups and spill the milk, they won't have any cups or milk left. But the children evidently did not believe her because they could not imagine "the extent of all the things available to them for use, and therefore could not imagine that that which they are destroying are the very things that they need for life.

"All this is granted," they thought, "there is nothing interesting or important about it because it has always been there and always will be. And it's always the same. We don't have to think about it, it's readily available; but we want to figure out something of our own, something new. So, we figured out to put raspberries in a cup and fry them over a candle, and squirt milk into each other's mouths. This is fun, and new, and no worse than to drink from cups."

"Isn't this the same thing that we do, I did, when I tried to reason out the meaning of forces of nature and the meaning of man's life?" Levin went on.

"And isn't this the same thing that philosophies do that lead man may be means of thinking, a means that is strange and alien to man, lead him to knowledge of that which he knew all the time, and knows well enough not even to want to live without this knowledge. Isn't it obvious from the development of every philosopher's theory that he knows in advance, just as surely as the peasant Fedor, and no better than he, what the main meaning of life is, and merely wants to arrive by dubious rational means at that which is already known to everyone."

"What would happen if we let loose the children, all by themselves, to find out how to make dishes, milk cows, etc. Would they still misbehave? If they did, they'd starve to death. And what happens if we are let loose in life, with all of our passions and ideas but without a knowledge of the one Lord and Creator! Or without a knowledge of what is good, without an explanation of what is moral evil."

"Just try to build anything without such concepts!

"We merely destroy because we are spiritually satiated. Children indeed!"

In a word, all doubts are gone and Levin is now a believer — in what? He hasn't quite figured it all out yet, but he already believes. However, is this faith? Joyfully, he asks himself the question "Could this be faith?" Presumably not quite yet. Moreoever, the ones who are like Levin could hardly even have a permanent kind of faith. Levin likes to think of himself as "the people" but he is not, he is a master, a young gentleman of the mid-upper circles of Moscow nobility, whose history Count Tolstoy has mostly been writing. Even though the peasant did not tell Levin anything new, still, he nudged Levin towards the idea, and this idea stirred his faith. That alone ought to have been enough to make Levin realize that he isn't quite yet the people and that he therefore mustn't constantly use the phrase: "the people — that's me." However, I'll come back to that later. I only want to say that those like Levin, no matter how long they may rub elbows with, or live next to, the people, will never completely merge with them, more than that — on many points they may never even understand the people at all. Mere conceit or an act of will, especially such a fanciful one, is not enough. It is not enough just to say so and expect to become immediately one with the people. So what if he is a squire, and a working squire, and knows all about the peasants' work, and does the mowing, knows how to hitch a horse to a cart, and knows that honey is served with fresh cucumbers. Nevertheless, and no matter how hard he tries, in his soul there will remain a shade of that thing that one may perhaps call *supercilious dalliance*, that very same attitude of idle curiosity, physical as well as spiritual, that he inherited, try as hard as he may to get rid of, and which the people detect in every gentleman, since they see things with an eye different from ours. But I'll come back to this, too, later. And his faith he will destroy again, all by himself. It won't last very long; a new hitch will develop and right away everything will collapse. Kitty went for a walk and stumbled, so why did she stumble? If she stumbled it means that she could not help stumbling; it's all too obvious that she stumbled because of this and that. It is clear that everything depended here on laws [of causality] that can be clearly determined. And if so, then science is everywhere. And where is [Divine] Purpose? What part does it play? Where does man's responsibility come in? And if there is no Divine Purpose, how can I believe in God and so on, and so forth. Take a straight line [of argument] and follow it to infinity. In a word, this honest soul is at the same time the most idle and chaotic soul, or else he would not be a modern Russian squire and an intellectual, especially if he also belongs to the mid-upper circles of the nobility.

He proves all this spectacularly a mere hour after having acquired his faith; he argues that the Russian people do not in the least feel what people feel generally, he destroys the people's soul in the most arbitrary fashion and, furthermore, declares that he himself feels no compassion for human suffering. He declares that "there is not, and cannot be any immediate feeling about the persecution of the Slavs," that is to say, not just he, but no Russian can have such feelings; the people, that's me. Levin and his ilk grossly undervalue the Russian people. This kind of valuation is not new, of course, coming from those kind of people. Less than an hour has passed, and again, raspberries are being fried over a candle.

Count Leo Tolstoi

Matthew Arnold*

In reviewing at the time of its first publication, thirty years ago, Flaubert's remarkable novel of *Madame Bovary*, Sainte-Beuve observed that in Flaubert we come to another manner, another kind of inspiration, from those which had prevailed hitherto; we find ourselves dealing, he said, with a man of a new and different generation from novelists like George Sand. The ideal has ceased, the lyric vein is dried up; the new men are cured of lyricism and the ideal; "a severe and pitiless truth has made its entry, as the last word of experience, even into art itself." The characters of the new literature of fiction are "science, a spirit of observation, maturity, force, a touch of hardness." *L'idéal a cessé, le lyrique a tari.*

The spirit of observation and the touch of hardness (let us retain these mild and inoffensive terms) have since been carried in the French novel very far. So far have they been carried, indeed, that in spite of the advantage which the French language, familiar to the cultivated classes everywhere, confers on the French novel, this novel has lost much of its attraction for those classes; it no longer commands their attention as it did formerly. The famous English novelists have passed away, and have left no successors of like fame. It is not the English novel, therefore, which has inherited the vogue lost by the French novel. It is the novel of a country new to literature, or at any rate unregarded, till lately, by the general public of readers: it is the novel of Russia. The Russian novel has now the vogue, and deserves to have it. If fresh literary productions maintain this vogue and enhance it, we shall all be learning Russian.

The Slav nature, or at any rate the Russian nature, the Russian nature as it shows itself in the Russian novels, seems marked by an extreme sensitiveness, a consciousness most quick and acute both for what the man's self is experiencing, and also for what others in contact with him are thinking and feeling. In a nation full of life, but young, and newly in contact with an old and powerful civilisation, this sensitiveness and self-consciousness are prompt to appear. In the Americans, as well as in the Russians, we see them active in a high degree. They are somewhat agitating and disquieting agents to their possessor, but they have, if they get fair play, great powers for evoking and enriching a literature. But the Americans, as we know, are apt to set them at rest in the manner of my friend Colonel Higginson of Boston. "As I take it, Nature said, some years since: 'Thus far the English is my best race; but we have had Englishmen enough; we need something with a little more buoyancy than the Englishman; let us lighten the structure, even at some peril in the process. Put in one drop more of nervous fluid, and make the American.' With that drop, a new range of promise opened on the human race, and a lighter,

*From *Essays in Criticism*, 2d ser. (New York: Macmillan, 1888), 253-99. First published in the *Fortnightly Review*, December 1887.

finer, more highly organised type of mankind was born." People who by this sort of thing give rest to their sensitive and busy self-consciousness may very well, perhaps, be on their way to great material prosperity, to great political power; but they are scarcely on the right way to a great literature, a serious art.

The Russian does not assuage his sensitiveness in this fashion. The Russian man of letters does not make Nature say: "The Russian is my best race." He finds relief to his sensitiveness in letting his perceptions have perfectly free play, and in recording their reports with perfect fidelity. The sincereness with which the reports are given has even something childlike and touching. In the novel of which I am going to speak there is not a line, not a trait, brought in for the glorification of Russia, or to feed vanity; things and characters go as nature takes them, and the author is absorbed in seeing how nature takes them and in relating it. But we have here a condition of things which is highly favourable to the production of good literature, of good art. We have great sensitiveness, subtlety, and finesse, addressing themselves with entire disinterestedness and simplicity to the representation of human life. The Russian novelist is thus master of a spell to which the secrets of human nature—both what is external and what is internal, gesture and manner no less than thought and feeling—willingly make themselves known. The crown of literature is poetry, and the Russians have not yet had a great poet. But in that form of imaginative literature which in our day is the most popular and the most possible, the Russians at the present moment seem to me to hold, as Mr. Gladstone would say, the field. They have great novelists, and of one of their great novelists I wish now to speak.

Count Leo Tolstoi is about sixty years old, and tells us that he shall write novels no more. He is now occupied with religion and with the Christian life. His writings concerning these great matters are not allowed, I believe, to obtain publication in Russia, but instalments of them in French and English reach us from time to time. I find them very interesting, but I find his novel of *Anna Karénine* more interesting still. I believe that many readers prefer to *Anna Karénine* Count Tolstoi's other great novel, *La Guerre et la Paix*. But in the novel one prefers, I think, to have the novelist dealing with the life which he knows from having lived it, rather than with the life which he knows from books or hearsay. If one has to choose a representative work of Thackeray, it is *Vanity Fair* which one would take rather than *The Virginians*. In like manner I take *Anna Karénine* as the novel best representing Count Tolstoi. I use the French translation; in general, as I long ago said, work of this kind is better done in France than in England, and *Anna Karénine* is perhaps also a novel which goes better into French than into English, just as Frederika Bremer's *Home* goes into English better than into French. After I have done with *Anna Karénine* I must say something of Count Tolstoi's religious writings. Of these too I use the French translation, so far as it is available. The

English translation, however, which came into my hands late, seems to be in general clear and good. Let me say in passing that it has neither the same arrangement, nor the same titles, nor altogether the same contents, with the French translation.

There are many characters in *Anna Karénine*—too many if we look in it for a work of art in which the action shall be vigorously one, and to that one action everything shall converge. There are even two main actions extending throughout the book, and we keep passing from one of them to the other—from the affairs of Anna and Wronsky to the affairs of Kitty and Levine. People appear in connection with these two main actions whose appearance and proceedings do not in the least contribute to develop them; incidents are multiplied which we expect are to lead to something important, but which do not. What, for instance, does the episode of Kitty's friend Warinka and Levine's brother Serge Ivanitch, their inclination for one another and its failure to come to anything, contribute to the development of either the character or the fortunes of Kitty and Levine? What does the incident of Levine's long delay in getting to church to be married, a delay which as we read of it seems to have significance, really import? It turns out to import absolutely nothing, and to be introduced solely to give the author the pleasure of telling us that all Levine's shirts had been packed up.

But the truth is we are not to take *Anna Karénine* as a work of art; we are to take it as a piece of life. A piece of life it is. The author has not invented and combined it, he has seen it; it has all happened before his inward eye, and it was in this wise that it happened. Levine's shirts were packed up, and he was late for his wedding in consequence; Warinka and Serge Ivanitch met at Levine's country-house and went out walking together; Serve was very near proposing, but did not. The author saw it all happening so—saw it, and therefore relates it; and what his novel in this way loses in art it gains in reality.

For this is the result which, by his extraordinary fineness of perception, and by his sincere fidelity to it, the author achieves; he works in us a sense of the absolute reality of his personages and their doings. Anna's shoulders, and masses of hair, and half-shut eyes; Alexis Karénine's updrawn eyebrows, and tired smile, and cracking finger-joints; Stiva's eyes suffused with facile moisture—these are as real to us as any of those outward peculiarities which in our own circle of acquaintance we are noticing daily, while the inner man of our own circle of acquaintance, happily or unhappily, lies a great deal less clearly revealed to us than that of Count Tolstoi's creations.

I must speak of only a few of these creations, the chief personages and no more. The book opens with "Stiva," and who that has once made Stiva's acquaintance will ever forget him? We are living, in Count Tolstoi's novel, among the great people of Moscow and St. Petersburg, the nobles and the high functionaries, the governing class of Russia. Stépane Arcadiévitch—

"Stiva" — is Prince Oblonsky, and descended from Rurik, although to think of him as anything except "Stiva" is difficult. His *air souriant*, his good looks, his satisfaction; his "ray," which made the Tartar waiter at the club joyful in contemplating it; his pleasure in oysters and champagne, his pleasure in making people happy and in rendering services; his need of money, his attachment to the French governess, his distress at his wife's distress, his affection for her and the children; his emotion and suffused eyes, while he quite dismisses the care of providing funds for household expenses and education; and the French attachment, contritely given up to-day only to be succeeded by some other attachment tomorrow — no never, certainly, shall we come to forget Stiva. Anna, the heroine, is Stiva's sister. His wife Dolly (these English diminutives are common among Count Tolstoi's ladies) is daughter of the Prince and Princess Cherbatzky, grandees who show us Russian high life by its most respectable side; the Prince, in particular, is excellent — simple, sensible, right-feeling; a man of dignity and honour. His daughters, Dolly and Kitty, are charming. Dolly, Stiva's wife, is sorely tried by her husband, full of anxieties for the children, with no money to spend on them or herself, poorly dressed, worn and aged before her time. She has moments of despairing doubt whether the gay people may not be after all in the right, whether virtue and principle answer; whether happiness does not dwell with adventuresses and profligates, brilliant and perfectly dressed adventuresses and profligates, in a land flowing with roubles and champagne. But in a quarter of an hour she comes right again and is herself — a nature straight, honest, faithful, loving, sound to the core; such she is and such she remains; she can be no other. Her sister Kitty is at bottom of the same temper, but she has her experience to get, while Dolly, when the book begins, has already acquired hers. Kitty is adored by Levine, in whom we are told that many traits are to be found of the character and history of Count Tolstoi himself. Levine belongs to the world of great people by his birth and property, but he is not at all a man of the world. He has been a reader and thinker, he has a conscience, he has public spirit and would ameliorate the condition of the people, he lives on his estate in the country, and occupies himself zealously with local business, schools, and agriculture. But he is shy, apt to suspect and to take offence, somewhat impracticable, out of his element in the gay world of Moscow. Kitty likes him, but her fancy has been taken by a brilliant guardsman, Count Wronsky, who has paid her attentions. Wronsky is described to us by Stiva; he is "one of the finest specimens of the *jeunesse dorée* of St. Petersburg; immensely rich, handsome, aide-de-camp to the emperor, great interest at his back, and a good fellow notwithstanding; more than a good fellow, intelligent besides and well read — a man who has a splendid career before him." Let us complete the picture by adding that Wronsky is a powerful man, over thirty, bald at the top of his head, with irreproachable manners, cool and calm, but a little haughty. A hero, one murmurs to oneself, too much of the Guy Livingstone type, though without the bravado and exaggeration. And such is, justly enough perhaps, the first impression, an impression which continues all through the first volume; but Wronsky, as we shall see, improves towards the end.

Kitty discourages Levine, who retires in misery and confusion. But Wronsky is attracted by Anna Karénine, and ceases his attentions to Kitty. The impression made on her heart by Wronsky was not deep; but she is so keenly mortified with herself, so ashamed, and so upset, that she falls ill, and is sent with her family to winter abroad. There she regains health and mental composure, and discovers at the same time that her liking for Levine was deeper than she knew, that it was a genuine feeling, a strong and lasting one. On her return they meet, their hearts come together, they are married; and in spite of Levine's waywardness, irritability, and unsettlement of mind, of which I shall have more to say presently, they are profoundly happy. Well, and who could help being happy with Kitty? So I find myself adding impatiently. Count Tolstoi's heroines are really so living and charming that one takes them, fiction though they are, too seriously.

But the interest of the book centres in Anna Karénine. She is Stiva's sister, married to a high official at St. Petersburg, Alexis Karénine. She has been married to him nine years, and has one child, a boy named Serge. The marriage had not brought happiness to her, she had found in it no satisfaction to her heart and soul, she had a sense of want and isolation; but she is devoted to her boy, occupied, calm. The charm of her personality is felt even before she appears, from the moment when we hear of her being sent for as the good angel to reconcile Dolly with Stiva. Then she arrives at the Moscow station from St. Petersburg, and we see the gray eyes with their long eyelashes, the graceful carriage, the gentle and caressing smile on the fresh lips, the vivacity restrained but waiting to break through, the fulness of life, the softness and strength joined, the harmony, the bloom, the charm. She goes to Dolly, and achieves, with infinite tact and tenderness, the task of reconciliation. At a ball a few days later, we add to our first impression of Anna's beauty, dark hair, a quantity of little curls over her temples and at the back of her neck, sculptural shoulders, firm throat, and beautiful arms. She is in a plain dress of black velvet with a pearl necklace, a bunch of forget-me-nots in the front of her dress, another in her hair. This is Anna Karénine.

She had travelled from St. Petersburg with Wronsky's mother; had seen him at the Moscow station, where he came to meet his mother, had been struck with his looks and manner, and touched by his behaviour in an accident which happened while they were in the station to a poor workman crushed by a train. At the ball she meets him again; she is fascinated by him and he by her. She had been told of Kitty's fancy, and had gone to the ball meaning to help Kitty; but Kitty is forgotten, or at any rate neglected; the spell which draws Wronsky and Anna is irresistible. Kitty finds herself opposite to them in a quadrille together: —

She seemed to remark in Anna the symptoms of an over-excitement which she herself knew from experience — that of success. Anna appeared to her as if intoxicated with it. Kitty knew to what to attribute that brilliant and animated look, that happy and triumphant smile, those half-parted lips, those movements full of grace and harmony.

Anna returns to St. Petersburg, and Wronsky returns there at the same time; they meet on the journey, they keep meeting in society, and Anna begins to find her husband, who before had not been sympathetic, intolerable. Alexis Karénine is much older than herself, a bureaucrat, a formalist, a poor creature; he has conscience, there is a root of goodness in him, but on the surface and until deeply stirred he is tiresome, pedantic, vain, exasperating. The change in Anna is not in the slightest degree comprehended by him; he sees nothing which an intelligent man might in such a case see, and does nothing which an intelligent man would do. Anna abandons herself to her passion for Wronsky.

I remember M. Nisard saying to me many years ago at the École Normale in Paris, that he respected the English because they are *une nation qui sait se gêner* — people who can put constraint on themselves and go through what is disagreeable. Perhaps in the Slav nature this valuable faculty is somewhat wanting; a very strong impulse is too much regarded as irresistible, too little as what can be resisted and ought to be resisted, however difficult and disagreeable the resistance may be. In our high society with its pleasure and dissipation, laxer notions may to some extent prevail; but in general an English mind will be startled by Anna's suffering herself to be so overwhelmed and irretrievably carried away by her passion, by her almost at once regarding it, apparently, as something which it was hopeless to fight against. And this I say irrespectively of the worth of her lover. Wronsky's gifts and graces hardly qualify him, one might think, to be the object of so instantaneous and mighty a passion on the part of a woman like Anna. But that is not the question. Let us allow that these passions are incalculable; let us allow that one of the male sex scarcely does justice, perhaps, to the powerful and handsome guardsman and his attractions. But if Wronsky had been even such a lover as Alcibiades or the Master of Ravenswood, still that Anna, being what she is and her circumstances being what they are, should show not a hope, hardly a thought, of conquering her passion, of escaping from its fatal power, is to our notions strange and a little bewildering.

I state the objection; let me add that it is the triumph of Anna's charm that it remains paramount for us nevertheless; that throughout her course, with its failures, errors, and miseries, still the impression of her large, fresh, rich, generous, delightful nature, never leaves us — keeps our sympathy, keeps even, I had almost said, our respect.

To return to the story. Soon enough poor Anna begins to experience the truth of what the Wise Man told us long ago, that "the way of transgressors is hard." Her agitation at a steeplechase where Wronsky is in danger attracts her husband's notice and provokes his remonstrance. He is bitter and contemptuous. In a transport of passion Anna declares to him that she is his wife no longer; that she loves Wronsky, belongs to Wronsky. Hard at first, formal, cruel, thinking only of himself, Karénine, who, as I have said, has a conscience, is touched by grace at the moment when Anna's troubles reach their height. He returns to her to find her with a child just born to her and Wronsky, the lover in the house and Anna apparently dying. Karénine has words of kindness and forgiveness only. The noble and victorious effort transfigures him, and all that her husband gains in the eyes of Anna, her lover Wronsky loses. Wronsky comes to Anna's bedside, and standing there by Karénine, buries his face in his hands. Anna says to him, in the hurried voice of fever: —

> "Uncover your face; look at that man; he is a saint. Yes, uncover your face; uncover it," she repeated with an angry air. "Alexis, uncover his face; I want to see him."
> Alexis took the hands of Wronsky and uncovered his face, disfigured by suffering and humiliation.
> "Give him your hand; pardon him."
> Alexis stretched out his hand without even seeking to restrain his tears.
> "Thank God, thank God!" she said; "all is ready now. How ugly those flowers are," she went on, pointing to the wall-paper; "they are not a bit like violets. My God my God! when will all this end? Give me morphine, doctor — I want morphine. Oh, my God, my God!"

She seems dying, and Wronsky rushes out and shoots himself. And so, in a common novel, the story would end. Anna would die, Wronsky would commit suicide, Karénine would survive, in possession of our admiration and sympathy. But the story does not always end so in life; neither does it end so in Count Tolstoi's novel. Anna recovers from her fever, Wronsky from his wound. Anna's passion for Wronsky reawakens, her estrangement from Karénine returns. Nor does Karénine remain at the height at which in the forgiveness scene we saw him. He is formal, pedantic, irritating. Alas! even if he were not all these, perhaps even his *pince-nez*, and his rising eyebrows, and his cracking finger-joints, would have been provocation enough. Anna and Wronsky depart together. They stay for a time in Italy, then return to Russia. But her position is false, her disquietude incessant, and happiness is impossible for her. She takes opium every night, only to find that "not poppy nor mandragora shall ever medicine her to that sweet sleep which she owed yesterday." Jealousy and irritability grow upon her; she tortures Wronsky, she tortures herself. Under these trials Wronsky, it must be said, comes out well, and rises in our esteem. His love for Anna endures; he behaves, as our English phrase is, "like a gentleman"; his patience is in general exemplary. But then Anna, let us remember, is to the last, through all the fret and misery, still Anna; always with something which charms; nay, with something, even, something in her nature, which consoles and does good. Her life, however, was becoming impossible under its existing conditions. A trifling misunderstanding brought the inevitable end. After a quarrel with Anna, Wronsky had gone one morning into the country to see his mother; Anna summons him by telegraph to return at once, and receives an answer from him that he cannot return before ten at night. She follows him to his mother's place in the country, and at the station hears what leads her to believe that he is not coming back. Maddened with jealousy and misery, she descends the platform and throws herself under the wheels of a goods train passing through the station. It is over — the graceful head is untouched, but all the rest is a crushed, formless heap. Poor Anna!

We have been in a world which misconducts itself nearly as much as the world of a French novel all palpitating with "modernity." But there are two things in which the Russian novel — Count Tolstoi's novel at any rate — is very advantageously distinguished from the type of novel now so much in request in France. In the first place, there is no fine sentiment, at once tiresome and false. We are not told to believe, for example, that Anna is wonderfully exalted and ennobled by her passion for Wronsky. The English reader is thus saved from many a groan of impatience. The other thing is yet more important. Our Russian novelist deals abundantly with criminal passion and with adultery, but he does not seem to feel himself owing any service to the goddess Lubricity, or bound to put in touches at this goddess's dictation. Much in *Anna Karénine* is painful, much is unpleasant, but nothing is of a nature to trouble the senses, or to please those who wish their senses troubled. This taint is wholly absent. In the French novels where it is so abundantly present its baneful effects do not end with itself. Burns long ago remarked with deep truth that it *petrifies feeling*. Let us revert for a moment to the powerful novel of which I spoke at the outset, *Madame Bovary*. Undoubtedly the taint in question is present in *Madame Bovary*, although to a much less degree than in more recent French novels, which will be in every one's mind. But *Madame Bovary*, with this taint, is a work of *petrified feeling*; over it hangs an atmosphere of bitterness, irony, impotence; not a personage in the book to rejoice or console us; the springs of freshness and feeling are not there to create such personages. Emma Bovary follows a course in some respects like that of Anna, but where, in Emma Bovary is Anna's charm? The treasures of compassion, tenderness, insight, which alone, amid such guilt and misery, can enable charm to subsist and to emerge, are wanting to Flaubert. He is cruel, with the cruelty of petrified feeling, to his poor heroine; he pursues her without pity or pause, as with malignity; he is harder upon her himself than any reader even, I think, will be inclined to be.

But where the springs of feeling have carried Count Tolstoi, since he created Anna ten or twelve years ago, we have now to see.

We must return to Constantine Dmitrich Levine. Levine, as I have already said, thinks. Between the age of twenty and that of thirty-five he had lost, he tells us, the Christian belief in which he had been brought up, a loss of which examples nowadays abound certainly everywhere, but which in Russia, as in France, is among all young men of the upper and cultivated classes more a matter of course, perhaps, more universal, more avowed, than it is with us. Levine had adopted the scientific notions current all round him; talked of cells, organisms, the indestructibility of matter, the conservation of force, and was of opinion, with his comrades of the university, that religion no longer existed. But he was of a serious nature, and the question what his life meant, whence it came, whither it tended, presented themselves to him in moments of crisis and affliction with irresistible importunity, and getting no answer, haunted him, tortured him, made him think of suicide.

Two things, meanwhile, he noticed. One was, that he and his university friends had been mistaken in supposing that Christian belief no longer existed; they had lost it, but they were not all the world. Levine observed that the persons to whom he was most attached, his own wife Kitty amongst the number, retained it and drew comfort from it; that the women generally, and almost the whole of the Russian common people, retained it and drew comfort from it. The other was, that his scientific friends, though not troubled like himself by questionings about the meaning of human life, were untroubled by such questionings, not because they had got an answer to them, but because, entertaining themselves intellectually with the consideration of the cell theory, and evolution, and the indestructibility of matter, and the conservation of force, and the like, they were satisfied with this entertainment, and did not perplex themselves with investigating the meaning and object of their own life at all.

But Levine noticed further that he himself did not actually proceed to commit suicide; on the contrary, he lived on his lands as his father had done before him, busied himself with all the duties of his station, married Kitty, was delighted when a son was born to him. Nevertheless he was indubitably not happy at bottom, restless and disquieted, his disquietude sometimes amounting to agony.

Now on one of his bad days he was in the field with his peasants, and one of them happened to say to him, in answer to a question from Levine why one farmer should in a certain case act more humanely than another: "Men are not all alike; one man lives for his belly, like Mitiovuck, another for his soul, for God, like old Plato."[1] — "What do you call," cried Levine, "living for his soul, for God?" The peasant answered; "It's quite simple — living by the rule of God, of the truth. All men are not the same, that's certain. You yourself, for instance, Constantine Dmitrich, you wouldn't do wrong by a poor man." Levine gave no answer, but turned away with the phrase, *living by the rule of God, of the truth*, sounding in his ears.

Then he reflected that he had been born of parents professing this rule, as their parents again had professed it before them; that he had sucked it in with his mother's milk; that some sense of it, some strength and nourishment from it, had been ever with him although he knew it not; that if he had tried to do the duties of his station it was by help of the secret support ministered by this rule; that if in his moments of despairing restlessness and agony, when he was driven to think of suicide, he had yet not committed suicide, it was because this rule had silently enabled him to do his duty in some degree, and had given him some hold upon life and happiness in consequence.

The words came to him as a clue of which he could never again lose sight, and which with full consciousness and strenuous endeavour he must henceforth follow. He sees his nephews and nieces throwing their milk at one another and scolded by Dolly for it. He says to himself that these children are wasting their subsistence because they have not to earn it for themselves and do not know its value, and he exclaims inwardly: "I, a Christian, brought up in the faith, my life filled with the benefits of Christianity, living on these benefits without being conscious of it, I, like these children, I have been trying to destroy what makes and builds up my life." But now the feeling has been borne in upon him, clear and precious, that what he has to do is to *be good*; he has "cried to *Him*." What will come of it?

> I shall probably continue to get out of temper with my coachman, to go into useless arguments, to air my ideas unseasonably; I shall always feel a barrier between the sanctuary of my soul and the soul of other people, even that of my wife; I shall always be holding her responsible for my annoyances and feeling sorry for it directly afterwards. I shall continue to pray without being able to explain to myself why I pray; but my inner life has won its liberty; it will no longer be at the mercy of events, and every minute of my existence will have a meaning sure and profound which it will be in my power to impress on every single one of my actions, that of *being good*.

With these words the novel of *Anna Karénine* ends. But in Levine's religious experiences Count Tolstoi was relating his own, and the history is continued in three autobiographical works translated from him, which have within the last two or three years been published in Paris: *Ma Confession*, *Ma Religion*, and *Que Faire*. Our author announces further, "two great works," on which he has spent six years: one a criticism of dogmatic theology, the other a new translation of the four Gospels, with a concordance of his own arranging. The results which he claims to have established in these two works, are, however, indicated sufficiently in the three published volumes which I have named above.

Note

1. A common name among Russian peasants.

Anna Karenina   Lionel Trilling*

When *Anna Karenina* first appeared, it was read with a special delight which had as its chief element an almost childlike wonder at recognizing in art what was familiar in life. This, people said, is the way things are, the way they really are, the way we have always known them to be, and no writer has ever represented them so before. The general feeling about the book was expressed by Matthew Arnold when he said in his essay on Tolstoi that *Anna Karenina* was not to be taken as a work of art but as a piece of life. In any strict sense, of course, Arnold's statement is quite illegitimate — art is art and life is life; we read novels and live life; and if we try to express the nature of our response to certain novels by saying that we "live" them, that is only a manner of speaking. But it is a manner of speaking which is necessary to suggest the character of Tolstoi's art.

The early response to *Anna Karenina* had in it, I have suggested, a certain naïvety. It was as if people up to then had had experience only of an art which was formal and conventional and were now for the first time confronting an example of naturalistic representation, as if they had never before had the opportunity to perceive what verisimilitude was. Yet of course this was not at all the case. Tolstoi originated no new genre. When *Anna Karenina* appeared — serially from 1875 to 1877 and as a volume in 1878 — the novel as an art form had reached a very high point in its development and had made great conquests of that part of life with which the novel is pre-eminently concerned, the part of life which we call the *actual*. To mention only the novelists of France, where the theory of the actual had been more consciously formulated than anywhere else, Balzac had completed his great canon of French social history nearly three decades before, Flaubert had published both *Madame Bovary* and *L'Éducation sentimentale*, and Zola was in the full tide of his production. Yet with all these masters of actuality already on the scene — not to speak of his own *War and Peace*, which, although in the nineteenth century it did not have its modern reputation, was nevertheless much admired — Tolstoi still made with *Anna Karenina* the effect I have described.

And he continues to make it. In our time Proust and Joyce have greatly extended the dominion of the novel of actuality; our culture as a whole is obsessively committed to fact; we have removed virtually every taboo that once stood in the way of our grasp of the way things are and have evolved bold and elaborate sciences of human behavior which would have delighted Balzac and Zola. Yet still, when we read *Anna Karenina*, we exclaim in the old naïve wonder and surprise, Why *this* is the way it is, this is life itself! And a contemporary critic, Philip Rahv, in effect says for us today what Arnold said for the nineteenth-century readers of the book.

*From *The Opposing Self* (New York: Viking, 1959), 66-75. Copyright 1951 by Lionel Trilling. Reprinted by permission of Harcourt Brace Jovanovich, Inc.

In Tolstoi, Mr. Rahv says, "the cleavage between art and life is of a minimal nature. In a Tolstoian novel it is never the division but always the unity of art and life which makes the illumination. . . . One might say that in a sense there are no plots in Tolstoi but simply the unquestioned and unalterable process of life itself; such is the astonishing immediacy with which he possesses his characters that he can dispense with manipulative techniques, as he dispenses with the bellestristic devices of exaggeration, distortion, and dissimulation."

This quality of lifelikeness, which, among all novelists, he possesses to the highest degree, does not make Tolstoi the greatest of novelists. Great as he is, there are effects which are to be gained by conscious manipulation and distortion, by plot and design, by sheer romancing, which he with his characteristic method cannot manage; there are kinds of illumination and delight which Tolstoi cannot give us but which Dickens, Dostoevski, and James can. But if Tolstoi is not the greatest of novelists—and that particular superlative, in any case, stands stupidly in the way of our free response to literature—he can be called the most *central* of novelists. It is he who gives to the novel its norm and standard, the norm and standard not of art but of reality. It is against his work that we measure the degree of distortion, exaggeration, and understatement which other novelists use—and of course quite legitimately use—to gain their effects.

Only one other writer has ever seemed to his readers to have this normative quality—what we today are likely to feel about Tolstoi was felt during the eighteenth century in a more positive and formulated way about Homer. It was what Pope felt when he said that Nature and Homer were the same.

One of the ways of accounting for the normative quality of Homer is to speak of his objectivity. Homer gives us, we are told, the object itself without interposing his personality between it and us. He gives us the person or thing or event without judging it, as Nature itself gives it to us. And to the extent that this is true of Homer, it is true of Tolstoi. But again we are dealing with a manner of speaking. Homer and Nature are of course not the same, and Tolstoi and Nature are not the same. Indeed, what is called the objectivity of Homer or of Tolstoi is not objectivity at all. Quite to the contrary, it is the most lavish and prodigal subjectivity possible, for every object in the *Iliad* or in *Anna Karenina* exists in the medium of what we must call the author's love. But this love is so pervasive, it is so constant, and it is so equitable, that it creates the illusion of objectivity, for everything in the narrative, without exception, exists in it as everything in Nature, without exception, exists in time, space, and atmosphere.

To perceive the character of Tolstoi's objectivity, one has only to compare it with Flaubert's. As the word is used in literary criticism, Flaubert must be accounted just as objective as Tolstoi. Yet it is clear that Flaubert's objectivity is charged with irritability and Tolstoi's with affection. For Tolstoi everyone and everything has saving grace. Like Homer, he scarcely permits us to choose between antagonists—just as we dare not give all our sympathy either to Hector or to Achilles, nor, in their great scene, either to Achilles or to Priam, so we cannot say, as between Anna and Alexei Karenin, or between Anna and Vronsky, who is right and who is wrong.

More than anything else, and certainly anterior to any specifically literary skill that we may isolate, it is this moral quality, this quality of affection, that accounts for the unique illusion of reality that Tolstoi creates. It is when the novelist really loves his characters that he can show them in their completeness and contradiction, in their failures as well as in their great moments, in their triviality as well as in their charm. And what other novelist than Tolstoi, without ever abating his almost sexual love for his heroine, can make us believe of her, as we believe of Anna, that she has become a difficult, almost impossible, woman? Or what novelist can tell us, as Tolstoi tells us of Vronsky, that his romantic hero is becoming increasingly bald without using the fact to belittle him? What we call Tolstoi's objectivity is simply the power of his love to suffer no abatement from the notice and accounts it takes of the fact that life usually falls below its ideal of itself.

It is a subtle triumph of Tolstoi's art that it induces us to lend ourselves with enthusiasm to its representation of the way things are. We so happily give our assent to what Tolstoi shows us and so willingly call it reality because we have something to gain from its being reality. For it is the hope of every decent, reasonably honest person to be judged under the aspect of Tolstoi's representation of human nature. Perhaps, indeed, what Tolstoi has done is to constitute as reality the judgment which every decent, reasonably honest person is likely to make of himself—as someone not wholly good and not wholly bad, not heroic yet not without heroism, not splendid yet not without moments of light, not to be comprehended by any formula yet having his principle of being, and managing somehow, and despite conventional notions, to maintain an unexpected dignity.

This is, of course, another way of saying that Tolstoi's reality is not objective at all, that it is the product of his will and desire (and of ours). And when we have said this, we must say more—we must grant that to achieve this particular reality Tolstoi omitted from it what some other realities include. Most notably he omitted the evil which is at the center of the vision of his great contemporary, Dostoevski. Tolstoi, to be sure, was anything but unaware of man's suffering. Levin, who, in *Anna Karenina*, is Tolstoi's representation of himself, is brought to a crisis of the soul by the thought that "for every man, and himself too, there was nothing but suffering, death, and forgetfulness," and he reaches a point where he believes that he "must either interpret life so that it would not present itself to him as the evil jest of some devil, or shoot himself." This is in form the very same idea that tortures Ivan Karamazov. But how different it is in tone, how different in intensity. Levin's sense of negation, though painful, is vague and perhaps merely melancholy; it has nothing of the specific horror and hideousness of Ivan's. And Levin can bring his crisis to resolution with relative ease, for he has conveniently at hand the materials of peace that Ivan does not possess and probably would not have accepted — piety, work, tradition, and the continuity of the family.

Nowadays the sense of evil comes easily to all of us. We all share what Henry James called the "imagination of disaster," and with reason enough, the world being what is is. And it is with reason enough that we respond most directly to those writers in whom the imagination of disaster is highly developed, even extremely developed. To many of us the world today has the look and feel of a Dostoevski novel, every moment of it crisis, every detail of it the projection of exacerbated sensibility and blind, wounded will. It is comprehensible that, when the spell of Tolstoi is not immediately upon us, we might feel that he gives us, after all, not reality itself but a sort of idyl of reality.

No doubt the imagination of disaster was not particularly strong in Tolstoi.[1] But perhaps it is just here that his peculiar value for us lies. For the imagination of disaster is a bold and courageous function of the mind but it is also exclusive and jealous — it does not easily permit other imaginations to work beside it; it more readily conceives evil than that to which the evil may befall; or, if it does conceive the thing that may be harmed, it is likely to do so in a merely abstract way. Our taste for the literature which arises from this imagination is a natural one, yet it has in it this danger, that we may come to assume that evil is equivalent to reality and may even come, in some distant and unconscious way, to honor it as such. Or it may happen that our preoccupation with evil will lead us to lose our knowledge, or at least the literary confirmation of our knowledge, of what goodness of life is. The literary production since Tolstoi has been enormously brilliant and enormously relevant, yet it is a striking fact that, although many writers have been able to tell us of the pain of life, virtually no writer has been able to tell us of pain in terms of life's possible joy, and although many have represented the attenuation or distortion of human relationships, scarcely any have been able to make actual what the normalities of relationships are. But in Tolstoi the family is an actuality; parenthood is a real and not a symbolic condition; the affections truly exist and may be spoken of without embarrassment and as matters of interest; love waxes and wanes, is tender or quarrelsome, but it is always something more than a metaphor; the biological continuity is a fact, not as in James Joyce's touchingly schematic affirmations, but simply and inescapably. It is, we may say, by very reason of the low pitch of his imagination of disaster that Tolstoi serves us, for he reminds us of what life in its normal actuality is.

I have said that it is chiefly Tolstoi's moral vision that accounts for the happiness with which we respond to *Anna Karenina*. That is why criticism, so far as it is specifically literary criticism, must lay down its arms before this novel. We live at a time when literary criticism has made for itself very bold claims which are by no means all extravagant. But the characteristic criticism of our time is the psychological analysis of language. This is a technique of great usefulness, but there are moments in literature which do not yield the secret of their power to any study of language, because the power does not depend on language but on the moral imagination. When we read how Hector in his farewell to Andromache picks up his infant son and the baby is frightened by the horsehair crest of his father's helmet and Hector takes it off and laughs and puts it on the ground, or how Priam goes to the tent of Achilles to beg back from the slayer the body of his son, and the old man and the young man, both bereaved and both under the shadow of death, talk about death and fate, nothing can explain the power of such moments over us — or nothing short of a recapitulation of the moral history of the race. And even when the charge of emotion is carried by our sense of the perfect appropriateness of the words that are used — Cordelia's "No cause. No cause"; or Ophelia's "I was the more deceived"; or Hamlet's "The rest is silence" — we are unable to deal analytically with the language, for it is not psychologically pregnant but only morally right; exactly in this way, we feel, should this person in this situation speak, and only our whole sense of life will explain our gratitude for the words being these and not some others.

In short, there are times when the literary critic can do nothing more than point, and *Anna Karenina* presents him with an occasion when his critical function is reduced to this primitive activity. Why is it a great novel? Only the finger of admiration can answer: because of this moment, or this, or this, mostly quiet moments, prosaic, circumstantial. Because of an observation of character: "Prince Kuzovlev sat with a white face on his thoroughbred mare from the Grabovsky stud, while an English groom led her by the bridle. Vronsky and his comrades knew Kuzovlev and his peculiarity of 'weak nerves' and terrible vanity. They knew he was afraid of everything, afraid of riding a spirited horse. But now, just because it was terrible, because people broke their necks, and there was a doctor standing at each obstacle, and an ambulance with a cross on it, and a sister of mercy, he had made up his mind to take part in the race." Or because of a fragment of social observation: "Vassenka Veslovsky had had no notion before that it was truly *chic* for a sportsman to be in tatters but to have his shooting outfit of the best quality. He saw it now as he looked at Stepan Arkadyevich, radiant in his rags, graceful, well-fed, and joyous, a typical Russian nobleman. And he made up his mind that the next time he went shooting he would certainly adopt the same get-up." Or because of Vronsky's unforgettable steeplechase and the almost tragic fall of the beautiful English mare; or Dolly's conversation with the peasant women about children and the business of being a woman; or Levin mowing with the peasants in the fields, the old peasant challenging him with "Once take hold of the rope, there's no letting it go!" and all the mowers watching for the master to break under the strain and on the whole glad that he does not; or the scene, taken from Tolstoi's own courtship of his wife, in which Levin and Kitty communicate by the initials of words written with chalk on a card table; or Alexei Karenin's determination to be a noble and Christian spirit and his inability to pursue his intention in the face of society's wish that he be ridiculous; or Anna's visit to her son on the morning of his birthday; or the passing of the moment in which Sergei, Levin's brother, might have proposed to Varenka, and the recognition by each of them that the moment had passed.

Part of the magic of the book is that it violates our notions of the ratio that should exist between the importance of an event and the amount of space that is given to it. Vronsky's sudden grasp of the fact that he is bound to Anna not by love but by the end of love, a perception which colors all our understanding of the relationship of the two lovers, is handled in a few lines; but pages are devoted to Levin's discovery that all his shirts have been packed and that he has no shirt to wear at his wedding. It was the amount of attention given to the shirts that led Matthew Arnold to exclaim that the book is not to be taken as art but as life itself, and perhaps as much as anything else this scene suggests the energy of animal intelligence that marks Tolstoi as a novelist. For here we have in sum his awareness that the spirit of man is always at the mercy of the actual and trivial, his passionate sense that the actual and trivial are of the greatest importance, his certainty that they are not of final importance. Does it sound like a modest sort of knowledge? Let us not deceive ourselves—to comprehend unconditioned spirit is not so very hard, but there is no knowledge rarer than the understanding of spirit as it exists in the inescapable conditions which the actual and the trivial make for it.

Note

1. Although strong enough to give us the character of Levin's brother Nicolai, whose despair of life is as entire and as deeply rooted as that of any of Dostoevski's characters.

Why Anna Kills Herself   Edward Wasiolek*

There are few scenes in world literature as painful to read as Anna's last day on earth. She is environed by emptiness. Within her is an abyss which she is helpless to fill. For her Vronsky alone can fill it, but he has left her—after the inevitable quarrel—to see his mother about business

*From *Tolstoy's Major Fiction* (Chicago: University of Chicago Press, 1978), 149–59. Reprinted by permission of the publisher and the author.

matters. As she waits for the word from the servant she had sent to summon Vronsky back, Anna attempts to fill the vacuum of time about her and in her. She cannot recognize herself in the mirror; she cannot remember whether or not she has done her hair. She can no longer coherently connect what she thinks with what she does and says. The world about her, including her own person, appears alien. The details that flash on the retina of her mind as she goes to see Dolly are, I believe, there to emphasize Anna's disconnectedness with the world about her. Life has become like a film that she watches but is not part of. She sees signs, people, dresses; someone bows to her; but none of what passes in front of her has any meaning to her. The visit to Dolly and the meeting with Kitty are as meaningless as everything else. Anna doesn't know why she has come or what to do. Tolstoy again projects Anna's inner state onto the world outside her, and what she sees is ugly. Back home, not knowing why she has returned, Anna sets off to the railway station in an effort to catch Vronsky. On the way to the railway station she has a moment of lucidity: she understands that Vronsky will not deceive her, that he has no schemes about Princess Sorokin, that he is not in love with Kitty, that he will not leave her. The moment of lucidity sets off the darkness of the irrational impulses that are overwhelming her. In that moment, Anna understands that what is driving her to destruction has nothing to do with the many pretexts she has given herself. *She even admits that a divorce and the return of her son would not really change anything.* The feelings that Vronsky and she have for each other would not change, the shame would be the same, the contempt of other women would not diminish.

When Anna gets out at the provincial station and the coachman gives her a note from Vronsky nonchalantly saying he will be home at ten, Anna is engulfed with a feeling of desperate aimlessness. The world recedes from her. She exclaims, "My God, where am I to go?" Tolstoy could not have chosen a more appropriate setting in which to dramatize Anna's desperate lack of goal. The station itself is a background for people who are going somewhere. Anna is going nowhere and has nowhere to go. People rush past her, greet each other, embrace, pursue their destinations, reach out for each other. But Anna stands on the platform with nothing inside her or outside her; she stands on the edge of her being. It is then that she sees the approach of a heavy freight train. The platform shakes, reflecting physically the dizziness Anna feels. Tolstoy increases the tension: as Anna tries to fling herself under the wheels of the first car, she is held back by the effort to get rid of the red bag she is carrying. On her second try, she succeeds, and the candle which had illuminated her brief life is extinguished forever.

Why does Anna kill herself? The question asks why Anna degenerated from the life-loving, generous and humane person we first meet to the tormented, punishing, strife-ridden and strife-giving person she becomes at the end. One will want to exonerate Anna—to blame society, her husband, Vronsky, and surely to blame the conditions of her love. Good reasons can be found to exonerate her; Tolstoy gives us many. But although he loves Anna and weeps for her, Tolstoy is convinced that she is wrong and that the love she bears for Vronsky is wrong. To show that she is wrong he gives us a picture of the right kind of love in Kitty's and Levin's love. The contrast between those two loves embraces the structure of the novel. Tolstoy has worked out the contrast in a deliberate way. While Anna is falling in love with Vronsky, Levin is being rejected by Kitty. When Kitty and Levin are falling in love, Anna is on her deathbed, attempting to reconcile herself to Karenin, struggling to give up Vronsky. As Anna and Vronsky leave Russia to begin their restless and aimless travels, Kitty and Levin are married. When Anna and Vronsky return to Moscow to make one desperate attempt to get a divorce and resolve their situation, Kitty is having a baby, finding new bonds of love and companionship with Levin. When Anna kills herself, Levin finds the secret of life in the words of an ignorant peasant. By and large the novel describes the deterioration of Anna's and Vronsky's love and the growth toward maturity of Kitty's and Levin's love. Both couples face some of the same situations, but the situations separate Anna and Vronsky and they bring Kitty and Levin together. Kitty, like Anna, experiences irrational outbursts of jealousy; like Anna, she feels unloved at times. Levin, like Vronsky, feels put upon by the demands of his beloved. Yet, while jealous outbursts increase the strife between Vronsky and Anna, they give Levin insight into the complexities of Kitty's soul. After Levin returns late and tells Kitty that he has been drinking at the club with Oblonsky and Vronsky and has met Anna, Kitty is convinced irrationally that her husband is in love with Anna. But the assurances of Levin assure Kitty, and the assurances of Vronsky that he is not in love with Princess Sorokin do not assure Anna. Later that night, when Kitty begins her labor, one of the important bonds between the couple becomes manifest.

To account for the difference between Kitty's and Levin's "right" love, and Anna's and Vronsky's "wrong" love, one may say that the former is "natural" and the latter "unnatural." But it is not so easy to say why one is natural and the other is unnatural. The good marriage for Tolstoy is free of the vanities of social life, fixed in mutual obligation of practical work, characterized by devotion of the partners to each other; most of all it is based on the birth and rearing of children. Levin's and Kitty's union fulfills, or at least comes to fulfill, all of these conditions. But in large measure so does the union of Vronsky and Anna. They are surely devoted to each other, at least before the union begins to sour; Anna has a contempt for society and Vronsky comes to say that he has; they have a child; and for a time at least they are both engaged in practical work— Vronsky, like Levin, with the circumstances of agricultural work, and Anna in helping him in his work. Yet each of these conditions comes to separate them rather than to unite them. Some incalculable element converts some of the same things into a warm, growing relationship for Kitty and Levin, and some incalculable element converts the love of Anna and Vronsky into a destructive, humiliating relationship. Kitty's and Levin's love ends, of course, in marriage and enjoys the approval of the society about them. There can be no doubt that the illicit relationship makes the love of Anna and Vronsky harder to maintain. But it is inconceivable that the legality of the one and the illegality of the other should explain the rightness and wrongness of the loves. Tolstoy makes it amply clear that he has nothing but contempt for much of what is approved by society. It is equally clear in his description of Anna's love that something deeper than the violation of convention lies at the basis of the destruction which overcomes that love.

This incalculable element cannot be the cruelty of the society in which Anna lives, nor the condition of irreconcilable love of son and lover, for the reasons I have already explained. Even less can it be what the epigraph suggests: that Anna suffers because she has sinned. Karenin thinks about God, but Anna does not. During her last day on earth Anna does not think about society, divorce, sin, or her son; she thinks only about Vronksy and his lack of love for her. Her last words are: "I will punish him and escape from everyone and from myself." She kills herself, at least as she explains it to herself, in order to punish Vronsky. This is not the first time that the thought of death has been linked in her mind with punishing Vronsky. It is, in fact, a repeated refrain. At the time of the quarrel about when to leave for the country, she solaces her "horrible shame" with the thought of death: how, if she died, Vronsky would repent, pity her, love her, and suffer for her. She smiles with satisfaction at the thought of his feelings after she is dead. If she is killing herself in order to punish Vronsky, then the motive is in keeping with what she has been doing to him throughout the affair. Since the consummation of their love, she has been punishing him by her fitfulness, her refusal to get a divorce and regularize this position, her jealousy, as well as by direct taunt and insult. "Where love ends hate begins," she tells herself as she prepares to end her life on earth, implying by this a necessary transition from one to the other. If Anna cannot have Vronsky by love, she will have him by hate. Many of her irrational actions are explainable as attempts, pleas, stratagems, by which to compel, if not Vronsky's love, at least his attention. If nothing else will turn Vronsky to her, perhaps the pain and guilt from her death will, if only in memory. All of this, while explaining why Anna acts and speaks as she does, does not explain why she would want to cling to Vronsky with such compulsive possessiveness. Nor does it explain why she hates herself as much as she hates Vronsky. For she is convinced that she is a shameful and corrupt woman. When, after the quarrel on the subject of when they should leave for the country, Vronsky comes to her tenderly and tells her that he is ready to go whenever she wants to, she cries out in tears, "Throw me over, get rid of me," for "I am a corrupt woman." Only the desperate, passionate caresses which she showers on him are able to still for a little while the hate she feels for herself. On the day before her suicide, after Vronsky's departure, she imagines his saying to her all the cruelest words that a coarse man would say. The next day, on her way to see Dolly, she catches herself in her thinking by noticing, "Again you want humiliation." The ugliness she sees around her on that day is surely the ugliness and hate she feels in herself.

The shame, as well as the desire to punish Vronsky and herself, come for Tolstoy from the nature of the love itself. It is the love that is wrong, not Anna or Vronsky or Karenin or society. And what is wrong with the love, for Tolstoy, is that it is contaminated and corrupted by sexual passion, whereas Kitty's and Levin's love is not so contaminated. Tolstoy insists rather coarsely on the physical basis of Anna's love. The imagery used to describe the suicide is sexual: the huge railway car throws Anna on her back; the peasant who appears at this point and who has appeared in her dreams is probably a symbol of the remorseless, impersonal power of sex. As he beats the iron, he pays no attention to her. In an early instance of the dream that she recounted to Vronsky, the bearded peasant (who mutters French phrases) runs into her bedroom. Vronsky too associates his dream of the peasant with the hideous things that he had to witness in conducting the visiting foreign prince about town. The last agonizing hours she spends on earth are also filled with sexual references. There is the explicit acknowledgment that she cannot live without Vronsky's caresses; she shudders with the imaginary physical caresses on her back as she stands in front of a mirror examining her hair. She sees the world about her as dirty, and such dirt is associated with shame and with the self-hate resulting from the slavery of sex. She reacts to children buying ice cream by the bitter acknowledgment that she has lived only for her dirty appetites, as do all people. On the train she mentally undresses a stout woman dressed in a bustle and finds her hideous.

It is the nature of physical passion that works for the destruction of Anna's and Vronsky's love, brings them to hatred of each other, brings Anna to hatred of herself, makes their relationship more and more spectral, breaks down the communication between them, brings them into a situation where they cannot speak frankly to each other, makes them avoid certain subjects, and forces them to surround themselves with other people so as to make each other's presence tolerable. Kitty's and Levin's relationship, on the other hand, is free of passion: they argue, work together; they feel close and at moments drift apart; they love each other and the love grows and prospers, but there is no indication on the part of either that the body of each is in some way the basis of their closeness. Kitty's and Levin's union is uncontaminated by sex. They draw closer to each other because they come to respect a certain distance; the constant refrain of Levin's understanding of Kitty is her difference from what he had imagined her to be. He comes to see and respect a center in Kitty

different from his own and he permits her to work out her own relationship to children, work, the household, and people, just as she permits him
his absorption in his agricultural theories and practice. The work of each
is serious in a way that the activities of Anna and Vronsky are not.
Vronsky's hospital, agricultural management, machinery, and painting
strike us as pretexts; and Anna's care of the English children, her writing
of a children's book and her absorption in agricultural books are patently
pretexts. Anna herself recognizes this in her scorching analysis of her
relationship with Vronsky on the last day of her life, when she calls their
activities pastimes (*zabavy*). Vronsky never enjoys the kind of total
absorption in work that Levin enjoys when he cuts hay with the peasants.

Tolstoy sees sex as a massive intrusion on a person's being and a
ruthless obliteration of the sanctity of personhood. Both Anna and
Vronsky feel coerced and manipulated by the other. The stronger Anna
loves, the more she coerces and the more she alienates. The corrupting
power of sex seems to be an extreme example of what Tolstoy has always
been against: the attempt of the individual to make the world one's own
and the consequent impoverishing and desiccating effect that such coercion
has on the world about one. The truth he reaches in *War and Peace*
consists of the consciousness of the plenitude of life that one attains when
one gives up one's control of the world. The centers of being of others with
all their radical uniqueness come into consciousness only when one
permits them to so arise. The right love also, for Tolstoy, comes into being
under the same conditions. And although it happens for Kitty and Levin,
one cannot avoid the feeling that the love is there to assure Tolstoy that
what he has believed in is still valid: that one can find wisdom, happiness,
peace, fulfillment, no matter how powerfully Anna's story seems to argue
the existence of something in nature that makes these things impossible.

Such an explanation of Anna's deterioration and death is consistent
both with Tolstoy's view of life and with the course of Anna's actions in the
novel. Anna's is a possessive love. Feeding on its possession, the love
alienates or destroys what it attempts to possess. Tolstoy signals this in the
seduction scene, when he compares the act of physical love to an act of
murder; this is for him no idle conceit, for possessive love does kill what he
considers to be the fount of a person' being—something sacrosanct,
radically individual, belonging to no man but only to the self-in-God.
Vronsky resents Anna's invasions of his personality, reacts unfavorably to
her attempts to coerce him into undivided attention to her; yet his very
resistance provokes Anna to demand more and more. The duel of control
and resistance leads Anna to more and more hysterical attempts and to
resentment too, because of his refusal to give himself entirely to her.
Suicide thus becomes the final attempt to control his being by way of guilt.
Tolstoy has built into the structure of the novel a fairly probable course for
Anna's actions that is in keeping with his personal distaste for sexual love.

He has in short been able to generalize what is personal and for many a bizarre view of sexual love, and to incorporate it into his general views about what desiccates life and what makes it flourish.

What is more, with his immense talent he has been able to dramatize the course of such a love so that it appears persuasive in its consequences. All this is Tolstoy's reading; yet it is not the only reading that the text will support. There is, of course, a presumptive validity to what the author has on some discernible level of structure led the reader to believe; yet the reader is not bound to accept—and, indeed, in some cases must not accept—the author's intentional structure as the definitive structure of the novel. I am talking about an intentionalism that one can discern in the novel, not one pronounced by the author in letter or diary. Wimsatt and Beardsley disposed of the latter some decades ago, but the "intentional fallacy" disposed of one kind of intentionalism and obscured another. The personal predilections, even eccentricities, shape the inner relations of the text in an inescapable way. The author's text is only one of many. Otherwise the text would be the prisoner of a special personality; no matter how great, it would still be limited and fixed in a special time. Anna's fate continues to provoke in us powerful feelings of compassion and mystery for reasons other than those Tolstoy has worked into the structure of the novel. Tolstoy has drawn a powerful portrait of a woman tortured and torturing, loving and hurting and being hurt. The portrait moves us as powerfully as it did Tolstoy's contemporaries, but for different reasons—reasons supported by structures in the text. Tolstoy's views on sex were already extreme at the time he wrote *Anna Karenina*; they are bizarre today. If Anna's terrible fate is the consequence of her sexual love and its evil nature, as Tolstoy would have us believe, and if this were the only explanation that the text could support, then I do not believe the novel would continue to move us as deeply as it does. There seems little doubt that in reading *Anna Karenina* we are in the presence of one of those great texts, the structure of which is multiple and which in its richness can support a great number—perhaps an inexhaustible number—of explanations.

The compulsive nature of Anna's love and the delusional nature of her mental life as the novel progressives would lead us, for example, to look for some psychoanalytic explanation of her motives. Anna is a driven person who becomes increasingly impervious to rational argument and objective evidence and increasingly incapable of discerning with reasonable accuracy the reality about her. It is some inner need that directs the course of her actions, feeding her delusions, and distorting the reality about her. Tolstoy has instinctively perceived that Anna uses the reality about her to camouflage a hidden reality. He gives us what appear, but only appear, to be explanations of why she acts as she does: the cruel society, the irreconcilable love of son and lover, the social shame before her actions, the conscious guilt at having hurt her husband, the fear of being abandoned by Vronsky. But Tolstoy has signaled that in the end these are all pretexts or rationalizations for something else.

Tolstoy explains the delusions as consequences that proceed from the nature of sex, which he looks upon as destructive of the sanctity of being. Perhaps, but not necessarily. A consequence in one system of explanation may be cause in another. What is painfully apparent on the last days of Anna's life is that Anna's misery does not come from the threat of abandonment by Vronsky, but that the threat of abandonment is a consequence of some other cause. Anna courts abandonment by insulting Vronsky and pushing him to hate her. Although Vronsky is not involved with other women, Anna insistently and obsessively needs to feel that he is in love with someone else. Vronsky does not hate her or see her as a corrupt creature (as she repeatedly charges him with thinking), but Anna needs to feel that she is hateful and corrupt. Why does Anna want to be hurt? to feel humiliated? and why does she court and propel the very things she fears and loathes? If not from external causes, then from inner causes, and from drives that seem unmodifiable by external circumstances. Nothing is more obvious than the "trapped" nature of Anna's feelings. If these destructive drives are so deep and powerful, they can only come from early experiences.

We know nothing about what led her to marry Karenin, but we do know that Karenin is twenty years older than she, and that his whole manner is one of public and private authority. One of the elders of society, he is something of a father to Anna. If Anna feels abused by Karenin's emotionless relationship to her, we might entertain the hypothesis that some psychic need was being satisfied when she chose him for her husband. This hypothesis takes on some credence when we see that Vronsky, for whom Anna abandons Karenin, in many ways resembles her husband. From Vronsky too Anna suffers from the threat of abandonment, and from a coldness that she discerns in him and projects onto him. That Anna should have been swept away by someone as unprepossessing as Vronsky—which astonished Matthew Arnold—becomes less mysterious when one entertains the hypothesis that Vronsky may be precisely the kind of person Anna needs: that she has chosen someone who will not meet the demands of her love and someone who will—with good form and a sense of honor—abandon her for social and political standing.

What I am suggesting is that Anna neurotically chooses someone who will hurt her, that she courts the feeling of being unloved, and chooses a situation in which she will feel shamed and corrupt. It matters not a bit that her sense of abandonment and emotional abuse is in good measure imaginary. The delusional nature of her hurt signal to us how compulsive and unchangeable her needs are. The need to be abandoned and hurt and the need to feel corrupt and hateful must come from sources deep in her being and early in her upbringing. Though we know nothing about her childhood, we do know that the sense of corruption precedes rather than follows upon the self-destructive acts she engages in. We also have some hints in the text itself that the drama in its most painful stages is related to her childhood; at least elements of childhood feelings invade her reflections at certain moments. On the night before her suicide, Anna waits in her room like a petulant child for Vronksy's return and for proof of his love by a visit to her before going to bed. She waits like a child waiting to be tucked in for the night. On the morning of the day of the suicide she kisses her hand as a mother will do to a hurt child. When she commits suicide her last thought is of herself as a child. We know also from the text that Anna suffers from the delusion that Vronsky loves another woman, who, in the last days, becomes increasingly his mother. Vronsky's mother, who becomes the obstacle to their moving to the country, is for that moment at least the cause of Vronsky's abandonment of her. It takes only the mildest of displacements to shift the cause of being unloved and abandoned by Vronsky from Vronsky's mother to her own mother. And if Vronsky represents for Anna's psyche a repetition of Karenin and the paternal image, then Anna in her last delusional hours reenacts a drama of terrified child facing abandonment by the father because of the intervening and hateful mother.

Once one begins to reason in this vein, a host of statements, actions, and ruminations begin to develop in a way different from the way Anna's fate is usually explained — whatever the range and variety of explanations — and different too from the way I have explained Anna's motives. I am not suggesting that *Anna Karenina* is best read as a psychoanalytic drama, but I am suggesting that one of the reasons the novel escapes the constricting force of Tolstoy's bizarre views on sex lies in the fact that multiple novels can be constructed from the order of dramatic events given. This is to say that the author's intentionalism — however deeply we see it imbedded in the text itself, and whatever term we wish to use for such a presence, whether "implied" or "realized" author — has a limited control over what we read and should have a limited control over what we accept. The emotions we give to *Anna Karenina* come from sources in part different from those that feed Tolstoy's passion.

We have, of course, an obligation to discern what the author has put into his work, but it will do his work and him no credit to limit its power to the sometimes eccentric views of the author himself. If a great work is "universal" — and I think *Anna Karenina* is universal — then it expresses and escapes even the deepest recesses of the author's creative being. This study is devoted to tracing out the special "mythology" of Tolstoy's view of reality and man's proper relationship to it, as Tolstoy has confronted this relationship in his fictive hypotheses. But I believe that such a "mythology" or personally structured experience is something that we must displace if we are to bring the structure into reasonable alignment with our understandings. *Anna Karenina* is powerful evidence for the spiritual and emotional biography of Tolstoy at this juncture of his life, for it shows how mightily Tolstoy attempts to integrate his increasing aversion to sex into a structure of experience that he had formulated so beautifully and coherently in the early works, especially in *War and Peace*. It is because he has trouble integrating Anna into his structured world that so much of her escapes his understanding and control. Kitty's and Levin's love is there to reassure us and especially Tolstoy himself that everything he believed in before *Anna Karenina* is still true. Tolstoy takes Levin to the fountain of truth again. But because it is a truth we have seen before it is less persuasive, especially when seen against Anna's fate.

The truth that Levin comes to is the truth that all the heroes of Tolstoy's novels come to: what Olenin glimpses and what Pierre and Natasha experience for a while, and what Karataev epitomizes: that one is in touch with reality when one empties oneself of wishes, desires, thoughts, plans, intentions. The world about one, incalculable in its movement and complexity, becomes one with oneself when one permits it to be. A good part of Levin's story, for example, has to do with plans and failures in his dogmatic attempts to bend life and people to his will. His plans are continually frustrated by the peasants, much as Pierre's reform intentions are sabotaged by the realities of peasant life. The peasants wreck Levin's machinery, disregard his instructions, steal his hay, and are uninterested in his reforms. They are like the recalcitrant element of life which refuses to give itself to the abstractions of Levin, as life had refused to give itself to the abstractions of Olenin, Prince Andrey, and most of Tolstoy's heroes up to this point. Levin comes to learn the most precious of Tolstoy's truths: that reality gives itself to one when one ceases efforts to possess it. Perhaps nowhere in the novel is this expressed more beautifully than in the "sacramental" scene of the hay mowing. In that scene Levin experiences, if only for a day, what the feel of reality is; and if the scene is no effective answer to the destructive impulses in people that Anna has introduced, Tolstoy's art is so great that one feels that it is an answer.

LATE NOVELS

Reviews

[Review of *Master and Man*]   Anonymous*

Tolstoy has warm admirers who could only under severe compulsion read *The Kingdom of God is Within You*, just as he has others who read *War and Peace* and *Anna Karénina*, in the rather vain hopes of extracting a gospel from them. The former had grown to think that the vein they valued was completely worked out; but the inventive faculty and the power of scenic representation, when they are as strong as they were in Tolstoy, are not easily exhausted or weakened. In his case an absorbing mission, and perhaps some ascetic principles, have had far more to do with the arrest of his artistic career than any decay of genius. The proof is, that now and again in his later peasant stories, written purposely for an uncultured audience, the old strength and beauty of phrase and incident refuse to be suppressed. Notably is this so in *Master and Man*; and surely we may be allowed to rejoice freely at the reappearance of the earlier Tolstoy. After all, next to life we learn most from art. Precept and homily have not half its reach. And the best reason for rejoicing he himself involuntarily provides. As a story-writer he is a fastidious artist; none more eager to search for the word, or, at least, the circumstance that will produce the desired effect on our imagination; there is nothing casual or haphazard in word or arrangement. He has plainly loved his imaginings, and tended them till they have become fair. In his books of precept, on the other hand, in spite of their striking thought, the form is as careless, and often as unsatisfactory as it could be. Unconsciously, and against his will, he has himself apportioned the respective values to be set on his two orders of books.

Master and Man begins in the dryest, most literal fashion, describing two commonplace persons, one a sordid country merchant, whose soul only stirs when he outwits a customer; the other, a ground-down, poverty-stricken peasant, a drunkard with fits of sour repentance. They take a winter journey together in a sledge, and get lost. The account of their wanderings and adventures is in its way masterly. But you are probably

*Review of *Master and Man*, trans. A. Hulme Beaman. From *Bookman* 1 (July 1895):409–10.

beginning to think you have had enough of their company — the tone and description being rigidly kept at their level, and their minds are not very lively — when the catastrophe occurs. While the deadly sleep is creeping over them they have each their own fears and visions. As a man knows his own heart best by his dreams, so these two different human hearts are revealed to us by theirs — the selfish, greedy man with his hopes still on gain, the overdriven peasant with desire for rest. Then Vassili the master makes a great effort for life, deserting the now unconscious Nikita; and if ever the terror of a desperate man in a wilderness of night and snow could be adequately suggested to the imagination, it is suggested here — by the simplest means, too. The dark spot, which might be a sheltering house, turning into a black strip of reeds, all whistling and bending before the merciless storm; the horse's tracks speaking of hope till they are discovered to be his own, and prove him to have been travelling in a circle: a few such glimpses in a short page or two keep the man's desperate case fast and vivid in our imaginations. Then comes the climax, or rather the revelation of the motive of the story. A central and sublime belief in the religion which Tolstoy literally accepts, declares that the soul, in great moments, by divine intervention, is made better than itself — a doctrine contradicted by our daily common life of sordid disappointments, but which a wider human experience, reaching beyond Christendom, faithfully corroborates. So Vassili, of the petty bargaining past, who, if a to-morrow were still granted him, would again overreach his neighbours and chuckle at his cleverness — Vassili goes back to Nikita, clasps him in his arms, wraps him in his coat, and gives him all his warmth. Thoughts and dreams crowd on him for long. "He remembered his money, his shop, his house, his buying, and his sales, and the Mironoff millions, and could not understand why the man they called Vassili Andreïtch Brekhunoff had worried over what he had worried over. . . . And he felt that he was free, and nothing further held him back. And these were the last things that Vassili Andreïtch saw, heard, and felt in this world."

Perhaps with the death of the master and the comparative safety of Nikita the tale should have ended. But we will not perversely seek for an artistic defect in a story so beautiful in conception, so masterly in development, so skillfully delicate in workmanship.

Tolstoi's *Kreutzer Sonata*   Isabel Hapgood*

What are the legitimate bounds of realism? To what point is it permissible to describe in repulsive detail the hideous and unseemly things of this world, simply because they exist, when it is quite impossible to say

*From the *Nation* 50 (17 April 1890):313–15.

what the effect will be upon thousands of people to whom such description conveys the first knowledge of the existence of evil? It has been proved that public executions, far from inspiring horror of the deeds which led to them, and deterring others from the commission of like deeds, through fear of the result thus presented, actually give rise to crimes copied after those which are thus brought to general attention. The same thing is true in the case of crimes which are minutely described in the newspapers. But books? On the whole, although a sensational realistic book may never reach as many people as an article published in the popular newspaper, it probably produces as much effect because of the weight and respectability which the binding and comparatively high price give to it.

One has occasion to reflect upon this topic rather frequently in these days of "psychological" romances; but it is not often necessary, I think, to meditate so seriously as one is forced to do over Count Lyoff Tolstoi's last story.

When I first reached Russia, in the autumn of 1887, I heard that Count Tolstoi was writing a new tale: it began on the railway, and a man murdered his wife, and it was to be of the searching psychological type exemplified by *Ivan Ilyitch*. So much seemed to be known in well-informed circles. I asked no questions when I made the Count's acquaintance a year later. But one evening last July, during a visit I made to Yasnaya Polyana, at the Countess's invitation, the Count spoke to me of his story as being near completion, and asked me to translate it when it should be finished. I promised, and inquired whether it was in a condition for me to read. "You may read the last version if you like," he answered, "but I would rather have you wait." His wife showed me sheets of the fourth version, which she was then copying, and advised me not to waste time in reading it, as it was quite likely that he might suddenly see the subject in a totally different light, and write it all over again from that point of view. So I read nothing, asked no questions, and waited, being informed from time to time that the book was progressing. How many different versions were finally made, I do not know, but this winter one of these versions began to make the rounds in Petersburg. The solitary manuscript flew rapidly from hand to hand. I was warned, however, that it or any copy from it would be imperfect, incomplete, and not approved by the author, who was at work upon the final version. I contented myself with the verdict of those who were too impatient to wait, and who had not been promised the first complete copy, as I had been. That verdict was, "Shocking!" "Beauties mingled with horrors," and so forth. It was said that it was not allowed to be printed—the usual cry; but, as there is nothing religious or political in it, its morality must have been the cause of the prohibition, if true.

At length I received the first copy of the genuine story (the second went to the Danish translator), with the information that, although the substance was nearly identical with that of the version which had already been circulating, and which was said to be in process of translation into foreign languages, the execution had been so altered that "not one stone was left upon another" in some places, while in others whole pages, and even chapters, had been completely rewritten by the author. My copy was corrected by the author especially with a view to translation, and was, therefore, to be regarded as the only one sanctioned by him for rendering into other tongues, and this version is yet unattainable in St. Petersburg.

Why, then, do I not translate a work from the famous and much-admired Russian author? Because, in spite of due gratitude to Count Tolstoi for favoring me with the first copy, and in spite of my faith in his conviction that such treatment of such a subject is needed and will do good, I cannot agree with him. It recalls the fable of his countryman, Kriloff, about the man who borrowed his neighbor's water cask, used it for wine, and returned it impregnated with vinous fumes to such a degree that the unfortunate lender was obliged to throw it away, after using every possible means, during the space of two years, to expel the taint so that the water should be pure once more.

"Too frank and not decent," was one of the Petersburg verdicts upon this *Kreutzer Sonata*. This is so true that, although thus forewarned, I was startled at the idea that it could possibly be beneficial, and, destroying the translation which I had begun, I wrote promptly to decline the task. It is probable that the author and his blindly devoted admirers will consider that I have committed an unpardonable sin. But they must remember that his "comedy," *The Realm of Darkness*, although it was acted in private, in high Petersburg society, and in public in Paris, has never been translated into English, so far as I am aware, at least. I yield to no one in my admiration for and appreciation of Tolstoi's genius, as displayed in certain of his works. I tried to get American publishers to bring out *War and Peace* and *Anna Karenin* in 1881, five years before American readers were treated to the mangled versions of those works through the French. They declined, and one noted Boston publisher said, with great frankness: "No one in Russia knows how to write except Turgeneff, and he is far above the heads of Bostonians." I predicted a change of opinion, and if I am now morally compelled to appear unfaithful to my own former admiration, my regret is certainly more deep and sincere than even the regret of those who merely repent their failure to grasp an opportunity for making money, or of those who, consciously or unconsciously, follow the literary fashion of the hour.

But I will turn to the book. After making due allowance for the ordinary freedom of speech, which has greater latitude in Russia (as elsewhere in Europe) than is customary in America, I find the language of the *Kreutzer Sonata* to be too excessive in its candor. At the same time I admit that if that subject was to be treated in that way, no other language would have answered the purpose. I mention this first because it is the first thing which strikes the reader, and because it is also the special thing which hovers over the horrors of the tale with an added dread, and lingers long behind in the reader's mind, like a moral bad taste in the mouth. Next, the style and construction. The construction is good, as is usual with the author. The style errs in the direction in which all his books are faulty, viz., repetition. The unnecessary repetition of words or phrases occurs in his greatest works, while in the later, the polemical, writings, it has become greatly exaggerated. It forms a feature of this book, and although it gives strength at times, it is too marked on the whole. One must think that this tautology is deliberate on the author's part, since he is never in haste to publish uncorrected matter; but the result is harshness, which increases with every fresh work. Nevertheless, the book is well written. And the story? It is that of a man who kills his wife out of jealousy for a semi-professional violinist, who plays Beethoven's *Kreutzer Sonata* with her one evening.

The author begins by narrating how he is making a long journey by rail. In the compartment with him are a lawyer and a lady, masculine in appearance and attire, who converse, and a gray-haired man with brilliant eyes, who avoids all attempts to talk with him and utters a peculiar sound from time to time. A merchant and a clerk enter the railway carriage at one of the stations. A partly inaudible conversation between the masculine lady and the lawyer about some woman who has fallen out with her husband, leads the lawyer to remark upon the amount of attention which is being bestowed all over Europe upon the question of divorce, and to say that there was nothing of the sort in olden days. The merchant answers him that there were cases even in old times, but they were less frequent; and people had become too "cultured" nowadays. In the discussion which ensues, the merchant advocates the old-fashioned arrangement of marriages by parents, and strict government on the part of the husband, as most conducive to wedded happiness, alleging that love will come in due season. The masculine lady argues that it is stupid to join in marriage two people who do not love each other and then feel surprised if discord ensues between them, and that the day for such unions is past. The merchant maintains that the day for obeying the New Testament rule, "Let the wife fear her husband," will never pass away; that although unfaithfulness, which is assumed to be impossible on the part of the wife, may happen in other classes, in the merchant class it does not happen, and that the carouses of married men at the fair, which the narrator has heard him relating, and of which he reminds him, form a special topic which must be excluded from the discussion.

Here the merchant leaves the train, but the conversation is continued by the passenger with gray hair and brilliant eyes inquiring to what sort of love the masculine lady has reference. What is "true love," and how long must it last — a month, two days, or half an hour — when it has been defined as the preference for some one man or woman above all other men or women in the world! He contends that only in romances does this preference last for a lifetime, as per theory; whereas in real life it endures for a year, generally much less, and is felt by every man for every pretty woman; also, that this love is never mutual, and if it were, and if it lasted a lifetime on one side, it would not on the other. Identity of ideals, spiritual likeness, he does not admit as a ground for entering upon marriage. He gives a brief sketch of the manner, in his opinion, in which marriages are entered upon, winding up: "And the result of this is that frightful hell which makes men take to drink, shoot themselves, poison, and murder themselves and each other."

The lawyer, with a view to putting an end to the unseemly conversation, replies that "there are undoubtedly critical episodes in married life." Whereupon the speaker remarks: "I see that you recognize me. I am Pozdnisheff, the man with whom occurred the critical episode of murdering his wife." In fact, no one knows anything of him, but the lawyer and masculine lady change into another compartment as soon as possible, while Pozdnisheff offers to withdraw if his presence is disagreeable to the narrator. Finding that it is not, he offers to while away the night by relating the story of his life. I may remark here, in view of the above, that the author gives not a hint of his own opinion as to which is preferable, a marriage of love or a *mariage de convenance*, and also that some of the points suggested do not seem to be answered thereafter.

Pozdnisheff begins his tale with his introduction to evil at the age of sixteen. Shorn of digressions, his story would be brief. But the digressions attack many accepted views of things — or views which he says are accepted. The present order of society and life, modes of marriage, dress, and so forth, form the topics of these digressions. Pozdnisheff states that he has taken to analyzing the subject since his own life reached a climax in his crime. Many of these remarks I recognize as substantially identical with attacks on those subjects contained in all the author's serious writings. The sentence, "I never see a woman clad in ball attire that I do not feel like shouting, 'Police!' and ordering her to be removed as dangerous," closely corresponds to former utterances upon low-necked dresses and so on. He repeats former denunciations of higher education for women, but, astonishing to relate, instead of winding up with the moral that women should devote themselves solely to becoming the mothers of the largest possible families, he praises the Shakers because they do not marry, and declares that woman will only rise to a higher plane, cease to rule in false ways as an offset to oppression, and acquire her full rights, when virginity shall have become the highest ideal of womanhood.

I am tempted to a personal digression at this point. Count Tolstoi one day praised the Shakers in this manner before a table full of people. I was afraid to ask him his meaning, lest he should explain in detail, so I questioned his wife in private as to whether this new departure was not somewhat inconsistent with his previously advocated views on woman's vocation. She replied: "Probably it is inconsistent; but my husband changes his opinions every two years, you know." The explanation which I venture to offer is, that just at that time he was reading Mr. Bowell's *An Undiscovered Country*, and that he is impressionable. At all events, however clearly one can understand from these too frank digressions what a man should not do, it is quite impossible to comprehend how he thinks a woman should dress, behave, and live.

Returning to the thread of his story, Pozdnisheff relates how he proposed for his wife after a very brief acquaintance, fascinated by her jersey, her well-dressed hair, and a boating excursion, and adds that, had it not been for the tailors who dressed her well, and the close jersey, etc., he should never have married. This does not agree with the statement that all through his vicious bachelorhood he had firmly intended to marry if he could find any one good enough for him. An interesting point here is that he shows his betrothed his bachelor diary, just as Levin shows his to Kitty in *Anna Karenin*, and with precisely the same effect, only less well told. The repetition of this incident and the probable rarity of such diaries seem to hint at a personal experience.

They are married. The description of the honeymoon and of their married life nearly up to the date of the final catastrophe is, like what precedes, unquotable. Suffice it to say that they quarrel promptly and continue to quarrel frequently and fiercely, eventually using their five children as moral battering rams, so to speak, against each other. This last is very well done. At about the age of thirty, his wife becomes plump and prettier, and begins to take an interest again in pretty clothes. His mad jealousy interprets this into a quest for a lover, though there are no proofs of such a thing even alleged. The description of his jealousy is, however, the best part of the book. Presently the object for jealousy for whom the husband has been on the lookout, makes his appearance in the person of a handsome young man, of good family, who has been educated in Paris by a relative, as he has no money, and who has become a very fine and semi-professional violinist. The young man comes to call on his old acquaintance, Pozdnisheff, on his return to his native land. Pozdnisheff instantly fixes upon him, in his own mind, as the fated lover. Nevertheless, or rather in consequence of this, he is unusually cordial, introduces the musician to his wife (quite unnecessarily), and begs him to bring his violin that very evening and play duets with her. The musician comes, behaves with perfect propriety, as Pozdnisheff admits, but jealousy causes him to see what he expects. He urges the musician to dine and play at his house on the following Sunday, still impelled by the fancies of his own disordered brain. The musician accepts; but, having called in the interim to decide upon the proper music to present to the company, he drives Pozdnisheff to such a pitch of unreason that the latter uses vile language to his innocent wife and throws things at her, whereupon she promptly retires and takes poison.

She is rescued, a reconciliation ensues, the dinner comes off, and the

Kreutzer Sonata in the evening is a great success upon the violin and piano. But the husband's jealousy and imagination are all alive, and interpret every glance of the players to suit himself. On taking leave that evening, the musician bids Pozdnisheff and his wife a final farewell. Pozdnisheff is going to the country on business, and the musician says that he shall leave Moscow himself before the former's return, intimating that he shall not call upon Madame during her husband's absence. Pozdnisheff goes to the country in a tranquil frame of mind, but a letter from his wife, in which she mentions that the musician has called to fetch her the music he promised, sets his jealousy aflame again. He hastens back to Moscow, finds the musician eating supper with his wife, and murders her. On trial he is acquitted on the plea of "justifiable homicide" and when the narrator of the story meets him in the train, he is on his way to a small estate in one of the southern governments, his children remaining with his dead wife's sister.

The whole book is a violent and roughly worded attack upon the evils of animal passion. In that sense, it is moral. Translation, even with copious excisions, is impossible, in my opinion, and also inadvisable. The men against whom it is directed will not mend their ways from the reading of it, even if they fully grasp the idea that unhappiness and mad jealousy and crime are the outcome of their ways, as Pozdnisheff is made to say in terms as plain as the language will admit of, and in terms much plainer than are usually employed in polite society. On the other hand, the book can, I am sure, do no good to the people at whom it is not launched. It is decidedly a case where ignorance is bliss, and where uncontaminated minds will carry away a taint which a few will be able to throw off, but which will linger with the majority as the wine of the fable lingered in the cask meant for pure water. Such morbid psychology can hardly be of service, it seems to me, much as I dislike to criticise Count Tolstoi.

Posthumous Works of Tolstoy   Abraham Cahan*

When Turgéneff, writing on his deathbed, addressed Tolstoy as "the great writer of our Russian land" and implored him to return to literary activity, he meant Tolstoy the objective artist, the portrayer of throbbing human life, not Tolstoy the author of tracts. But the two Tolstoys were inseparably blended, in fact. Vengeroff, the literary historian and critic, has described the creator of Anna Karénina as "Russia's great conscience,"

---

*Review of *Hadji Murad, Father Sergius and Other Stories, The Forged Coupon and Other Stories, The Man Who Was Dead (The Living Corpse)*, and *The Light That Shines in the Darkness*. From *Bookman* 35 (April 1902): 209-12.

and this conscience manifests itself in Tolstoy's best artistic productions as well as in his essays on religion or morals.

Indeed, it takes a truly great artist to unite the two elements with impunity. In most cases it is apt to defeat both purposes at once. The novel which is intended to be a sermon in the form of a story usually hits neither of the two birds. Occurrences are marshalled and characters are trimmed to fit the preconceived moral, and the moral reflects the artificiality of the picture.

Life, however, is full of its own sermons. They are songs without words, these sermons, and an artist of Tolstoy's order does not have to sacrifice aesthetic sincerity to his sense of right and wrong. On the contrary, the more faithful he be to his art, the keener will be the human sympathy which his work will arouse, the more effective the moral lesson he will inculcate. Born with an extraordinary gift for listening to and conveying Life's unvarnished tale of our complex existence, with its lights and shades, joys and woes, poetry and squalour, with its iniquities, cruelties, irrelevancies, martyrdoms, self-sacrificing altruisms, Tolstoy was in a position to achieve the reconciliation of moralist and painter without as much as being aware of the feat. This he did in a wonderful manner, but not invariably.

Sometimes a lifelike picture of his would, by its very reality, belie the tenet which it was intended to vivify. On other occasions his marvellous art would simply be intruded upon by long-winded moralisings and theorisings which fused with the situations depicted no more than water would with oil. Or, he might introduce into the story his own personality under the guise of a Pierre Besoukhoff (in *War and Peace*), a Levin (in *Anna Karénina*), or a Nekludoff (in *Resurrection*) and take up page after page with his own meditations and "self-lashings."

In the several volumes of his posthumous stories and dramas, one sees the detachment between the missionary and the artist more often than in the best known of his former works, yet they contain much that bears the stamp of the master-hand which produced those works.

Every story or drama in the five volumes before us is interesting, and — in spite of limitations, due for the most part to lack of finish — full of the invigorating ozone of real art. The absolute simplicity, unsophisticated clarity and unembellished directness which are among the qualities of Tolstoy's method are characteristic of every one of these offerings. The appeal is made at once and is sustained to the last line. A simple human appeal it is, and it enthralls the reader's attention irresistibly. Here and there one comes across an unconvincing bit of narrative, some crudity or gap, which tend to indicate that the story was a rough first-sketch rather than a finished product. One feels that in order to make the tale as profoundly true as Tolstoy's stories usually are the author would have had to bestow far more time and space upon it. But it charms us as it is. We are always in the presence of a master with a penetrating eye and with an uncompromising prophet-like passion for truth, always in the presence of "the great conscience of Russia."

Whatever may be the relative merit of these posthumous productions when placed side by side with such works of their author as *War and Peace*, *Anna Karénina*, *The Death of Ivan Ilytch*, *Childhood and Youth*, *Family Happiness* or *Master and Man*, they certainly take rank with the best things we have received from any source since the publication of *Resurrection*.

Hadji Murad, which occupies one of the five volumes under consideration, has been characterised as a novel of action. But the term has been too woefully abused to suit a piece of literature of this type. It is usually contrasted with the "novel of character," and is meant to apply to "plot novels," in which the plot is the chief source of interest, animating detail being sacrificed to the rapidity with which events pass in review. *Hadji Murad* is certainly full of action, but it is the kind of action which is alive with the blood of reality. The story is peopled with characters every one of which appeals to one's imagination with the certainty of an acquaintance in actual life, and every scene in it makes the reader feel as though he had personally taken part in it. It is a romantic story, thrillingly so, but here again a word of special comment seems to be needed in order to save the term from misconstruction. Indeed, so deep-rooted is our habit of regarding romance as the antithesis of realism, that we are apt to forget that real life is rich in the wildest happenings which the boldest imagination could conceive; that fact is often really stronger than the most far-fetched fiction. *Hadji Murad* is an entrancing piece of romance, full of colour, but real, true, absolutely convincing. It is semi-historical, in fact, the author having met the central figure of the tale in the fifties and the events described being largely actual occurrences in the history of Russia's subjugation of the Caucasus.

Hadji Murad, a Tartar chieftain, was "the leading dare-devil and 'brave' " of the mountainous region. Tolstoy contrasts the naturalness and unsophisticated impulsiveness of this dauntless barbarian with the insincerities and varnished barbarities of his civilised conquerors. The following passage, which is distinctively Tolstoyan, is representative of the whole work:

> That evening, at the New Theatre, which was decorated in oriental style, an Italian opera was performed. Vorontsov was in his box when the striking figure of the limping Hadji Murad, wearing a turban, appeared in the stalls. He came in with Lovis Melikov (Count Louis Melikov, who afterward became Minister of the Interior and framed the Liberal ukase which was signed by Alexander II. the day that he was assassinated, but who was then Vorontsov's aide-de-camp). Having sat through the first act with oriental, Mohammedan dignity, expressing no pleasure, but only obvious indifference, he rose and looking calmly

around at the audience went out, drawing to himself everybody's attention.

The next day was Monday and there was the usual evening party at the Vorontsovs'. In the large, brightly lighted hall a band was playing hidden among the trees. Young and not very young women in dresses displaying their bare necks, arms and breasts, turned around in the embrace of men in bright uniforms. As the buffet footmen in red swallowtail coats and wearing shoes and knee breeches, poured out champagne and served sweetmeats to the ladies, the "Sirdar's" wife also, in spite of her age, went about half-dressed among the visitors, affably smiling, and through their interpreter said a few amiable words to Hadji Murad, who glanced at the visitors with the same indifference he had shown yesterday in the theatre. After the hostess, other half-naked women came up to him and all of them shamelessly stood before him and smilingly asked him the same question: How he liked what he saw? Vorontsov himself, wearing gold epaulets and gold shoulder-knots with his white cross and ribbon at his neck, came up and asked him the same question, evidently feeling sure, like all others, that Hadji Murad could not help being pleased at what he saw. Hadji Murad replied to Vorontsov, as he had replied to them all, that among his people nothing of the kind was done. He said it without expressing an opinion as to whether it was good or bad that it was so.

Father Sergius, the leading figure in a story by that name, was originally a courtier with a splendid future before him. Discovering a liaison between his betrothed and the Czar, he suddenly cuts short his worldly career and enters a monastery, where, in a desperate struggle for moral perfection, he is faced by a series of temptations in the form of the sex. It is a most original story, full of unique interest; and it is only to be deplored that the author died without having had an opportunity to develop the various parts more fully. As it is, and when one bears in mind the high finish, full of life-giving detail, which characterise Tolstoy's celebrated novels, the story strikes one as a somewhat crude, though a fascinating study intended to serve as a basis for a novel rather than the novel itself.

The Man Who Was Dead, a drama in five acts, is perhaps the most interesting piece of histrionic literature that ever came from Tolstoy's pen. Not that the drama was his most natural vehicle of expression. For Tolstoy was primarily a painter of the inner man, a department of literary art which cannot very well be restricted by the trammels of dialogue. Tolstoy's strongest effects are achieved by introducing the reader to the mental processes of his characters, and while it is certainly true that the best characterisation is often attained by hearing him or her talk, it is equally true that conversations alone would be powerless to admit us to those psychological depths and that vividness of portraiture which more than anything else places Tolstoy at the head of modern novelists. Yet the few dramas which he has left us are a notable contribution to this branch of literature, and among these *The Man Who Was Dead* will be found a most irresistible production. Indeed, it has met with singular success wherever it was produced, whether in the original or in translation; and the book is as thrilling to the reader as the play is to the theatre-goer.

The story of the play is practically the story of a case which came up in the criminal court of Moscow and the details of which were conveyed to Tolstoy by the judge who presided at the trial. In order to enable his wife to marry the man she loves, the prisoner had caused a false report to reach her to the effect that he, her legal husband, is dead. This he backed up by changing his name and completely withdrawing from his former world. The deception was discovered many years after the supposed widow celebrated what she thought was her second wedding.

Tolstoy was always fond of "plagiarising reality," as Jack London would put it. He preferred to borrow his plots from actual life. With such a story for a skeleton he would proceed to clothe it with flesh and blood and a delicately complicated nervous system. This he did with the above criminal case, as far as the limitations of the dramatic form would permit.

Protassoff, the leading character in the play, is easily one of the most engaging and pathetic personalities ever seen on any stage. It is a distinctively Russian type, the embodiment of conditions in a country where the nobility has been effeminated and rendered unfit for practical action by many centuries of the serf-system, on the one hand, and by the complexities of an iron-handed hierarchy on the other. Protassoff is the possessor of that "broad Russian soul" which often leaves little room for sober prosaic common sense. The so-called "Russian unpreparedness," of which one heard so much during the late Russo-Japanese conflict, was, in fact, to a large extent at least, the result of the same conditions. The Russian officers, sons of the same nobility to which Protassoff belongs, were no match for their hardy and practical opponents. It was simply a case of the history of the Crimean War repeating itself. It was the outcome of that war — by the way, an outcome disastrous for Russian arms — which was the most potent cause that led to the abolition of serfdom. The helplessness of the Russian, when pitted against an Englishman, made the effect of that system manifest to the then ruling spirits of the country. But then the abolition of serfdom is of too recent origin for all its traces to have vanished. The types which it produced persist.

Pure, high-minded, impatient of the cruelties and hypocrisies of the life that surrounds him, Protassoff is too weak to join in a crusade against these conditions. As an upshot, his own existence is abhorrent to him. He hates himself for what he regards as an iniquitous life, and he hates himself for his lack of fibre.

Here we at once recognise the spirit of "Russia's great conscience," but Protassoffs are a rather common occurrence in that country, and the central figure of the play is as real as was its author.

Protassoff seeks to drown the voice of his conscience in the Wine,

Woman and Song of a Moscow café, where there is a gypsy girl with a voice that "turns his whole inner life upside down," whose songs are as full of fire as her eyes. The girl is an interesting combination of traits inherited partly from her roving parents and partly from the civilisation which surrounds her. She is sincerely in love with Protassoff, but his is a sort of platonic interest.

His self-disgust grows in proportion as he sinks lower and lower economically and socially. Yet the inner-man in him remains as pure and attractive as ever, so that while we are repelled by his outer metamorphosis, we are overcome by a heart-breaking sense of commiseration for the spiritual man, coupled with a keen condemnation of the conditions which we hold responsible for his degradation.

Protassoff pities his wife, and it is in order to free her from himself and to enable her to be happy with his best friend, that he decides to become a "living corpse." When the multilated drowned body of an unknown man is picked up floating in the river, Protassoff avails himself of the incident. He sets a report on foot that the dead man is no other than he.

The Light That Shines in the Darkness is a play which is generally supposed to depict Tolstoy's own conflict with his family in endeavouring to live up to his high moral principles.

Two of the strongest and most touching stories in the volume headed by the *Forged Coupon* are "My Dream" and "After the Dance."

They are remarkable tales, both of them, reminding us of their author's best vein and of the most characteristic trend of his genius.

Articles and Essays

Master and Man and *The Death of Ivan Ilych*

N. K. Mikhaylovsky*

How does one preserve life without the thought of death that poisons one's existence? How does one burn out, destroy this fear of death that, as we have seen, "is put into everyone?" This is Tolstoy's main task lately. Although it concerned him before, now he is exclusively concerned with it, and all his writings are merely peripheral to it, connecting the various points of his outlook with this fear of death at its center.

All of his discussions of physical labor, about "harness," pure air of the fields and woods, and other hygienic features of his moral doctrine belong here in the first place. However these things merely guarantee health and longevity, death is only postponed, while still remaining the dreadful, inevitable end. Couldn't it be made at least not so dreadful? For this there is a prescription, already worked out to perfection by the buddhists: without repudiating life, one must reduce its budget as much as possible, so that when one reaches the inevitable end, one can pass without fear and regret into that area of nirvana, which, strictly speaking, is neither life nor death. If this is so, then the end may be not only free of fear but not even inevitable. I refuse to follow the fantastic leap of thought or the just as fantastic crawl of the willowy syllogisms with which Tolstoy arrives at the conclusion that the right kind of life will preserve us from death. I will merely remind the reader of the ending of the *Death of Ivan Ilych*. This ending is, artistically, an unpleasant blot on the story — to such a degree it is arbitrary, unmotivated, lacking in that bright and pitilessly authentic realism Tolstoy is justly famous for. Ivan Ilych didn't do anything particularly bad, but lived his entire life as a limp, shallow egotist and, having fallen ill, began to suffer from the fear of death. But just before the very end, having realized that his wife and son are really feeling sorry for him, becomes imbued with pity and love himself.

> And suddenly it became clear to him that what had been oppressing him and would not leave him was all coming out suddenly, and from both sides, from ten sides, and from all sides. He felt sorry for them, felt

*From *Otkliki* 2 (St. Petersburg: Russkoe bogatstvo, 1904): 63-68. Translated for this volume by Boris Sorokin.

the need to do something so that they would not suffer; to free them, and himself as well, from this suffering. "How nice and how simple," he thought. "And the pain?" he queried himself, "Where shall I put it?" "So, where are you, pain?"

He turned his attention to it.

"Ah, here it is. Well, what of it? Let the pain be."

"And death? Where is it?"

He was looking for his former habitual fear of death and could not find it. "Where is it? What death?" There was no fear, because there was no death. Instead of death there was light.

"So that's what it is!" he suddenly said out loud. "What joy!"

I think that this exclamation "What joy!" must strike any artistically somewhat sensitive person as a dissonant note that pains the ear. And if such a great artist like Tolstoy introduced this false chord into his story, then it must have been because he was so very eager to show that death may not be so dreadful after all, that it may not even exist. He is trying to console us as well as himself here. We appreciate it, of course. We thank him, particularly, for saying that in order to conquer the fear of death one needs to practice not just Buddhist asceticism but love, active love, love in the form of good deeds, even though this love might have been presented as having another, more solid and less speculative basis.

Ivan Ilych didn't do anything very bad, he lived more or less like everybody: went to work, played cards, went visiting, and had people come to his house, had a wife and a son with whom he more or less got along. But it was only at the very end that a spark of real love ignited in him that hitherto had had almost no chance to express itself in a good deed. But even that was enough to free Ivan Ilych from the fear of death and make him partake of a joyous death, even an absence of death. In this new story, "Master and Man," Tolstoy apparently makes a considerably greater demand upon one of his protagonists in terms of active love.

I said earlier that the new story reminds one of Tolstoy's peak years of literary production. One newspaper account even had it that "this story is a masterpiece even among the works of the famous writer himself." This, I believe, is going a little too far. The same paper asserted that the story was "almost four signatures long." This is not true: the story is less than two and a half signatures long, and if in reading it someone has felt that it was almost twice as long, then we have here a clear indication of one of the shortcomings of Tolstoy's new work: it is stretched too much with numerous and unnecessary details. It does remind one of Tolstoy's peak years, but that's all it does. The inner suspense of the story is concentrated in the last two chapters, which I shall quote here fully, especially since they are, artistically, the best too. As already mentioned, the master and man went in winter to take care of the master's pretty ordinary, everyday, yet not quite clean business, typical of the sort of man he was. To conduct this business the master, a well fed, rich, self-satisfied peasant-business-man and sweatshop owner who, by the way, was also a church warden, took along a sum of 2,300 rubles belonging to the church. Along the way they got lost and, after a number of misadventures, the man realized that he was freezing to death and was about to submit uncomplainingly to the will of the higher power. Meanwhile the selfish master decided to leave him to perish, while he himself rode away on horseback wherever the horse would take him. But the horse, after having circled aimlessly a few times, brought him back to the same place where his man was slowly freezing to death in the sleigh. In order to get warm, he lies down on the man's body and warms him up in this way. In his own terminal delirium he imagines that:

> And he lay on the bed, still unable to rise, waiting, and the waiting filled him with dread and also with joy. And suddenly his joy was complete: the one he was waiting for came, and it was not the policeman, Ivan Matveich, but someone else, but it was the one he was waiting for. He came and is calling him, and the one who is calling him is the same one who told him to lie on top of Nikita. And Vasilii Andreich is glad that this someone has come for him. "I'm coming!" he shouts joyfully. And his own shout wakes him up . . .
>
> And he wakes up, but now he is a different person from who he was when he fell asleep. He wants to get up but can't; wants to move his arm, and can't; his leg, too, would not move. He wants to turn his head, and can't do that either. And he feels surprise but is not in the least worried about this. He understands that this is death, but this does not worry him in the least either. He understand that Nikita is lying underneath him and that he is now warm and alive, and it begins to seem to him that he himself is Nikita, and Nikita is him, and that his own life is now not in him but in Nikita. He strains his hearing and hears Nikita breathing, even snoring faintly. "Nikita is alive, therefore I am alive too," he says triumphantly to himself. And something quite new, a feeling that he never knew all his life, is now descending upon him.
>
> And he remembers all about his money, his shop, his house, buying and selling, and the Mironov millions, and he is now at a loss to understand why this man whom they call Vasilii Brekhunov used to do all those things he was doing. "Well, he did not really know what was what, that's why," he thought about Vasilii Brekhunov. He didn't, but now I know. I know for sure that I *know now*. And again he hears the one who is calling him, and his whole being responds joyfully, "Coming, coming!" And he feels that he is now free and that nothing keeps him back any more.
>
> And indeed, Vasilii Andreich neither saw nor heard not felt anything any more in this world.
>
> . . . .
>
> But Nikita died only this year — at home, as he wished, lying below the icons and with a burning wax candle in his hands. Before he died he asked forgiveness of his wife, and forgave her her affair with the cooper;

he also took leave of his son and his grandchildren, and died, genuinely glad that his death relieves his son and daughter-in-law of the need to feed an extra mouth, and that now he really was passing from this wearisome life into that other life which with each passing year and hour had become for him more and more comprehensible and attractive. Is he better or worse off in that place where he awoke after this his real death? Was he disappointed, or did he find there whatever he expected? That we shall all soon know.

So there we have two more deaths (not counting the horse) in Tolstoy's rich collection. The master's death strongly reminds one of the death of St. Julian the Hospitalier in a well known legend by Flaubert, translated by Turgenev. St. Julian, too, lies down on a dying man in order to warm him, and, dying himself, also feels "an abundance of happiness, a superhuman joy." In his terminal delirium the person of the leper whom he was warming, also fuses with the higher being who, admittedly, does not call on St. Julian to join him but directly carries him off into the wide blue yonder. The master is not guilty of any of those terrible sins and evil deeds that burden St. Julian's soul, but on the other hand, St. Julian atones for his sins by years of achievement, and his final selfless deed is merely the last link in a chain, which lends the story a naturalness insofar as this is possible in a legend. The master, on the other hand, did not spill any blood, like St. Julian, nor did he kill his parents, yet he was a crook and probably responsible for the ruination of dozens of people in order to advance his own well being. Let us say, all this can be atoned for by his last minutes, but it seems to me that only one of two things is possible: if the master saved his man unconsciously, inadvertently, hoping to save himself by warming himself with the man's body, then this is hardly a self-sacrifice, and the moral value of the master's last few minutes is not great; but if he really did forget about himself and his only thought was to save the man, then this would seem to be too sudden a turnaround, too unmotivated an act — since only a short time before he was ready to betray and abandon the man to his fate in order to save himself. The "joyous" death that St. Julian *earned*, the master got as a real bargain: with an almost unconscious and in any case semi-conscious deed, the result of which was a rescue of his fellow man immediately after a heartless deed toward this selfsame fellow man. And yet his deed is somewhat more substantial than the terminal flareup of love in Ivan Ilych. As regards the man, Nikita, here we have an uncomplicated man, hardly a saint, a drunkard, but a goodnatured one, servile and hardworking, nonresistant to evil and completely satisfied with his lot, as opposed to his master who wants more and more money, no one knows why. Nikita knows that besides the "master" in the story he also has another "Master" in heaven, whose will be done. So, these are, then, the two roads that lead to a joyous death. . . .

As any other work of Tolstoy, his new story lends itself to drawing several conclusions from it, besides the main one concerning death; among others, one may, for example, conclude that it is better to be a man than a master. This conclusion would not be news for Tolstoy. In one of his fairy tales, "Ilias," the man and his wife, who used to be masters themselves, praise their present status. They say: "For fifty years we were looking for happiness and did not find it, and only now, for the second year that we are left with nothing and live as laborers, have we found real happiness and don't need any other . . . We used to live from one worry to another, one sin unto another, and saw no happiness in life . . . Now we get up, chat a little with each other lovingly, always agreeing, have nothing to argue about, nothing to worry. All we need to think about is how to serve the master." I'm afraid that neither masters nor men will believe Tolstoy.

The Later Stories   R. F. Christian*

"One usually thinks that most conservatives are old men and most innovators young men. This is not quite so. Most conservatives are young people who want to live, but who neither think nor have the time to think how one *should* live, and so choose as their model the life they have always known." These controversial words from *The Devil* have an unmistakably autobiographical ring, for Tolstoy as an old man was not a little proud of his nonconformity. The themes of nearly all his late stories were chosen to enable him to express his iconoclastic attitude to the organisation of society, the administration of justice and the relation between the sexes. Those on the subject of sex have attracted the greatest publicity. Uncompromising, perverse and uncharitable, they share a common loathing of the sexual act, whether lawful or unlawful, committed or merely meditated. The premise of *The Kreutzer Sonata* is that carnal love is selfish and that unselfish love needs no physical consummation. Do people go to bed together, asks its "hero" Pozdnyshev, because of their spiritual affinities or the ideals they have in common? The knowledge and recollection of his own sexual indulgence in the past dominate his thinking to the exclusion of all else. He assumes that his wife's musician friend has only one thought in mind, and as the text for *The Kreutzer Sonata* (and *The Devil*) reminds us: "But I say unto you that everyone who looketh on a woman to lust after her hath committed adultery with her already in his heart." Pozdnyshev murders his wife because he is tormented by jealousy. It follows for him that all husbands must be jealous, all wives unfaithful. His thoughts are controlled by the assumption that every possibility of evil must result in evil. The potential for good is simply discounted. Music is potentially evil

*From *Tolstoy: A Critical Introduction* (Cambridge: Cambridge University Press, 1969), 230-46. Reprinted by permission of the publisher.

because, like the presto in *The Kreutzer Sonata*, it may arouse feelings which cannot be satisfied by the music itself. Sexual passion is the root of all evil. Social conventions, low-cut dresses and the medical profession are accessories before the fact. By the second chapter of the story we already know Pozdynshev's opinion of love and marriage and we know that he has murdered his wife. The narrator's role, apart from occasional interruptions, is negligible; he is not important enough to form a barrier between Pozdnyshev and the reader, or between the author and his hero.

> In *The Kreutzer Sonata*, Tolstoy adopted Turgenev's method, putting a first-person narrative in the thin frame of a third-person setting. Just as, in many of Turgenev's novels, a party of gentlemen converse at dinner until one of them begins to recount an episode of his youth, which thereupon becomes the novel, so, in *The Kreutzer Sonata*, the general conversation in a railway-carriage resolves itself into a personal confession.[1]

Pozdnyshev dompletely cominates the scene with his powerful, polemical monologue, which by its very nature is unable to actualise the character of his wife and her suspected lover or to consider them from any point of view except his own. His wife has no opportunity to state her case. Her friend is treated with the same contempt which Tolstoy reserves for Napoleon, the bureaucrats and the intelligentsia: "He had an unusually well-developed posterior like a woman's, or like a Hottentot's, so they say." Of course Pozdnyshev is his own prosecutor, and one who shows no mercy. As he says to himself when he decides to go and see his dying wife, whom he has stabbed: "Yes I expect she wants to repent. . . ." He is given

> the thankless task of acting as Tolstoy's agent in the story. He is required to express Tolstoy's views, but with a pathological violence and peculiarity supposedly his own. It is as if we knew that Shakespeare hated sex, but not so much as Hamlet does; and was disgusted with human beings, but not in quite so sensational a fashion as Timon. Tolstoy can neither release Pozdnyshev nor conceal himself behind him.[2]

Pozdnyshev's arguments are absurdly exaggerated and inconsistent and flavoured with Tolstoy's addiction to percentage generalisations — 90% do this, 99% do that; music is responsible for "most cases" of adultery in our society. The body is the ever-present villain, the animal the symbol of unbridled incontinence, for all that it compares favourably with the human species in refraining from intercourse during pregnancy and suckling.

Significantly enough, in the light of Tolstoy's own prejudices, the whole story takes place in a railway carriage. Pozdnyshev himself comments on the emotional upheaval caused by railways. He claims to be afraid of railway carriages. He acknowledges a temptation to lie down on the rails — all this with reference to another train journey he is describing on his way to catch his wife, as he hopes, *in flagrante delicto*, a train journey within a train journey, as it were, which provides a structual basis for the story. And structurally speaking, it is taut, powerful and gripping, despite its occasional inept dialogue and its motley material culled from Tolstoy's letters to Chertkov and the books and letters he received from the American Shakers. A sensitive and, on the whole, convincing attempt has recently been made to relate the structure of the story to Beethoven's sonata itself.[3] It is an approach which is capable of further exploration. Put briefly, the argument is that Tolstoy's story appeals mainly to the ear; that the human voice is the literary equivalent of the solo instruments; that one's attention in reading (or listening) is constantly being drawn to sounds; and that the "confessional" form of the narrative is the nearest literary approach to the music of piano and violin, "two voices that strive through the sonata to become one." We are reminded that Beethoven's sonatas are characterised not only by intensity of dramatic feeling, but also by violent contrasts of moods and emotion. The structure of the story can plausibly be shown to correspond to general sonata form, and the Presto of the first movement — following an opening Adagio — which is so important for Pozdnyshev, is peculiarly important for the theme of the story as a whole. The author of the article observes that "the violin is the dominating instrument, the inviting instrument" in the Presto; "the piano changes key and sidesteps the issue. There is an extraordinary progressive ascending movement at the end, which strongly suggests a dragging away by force; there is a significant silence, a kind of consent, and a haunting passage which could suggest shame, and the movement ends with a burst of passion from both instruments, with the violin in control." Like the sonata, Tolstoy's story falls naturally into three movements with a slow introduction. "The subject of the first movement concerns the general notion of solicitation between the sexes and the particular instance of this in Pozdnyshev's own courtship, wedding and honeymoon. As in the sonata, there are false starts, the subject is introduced, dropped, hinted at. . . . Pozdnyshev at first is dominant, the narrator parries the question he raises and Pozdnyshev finally becomes the narrator. . . . The first movement of the sonata is disturbing, passionate and at times violent, and so is the story." The second movement (Chapters 13-19) corresponds to Pozdnyshev's married life and his growing jealousy, with each of the two partners contending for power, "or rather striving to be free from the dominance of the other." The third movement introduces the musician, and its pivotal point is the Kreutzer Sonata itself, the final chapter (28) rounding it off like a coda, and returning us to the mood of the Adagio opening. In musical terms the analogies could be pressed further without doing violence to the thesis which, when retailed in this eclectic manner, does less than justice to an article which is stimulating and well argued. Tolstoy's well-known receptivity to music and his intuitive feeling for musical form lend point to the musical analogies already made in the context of the Sevastopol sketches and developed further with reference to the composition, tempo and progression of *The Kreutzer Sonata*.

Structural considerations apart, few other novelists could have made compelling reading out of sentiments and arguments which are irritating and manifestly unjust. Few other novelists could have given pathos and poignancy to the ending of a story whose limits appear to be laid down by the advice proffered in its opening chapter: "Do not trust your horse in the field, or your wife in the house."

The Devil, by contrast, is not a story of obsessive jealousy or marital discord. The tragedy, which Tolstoy resolves variously in two different endings (in one the man commits suicide, in the other he kills his wife), stems solely from the husband Irtenev's lapse before marriage — an affair described with typically Tolstoyan reticence, which eschews naturalistic detail and leaves everything to the imagination. Happily married, he fears that his self-control will fail him against his will and his better judgment. His wife is good, kind and loving, but she is not realised as a person. His former mistress, the potential threat to Irtenev's fidelity, is hardly less nebulous. Irtenev monopolises the story. The women are merely A and B, the necessary bases of the triangle of which he is the apex. Had *The Devil* been cast in the form of a first-person monologue this would have mattered less. But narrated as it is by an omniscient and ostensibly impartial author, its balance is inexcusably upset and it is distinctly inferior to *The Kreutzer Sonata*.

Father Sergei, the third of the major stories on the theme of sex was, like *The Devil* and *Resurrection*, completed by Tolstoy after years of neglect in order to raise funds for the Dukhobors. Its powerful and moving plot combines the motif of the Prince who renounces the world, the theme of the saint who is tempted and falls and the idea of the false (rationally motivated) conversion and the true conversion which springs from the heart. Prince Kasatsky, a handsome, successful and ambitious aristocrat, leaves the world to enter a monastery on discovering that his fiancée had been the Emperor's mistress. He struggles against pride and sexual desire, is tempted, resists and eventually succumbs, only to be spiritually reborn on witnessing the example of a woman who lives for other people, for whom good is something to be done, not to be seen to be done. This is how Tolstoy expressed the idea of his story in his diary:

"There is no peace of mind either for the man who lives a secular life in the world or for the man who lives a spiritual life on his own. Peace of mind only comes when man lives to serve God in the world."[4] Spiritual pride is no less insidious than its secular variety.

The pattern of the story is provided by the parts played in the life of the Prince-monk by three different women: the first, whose determined assault he withstands by mortifying the flesh, the second who wins an easy and unpremeditated success, the third who is the passive instrument of his spiritual resurrection. There are many recognisably Tolstoyan touches: the description of a May evening, the trees in bloom, the nightingales singing, which plays the same anticipatory and contrasting role in Kasatsky's seduction as the Easter service does in the seduction of Maslova in *Resurrection*; the laconic entry on the sexual act; the moment of crisis issuing into reminiscences of childhood; the significant physical details ("the thin withered neck with prominent veins behind the ears"); and the occasional arresting metaphor ("He replaced his faith on its shaky pedestal, as one replaces an object of unstable equilibrium, and carefully stepped back from it so as not to knock and upset it"). Typical, too, is Tolstoy's habit of imparting unflattering physical attributes to a person antipathetic to his hero — the abbot of the monastery, for example, who has, almost predictably, a fat body, a protruding stomach, short plump hands and a bald head.

The fact that *Father Sergei* was never published in Tolstoy's lifetime, and not therefore finally revised, no doubt accounts for some of the minor narrative inconsistencies — whether in the colour of the Prince's hair which at first is grey but much later is "still black," or in the charge of murder which he brings against himself, an unexpurgated allusion to a discarded episode. More serious is the feeling that Father Sergei is not basically a changed man. It is true that the motive for his conversion — a woman who takes little or no part in church life, regards her prayers as mechanical and claims to lack any real religious feeling — is not unconvincing; and she is no less abruptly introduced than Karataev or Levin's peasant. "The only thing is," she says, "that I know how bad I am." But Sergei is only allowed one brief appearance after his change of heart when, as a wandering pilgrim, he accepts alms from a French traveller and gives it away to a blind beggar and "rejoiced particularly because he had despised the opinion of men"; when in fact he had behaved in a way which was entirely consistent with what would have been expected of him in the situation if he had *coveted* "the opinion of men." Tolstoy does not succeed in showing a new man in action, no doubt because human nature stubbornly resists the attempt to change it, no doubt also because Tolstoy himself was too much in the grip of egotism to create a character who had mastered it — if indeed any exist outside the pages of hagiography. Kasatsky cannot cease to be Kasatsky — he resumes his old name towards the end of the story — any more than Tolstoy, for all his novel theories and practices, could cease to be Tolstoy.

Vanity and sexual desire tormented Tolstoy almost to the end of his days — but not more insistently than the fear of death. Two of his finest stories of the later period are devoted to this theme. *The Death of Ivan Il'ich* is a harrowing account of the agonising end of an ordinary man who has achieved worldly success as a judge, but when faced with the dreadful inevitability of death, reviews his past and comes to the realisation that what he had valued then is of no significance now, that summoned before the highest court his case is a hopeless one, and that all he can do is, by dying, to rid his family of an unwanted encumbrance. In reaching this conclusion he loses his fear of death. An interesting parallel has been drawn between Tolstoy's story and Kafka's *The Trial*.[5] In the midst of ordinary and, to them, wholly satisfactory lives, Ivan Il'ich and Joseph K. are struck down by mysterious catastrophes. K. fails to win his case in an unknown court which tries him on an unspecified charge and he is executed. Ivan Il'ich fails to recover from an "unheard of " illness which the doctors cannot diagnose. The "case" and the "illness" are variations of the same device which allows the author to play God so as to confront an ordinary self-satisfied mortal with an extraordinary situation, rout his confidence and reason, and destroy him. Much closer to the text, however, is Maxim Gorky's use of Tolstoy's theme in his play *Yegor Bulychov and the Others*, in which the nearness of death compels the hero to look back over his apparently successful life, and to find it wanting.

Like several of Tolstoy's later stories, *The Death of Ivan Il'ich* incorporates the confessions of an ordinary commonplace individual, a man like many other men, who is overwhelmed by a crisis which shatters his whole outlook on life and forces him, however late in the day, to see the light — or at least a chink of it. Ivan Il'ich is a successful bureaucrat, a conformist, a creature of habit (could it be significant that his surname Golovin is, like Karenin's, derived from the word for a "head" — the one in Russian, the other in Homeric Greek?). He excludes his own emotions, his own personal opinions, his individuality; he is characterless and feature-less except in so far as he resembles other people in what he does and where he lives. His tragedy is — to be mortal. "Why this torture?" he asks himself when gravely ill. And he answers: "for no reason. It just is so." By a supreme irony, he receives the same treatment from his doctor, when on trial for his life, as he himself has been accustomed to mete out to others in court. Before he dies, it has been said, "he sees the inner light of Faith, renunciation and love."[6] But faith in what? And whom does he love? And how can he help renouncing life when he is at death's door? The fear of imminent death may explain his reappraisal of the values he has lived by: but it must be cold comfort to believe that the only purpose in his life is to cease to be — and so cease to be a burden to other people. Tolstoy resists a facile "religious" conclusion — the light he sees at the bottom of his imaginary sack is not God's love or immortality, but only a release from suffering. The "positive hero," the healthy peasant lad who waits cheer-fully on his dying master, is a shadowy stereotype. Life is stripped of all its poetry. We are offered only the sordid flesh, physical pain, exposed breasts, human excreta. We are told that Ivan Il'ich was once capable, cheerful, lively and agreeable, but we never see him in this happy state where at least the daily round of work is a compensation for the inevitable disappointments of life. The story begins with his death. After a flash-back to his early life, it proceeds with ever narrowing focus to his last excruciating moments. There are narrative touches of which Chekhov or Maupassant would have been proud. The scene at the onset of Ivan Ilich's illness, when he overtrumps his partner at cards, calls vividly to mind the passage in Chekhov's *Gusev* where the dying soldier gets his cards confused, calls hearts diamonds and muddles up the score. As a whole the story is so constructed technically that the chapters become increasingly shorter, with rare exceptions, as the climax approaches and the range of vision becomes more and more restricted (so much is telescoped, in fact, that the passage of time is blurred and the characteristic Tolstoyan discrepancies of age appear as the years fly by). Characteristically Tolstoyan too are the description of the thoughts aroused in his colleagues and friends by Ivan Il'ich's death — the prospects of unexpected promotion, the sense of relief that it is someone else who has died — the polemic against the medical profession or the observance of the proprieties; and indeed the thoughts about death which are ascribed to Ivan Il'ich himself are phrased in much the same way as those of Prince Andrew in *War and Peace* when faced with the almost certain prospect of extinction.

The Death of Ivan Il'ich, which Bunin may have had in mind when he wrote *The Gentleman from San Francisco*, has a modern existentialist flavour. In Sartre's words, "nothing can save man from himself, not even a valid proof of the existence of God."[7] Man's situation is tragic and absurd — but not hopeless. For Ivan Ilich the ray of hope comes too late to compensate for what he comes to regard as the futility of his past existence.

Tolstoy's short tale *Master and Man* is also on the theme of an eleventh-hour act of "unselfishness" in the face of death; it is, however, more conventional. A merchant and a peasant lose their way in a snowstorm. The merchant tries to escape and leaves the peasant to his fate. Chance brings him back to the place where the peasant is lying in the snow. On the impulse of the moment he throws himself on top of him, sheltering him with the warmth of his coat and body. When the two are found, the master is dead, but the peasant is still alive, saved by the seemingly unselfish act of an otherwise selfish man — in some respects the characters and relationships of the two men are a variation on the theme of Ivan Il'ich and his "man" Gerasim.

In his diary Tolstoy expressed himself dissatisfied with the poverty of content of the story, but was pleased with its artistic form.[8] Perhaps this provided the impulse for formalistically inclined scholars to subject it to a "close-reading" technique and to extract from it not only the recurring symbol of the circle and the repetition of the number three, but also symbolic overtones of Christ's passion.[9] Casual names and incidents are thus made to bear a heightened importance. There is of course no doubt that the merchant Brekhunov's name has a derogatory sound in Russian (*brekhun* means a "braggart" or "liar"). But when it is pointed out that he comes from the village of Kresty (The Crosses), and lives "in the shadow of the cross"; that when he stops to rest at a house on his journey he sits down at the head of the table for what is his last supper; that he overtakes a sledge driven by one Simon; that he is guided on his way by a certain Peter who turns back and leaves him to his fate; that he thinks he hears a cock crow; that there are several allusions to wormwood; and finally that he lies down on his servant with arms spread out in cruciform fashion – one's reaction is one of incredulity tempered by a sneaking admiration for the critic's ingenuity. The crucial moment of the story is the decision of an ordinary and by no means charitable man to perform an act which seems to be the embodiment of Christian charity. It is here that Tolstoy's innate sense of artistry comes to his aid, and while I do not share the view that *Master and Man* is on a higher artistic plane than the *Death of Ivan Il'ich*, I believe that Mr. Bayley puts his finger on the essential point when he writes:

> The motives of the merchant, his businesslike vigour and his desire to share his self-satisfaction with someone else, as if it were a bargain; the obvious calculation that in keeping Nikita (the peasant) warm he will be keeping himself warm too – all this makes the impulse to help the servant both moving and convincing. The moral of the story works without strain because the nature and personality of Brekhunov is fully established and he is allowed to remain true to it throughout.[10]

Most of Tolstoy's later fiction, whether published in his lifetime or posthumously, whether on the themes already illustrated or on such subjects as physical violence (*After the Ball*), guilt and repentance (*The False Coupon*) or prostitution (*Françoise*), are frankly edifying, admonitory and polemical. Their language is less varied and supple than that of the great novels. *Hadji Murat*, however, falls into a rather special category. Its ten principal drafts were written over the years 1896–1904, but no definitive version was completed by the author. It is worth emphasising that Tolstoy chose for his last major work a theme which took him back to his youth and to the fighting in the Caucasus in which he had himself been involved. Its subject matter and his treatment of it run directly counter to his professed belief in the doctrine of non-resistance, and his appeal to men to love their enemies and to turn the other cheek. He recognised this anomaly when he confessed to his daughter that he was ashamed of himself and was writing his story "on the quiet"![11] For the historical Hadji Murat was one of the leaders of the mountain tribesmen who fought under Shamil to resist the Russian conquest of the Caucasus in the 1850s. Having deserted to the Russians to avenge himself on Shamil, he changes sides again out of concern for the safety of his family, and is killed after a most desperate and tenacious resistance. Tolstoy records in his preface how he was reminded of an old Caucasian story "part of which I saw, part heard from eyewitnesses and part imagined to myself". Taking as his starting-point the death of a hero, he expands his subject into a broad panorama of life in the Caucasus and European Russia, ranging from the primitive mountain villages to the court of the Emperor Nicholas I. Much of his material is borrowed wholly or in part from the many works of reference which he consulted assiduously: articles and memoirs in historical journals, the letters of the Russian colonel Prince Vorontsov, the reminiscences of Poltoratsky, an officer who also figures in Tolstoy's story, and various ethnographical treatises on the Caucasus. His respect for the surface "facts" of history is shown by his diligent quest for the historical Hadji Murat. Did he have a noticeable limp? Did his house have a garden? Did he faithfully observe Muslim ritual? Did he speak any Russian? These questions, and many similar ones, he tried to answer accurately and conscientiously. As with his early Caucasian stories, he also drew on his own diary, which provided the rough basis of the first draft of *Hadji Murat*, entitled *The Thistle*, and supplied the metaphor of the sturdy and tenacious plant which survives the cart wheel and the plundering hands of man, and which is the symbol Tolstoy chose to frame his narrative:

> I was going home through the fields. It was midsummer. The meadows were mown and they were just about to cut the rye.
>
> There is a wonderful assortment of flowers at this time of the year; red, white and pink clover, fragrant and fluffy; pert, milk-white daisies with bright yellow centres and a musty, spicy smell; sweet-scented yellow charlock; tall, pink and white harebells; creeping vetch; prim scabious; yellow, red, pink and lilac; plantain with a suspicion of pink down and a faintly pleasant scent; cornflowers which are bright blue in the morning sun and pale blue with a rosy blush as they fade in the evening; and tender, almond-scented, drooping bindweed flowers.
>
> I had picked a large bunch of different flowers and was on my way home when I noticed a magnificent purple thistle in full bloom in a ditch. It was the sort we call a "Tartar," which the mowers are careful not to scythe; if they should accidentally cut it, they throw it out of the hay so as not to cut their hands on it. I thought I would pick this thistle and put it in the middle of my bunch. I clambered into the ditch, chased away a shaggy bumble-bee that had embedded itself in the heart of the flower and was blissfully dozing there, and tried to pick the flower. But it was very difficult; the stem pricked me on every side, even through the handkerchief which I had wrapped round my hand, and it was so terribly strong that I struggled with it for a good five minutes, breaking the fibres one by one. When I finally plucked the flowers, the stalk was all tattered and even the flower did not seem so fresh and beautiful. Moreover, its coarse and rough appearance made it a poor match for the other flowers in the bunch. I regretted having foolishly spoilt a flower which looked fine where it was, and threw it away. "But what energy and vitality," I thought, as I remembered the efforts I had made to pluck it. "How desperately it defended its life and how dearly it sold it."
>
> The way home lay through a freshly ploughed, fallow field of rich, black earth. I walked up along a dusty path. The ploughed field, which

was in private hands, was very large, and nothing was visible on either side or up the hill in front except the black, evenly furrowed, but still unharrowed earth. It had been well ploughed and not a single plant or blade of grass showed up — everything was black." What a cruel, destructive creature is man, how many living creatures and plants of every kind he has destroyed in order to support his life!" I thought, involuntarily looking for something alive in the midst of this dead, black field. Then I saw a clump of something to the right of the path in front of me. When I came closer, I saw it was another clump of "Tartar" thistle, whose flower I had idly plucked and thrown away.

The "Tartar" bush had three branches. One had been broken off and the part that was left stuck up like the stump of a severed arm. The other two each had a single flower. These flowers had once been red, but were now black. One stem was broken, and the top half dangled down with a dirty flower at the end; the other still pointed upwards, though coated with a film of black earth. It was obvious that the whole bush had been crushed by a wheel and had sprung up again, crooked but still standing. Part of its body, so to speak, had been shorn off, its bowels ripped out, an arm cut off, an eye gouged out. But it still stood there, refusing to surrender to man, who had destroyed all its brethren round about.

"What energy!" I thought. "Man has conquered everything, destroying millions of blades of grass, but this fellow has still not surrendered."

Then I remembered an old story of the Caucasus, part of which I saw, part heard from eyewitnesses and part imagined to myself. This story, as it has taken shape in my memory and imagination, is as follows.[12]

This vividly evocative and memorable passage is a good illustration of both the moral flavour and the metaphorical associations of the better stories of Tolstoy's last years. There is the same intimate knowledge of the countryside and the same power of minute observation which distinguished his earlier landscape descriptions; but there is also something obtrusive and too consciously "literary" about the simile of the severed arm or the body metaphors. In *War and Peace* one seldom feels that here is a professional writer practising his art. In the passage above, good as it is, one can sense a certain striving for effect.

There is more than a hint of Tolstoy's early Caucasian stories in the chapters about the death of an ordinary Russian soldier, Avdeev, who is wounded in a Chechen attack, the report sent back to headquarters and the reception of the news by the soldier's family. In Avdeev himself there are overtones of Platon Karataev. The familiar Tolstoyan note of denunciation is clearly audible in *Hadji Murat*, nowhere more so than in the merciless attack on Nicholas I and his entourage; while the assault on "the two despotisms, European and Asiatic," of Nicholas and Shamil (to quote Tolstoy) reinforces the opposition to autocracy and brutality so marked in the stories *After the Ball* and *What For?*, which are also set in the reign of Nicholas I.

While writing *Hadji Murat*, Tolstoy spoke of the need to convey in art the changing and contradictory aspects of human beings; change the context, and the same man appears in a different light. "How good it would be," he said, "to write a work of art which would clearly express the shifting nature of man; the fact that he is both villain and angel, wise man and fool, strong man and most helpless of creatures."[13]

One recalls the passage from *Resurrection*:

> One of the commonest and most widespread superstitions is that every man has certain definite qualities of his own: that a man is good, evil, wise, stupid, energetic, apathetic, and so on. People are not like that. We can say of a man that he is more often good than evil, more often wise than stupid, more often energetic than apathetic, or the reverse; but it would not be true if we were to say of one man that he is good or wise, and of another that he is evil or stupid. But we always classify people like this, and it is wrong. People are like rivers: the water in them is always the same, but every river is now narrow, now rapid, now broad, now slow, now clear, now cold, now muddy, now warm. So it is with people. Every person carries in him the seeds of every human quality, and sometimes he manifests some qualities and sometimes others, and it often happens that he appears unlike himself while still remaining one and the same person.[14]

In a somewhat similar vein Tolstoy emphasised the need to present his hero, Hadji Murat, in many different guises as warrior, family man, enemy and friend. "There is an English toy called a 'peepshow' (Tolstoy uses the English word), and under its glass, first one thing is shown and then another. That's the way to show Hadji Murat — as a husband, as a fanatic and so on. . . ."[15] On yet another occasion Tolstoy noted in his diary: "I dreamt about an old man — Chekhov has already anticipated me. The old man was particularly good because he was practically a saint, but at the same time he drank and swore. For the first time I clearly understood the force which characters acquire from having shadows boldly superimposed. I'll do this with Hadji Murat and Mar'ya Dmitrievna" [the mistress of an officer in the story].[16] Reading through some of the draft versions of the story, one realises the considerable labour Tolstoy expended in making Hadji Murat a rounded character by applying chiaroscuro effects and by the "peepshow" technique of using a rapid succession of different pictures. In a slightly different sense the expression "peepshow technique" can be applied to the composition of the book as a whole, with its rapid glimpses not merely of Hadji Murat, but of a cross-section of Russian life from Petersburg to the Caucasus. These glimpses are not haphazard. There is a striking symmetry about the order and arrangement of the twenty-five chapters, which start with a description of nature, progress through the ranks of the Russian army to the provincial society life in miniature of the Caucasus, to the court aristocracy and finally to the Emperor himself, then back in the reverse direction through the officer class to the ordinary soldier who tells the story of Hadji Murat's heroic death; while a final coda recalls the crushed thistle in the ploughed field and the inanimate world of nature of the preface. A judiciously used and characteristic subject inversion enables one to see the dead man's severed head and to hear the reactions of witnesses before the events leading up to the death are themselves described. Unlike Tolstoy's greatest fiction, however, there is little scope in *Hadji Murat* for psychological complexity or the exploration of mental states and processes. Much is on the surface. There is much narrative action. The omniscient author only withdraws to the extent of allowing his hero to relate the story of his early life to Prince Vorontsov's *aide*. And yet there is no mistaking the Tolstoyan stamp. Eyes talk, dreams and reality coincide at the moment of awakening, the nightingales, silent during the firing, burst into song again after Hadji Murat's death to signify the ceaseless continuity of life. Even the inaccuracies of language and the misuse of gerunds ("having had a smoke, conversation started up again between the soldiers") betray the author.

Hadji Murat has been unjustly neglected by foreign readers, no doubt because of the infelicitous rendering of the colloquial speech of soldiers and tribesmen which mars the standard translations, and the lack of polish which a final revision for the press would have ensured. Crystal-clear, exciting and supremely well narrated, it has claims to belong to that category of universal literature which Tolstoy prized so highly in his treatise *What is Art?*; for although on the one hand it acknowledges the driving force of vengeance and ambition, and although it does nothing to further the cause of passive resistance, its pathos is grounded in what Tolstoy called "those very simple, everyday feelings accessible to all" — the feelings of family solidarity and of compassion for human life.

Notes

1. D. Davie, *Russian Literature and Modern English Fiction* (University of Chicago, 1965), p. 190.

2. J. Bayley, *Tolstoy and the Novel* (London, 1966), p. 283.

3. Dorothy Green, "The Kreutzer Sonata: Tolstoy and Beethoven," *Melbourne Slavonic Studies*, I (1967).

4. L. N. Tolstoy, *Polnoe sobranie sochinenii*, ed. V. G. Chertkov et al., XXXI (Moscow 1928–58), p. 264.

5. P. Rahv, *Image and Idea: The Death of Ivan Il'ich and Joseph K.* (New Directions, 1957).

6. D. S. Mirsky, *A History of Russian Literature* (London, 1949), p. 305.

7. J. P. Sartre, *L'existentialisme est un Humanisme* (Paris, 1946).

8. Tolstoy, *Polnoe*, LIII, 3.

9. See "Tolstoy's *Master and Man* — Symbolic Narrative," *Slavic and E. European Journal*, III (1963).

10. Bayley, p. 95.
11. Tolstoy, *Polnoe*, LXXIV, 124.
12. *Hadji Murat*, Introduction.
13. Tolstoy, *Polnoe*, LIII, 187.
14. Tolstoy, *Polnoe*, LIII, 188.
15. *Resurrection*, Pt. I, Ch. 59.
16. Tolstoy, *Polnoe*, LIV, 97.

SELECTED
BIBLIOGRAPHY

Editions of Tolstoy's Works

The standard edition of Tolstoy's works in Russian is the Jubilee edition, published between 1928 and 1958, in ninety volumes. This edition contains forty-one volumes of letters and thirteen volumes of diaries, as well as rough drafts of some of the novels. The most complete edition in English of selected works is the Centenary edition in eleven volumes, translated by Louise and Aylmer Maude (London, 1929–37).

Bibliographical Material in Russian

Bitovt, Yury. *Graf L. Tolstoy v literature i isskustve* [Count L. Tolstoy in literature and art]. Moscow, 1903. Contains a listing of translations of Tolstoy's works before 1900.

Motyleva, T. I., et al., eds. *Khudozhestvennye proizvedeniya L. N. Tolstogo v perevodakh na innostrannye yazyki* [L. N. Tolstoy's artistic works in translations and in foreign languages]. Moscow, 1961. List of translations of Tolstoy's fiction into major foreign languages.

Shelyapin, N. G., et al., eds. *Bibliografiya literatury o L. N. Tolstom, 1917–1958* [Bibliographical literature about L. N. Tolstoy]. Moscow, 1960. The first in a series of updated volumes of secondary criticism on Tolstoy since the revolution. This volume contains more than 5,000 pieces, and the total entries of updated volumes now numbers more than 20,000 pieces.

Bibliographical Material in English

There are selective bibliographies of secondary works on Tolstoy (and other bibliographical aids) in studies by Simmons, Wasiolek, and Christian. The most complete listing of secondary criticism on Tolstoy in English is David R. Egan and Melinda A. Egan, eds., *Leo Tolstoy, an Annotated Bibliography of English-Language Sources to 1978* (Metuchen, NJ, and London: Scarecrow Press, 1979). Russian prerevolutionary criticism may be consulted in Boris Sorokin, *Tolstoy in Prerevolutionary Russian Criticism* (Columbus: Ohio State University Press, 1978).

Early Criticism

Ellis, H. Havelock. *Tolstoi, a Man of Peace*. Chicago, 1900.

Garnett, Edward. *Tolstoy: His Life and Writings*. London and New York, 1914.

Howells, William Dean. "The Philosophy of Tolstoy." In *The Library of the World's Best Literature*. Boston, 1897. Distinguished American man of letters deeply taken with Tolstoy.

James, Henry. Preface to *The Tragic Muse*. Reprinted in *The Art of the Novel*, ed. R. P. Blackmur, 79–97. New York and London, 1934. James's brief but immensely influential negative remarks about Tolstoy's art.

Redfern, Percy. *Tolstoy: A Study*. London, 1907. An early statement about the "two Tolstoys."

Turner, Charles Edward. *Count Tolstoi as Novelist and Thinker*. London, 1888.

de Vogüé, E. M. *The Russian Novel*. Translated by M. A. Sawyer. London, 1913. One of the earliest reactions in the West to Russian writers, including Tolstoy.

General Criticism

Abraham, Gerald. *Tolstoy*. New York, 1974. Reprint of 1935 edition. Short and intelligent.

Bayley, John. *Tolstoy and the Novel*. London, 1966. General review of Tolstoy's novels. Henry James's influence on his conception of the novel is evident.

Benson, Ruth Crego. *Women in Tolstoy: The Ideal and the Erotic*. Urbana, Ill., Chicago, and London, 1973.

Christian, R. F. *Tolstoy: A Critical Introduction*. Cambridge, 1969. A balanced view of Tolstoy's work. Approach is largely by way of sources and influences.

Edel, Leon. "Dialectic of the Mind: Tolstoy." In *The Modern Psychological Novel*, 147–53. Gloucester: Smith, 1972.

Edgerton, William B. "Tolstoy, Immortality and Twentieth Century Physics." *Canadian Slavonic Papers* 21 (1979):289–300.

Eikhenbaum, Boris. *The Young Tolstoy*. Translated by Gary Kern. Ann Arbor, Mich., 1972. Translation of the great Russian formalist 1922 study. Excellent study of Tolstoy's craft.

Gide, André. *Journals*. Vol. 3, *1928–1939*. New York: Knopf, 1948.

Goldenweizer, A. B. *Talks with Tolstoy*. Translated by S. S. Koteliansky and Virginia Woolf. New York, 1949. An abridged edition of the Russian *V blizi Tolstogo*. Rich in remarks and quotations of Tolstoy's comments on art.

Gorky, Maxim. *Reminiscences of Tolstoy, Chekhov, and Andreev*. New York, 1959. Published earlier in London, 1934. Eloquent and penetrating view of Tolstoy's personality and views.

Lavrin, Janko. *Tolstoy: An Approach*. New York, 1946.

Lednicki Waclaw. *Tolstoy between War and Peace*. London and The Hague, 1965. Tolstoy's relationship with Poland. Well done.

Lubbock, Percy. *The Craft of Fiction*. New York: Viking, 1964. Several chapters on Tolstoy. Lubbock is an apologist for Henry James, and though more sympathetic to Tolstoy than James, he still is highly critical of Tolstoy's craft.

Lukacs, Gyorgy. *Studies in European Realism*. Translated by Edith Bone. London, 1950. Lukacs is a respected Marxist critic, with a vast knowledge of the Western novel. Two chapters in this study are about Tolstoy: "Tolstoy and the Development of Realism" and "Leo Tolstoy and Western European Literature."

Mann, Thomas. *Essays of Three Decades*. New York, 1947. Contains essay "Goethe and Tolstoy."

Matlaw, Ralph, ed. *Tolstoy: A Collection of Critical Essays*. Englewood Cliffs, N.J., 1967. A representative selection of important essays on Tolstoy, not easily found elsewhere.

Morson, Gary Saul. "Tolstoy's Absolute Language." *Critical Inquiry* 7, no. 4 (Summer 1981):667–87. Bakhtinian approach.

Muchnic, Helen. *An Introduction to Russian Literature*. New York, 1964.

Muir, Edwin. *The Structure of the Novel*. New York, 1929. Excellent study of Tolstoy's use of time and of his craft in general.

Simmons, Ernest. *Introduction to Tolstoy's Writings*. Chicago and London, 1968. Helpful survey of Tolstoy's works.

Steiner, George. *Tolstoy or Dostoevsky*. New York, 1957. Very readable and original interpretation of Tolstoy. Intelligent and provocative.

Troyat, Henri. *Tolstoi*. Paris, 1965. English translation by Nancy Amphoux is in Doubleday 1967 edition. Very readable, somewhat fictionalized biography of Tolstoy.

Wasiolek, Edward. "Design in the Russian Novel." In *The Russian Novel from Pushkin to Pasternak*, edited by John Garrard, 51–66. New Haven: Yale University Press, 1983.

— — —. *Tolstoy's Major Fiction*. Chicago, 1978. Analysis of most important works with the view to formulating central structural truth of Tolstoy's vision.

Wilson, Edmund. "Notes on Tolstoy." In *A Window on Russia*, 160–83. New York: Farrar, Straus & Giroux, 1972.

Studies of Early Works

Dieckemann, Eberhard. *Erzählformen in Frühwerk L. N. Tolstojs, 1851–1857* Berlin, [Narrative form in L. N. Tolstoy's early work, 1851–1857]. 1969. Study of the narrative point of view of early works, especially of the *Childhood* trilogy and the *Two Hussars*.

Eikhenbaum, Boris. *The Young Tolstoi*. Translated by Boucher et al. Ann Arbor, Mich.: Ardis, 1972.

Forster, E. M. "Three Stories by Tolstoy." In *Two Cheers for Democracy*, 208–12. New York: Harcourt, 1941. Discussion of *The Cossacks*, *The Death of Ivan Ilych*, and *The Three Hermits*.

Hagan, John. "Ambivalence in Tolstoy's *The Cossacks*." *Novel* 3 (1969):28–47. Study of Tolstoy's ambivalence about the Cossack way of life.

Jackson, Robert L. "The Archetypal Journey; Aesthetic and Ethical Imperatives in the Art of Tolstoj: The Cossacks," *RusL*. 11, no 4 (1982):389–410.

Jones, W. Gareth. "The Nature of the Communication between Author and Reader in Tolstoy's *Childhood*." *Slavic and East European Journal* 55 (1977):506–16.

Lee, Nicholas. "Dreams and Daydreams in the Early Fiction of L. N. Tolstoy." In *American Contributions to the Seventh International Congress of Slavists*. Vol 2, *Literature and Folklore*, edited by Victor Terras. The Hague, 1973.

Poggioli, Renato. "Tolstoy's Domestic Happiness; Beyond Pastoral Love." In *The Oaten Flute: Essays on Pastoral Poetry and the Pastoral Ideal*, 265–82. Cambridge, Mass.: Harvard University Press, 1975.

Zweers, Alexander. *Grown-up Narrator and Childlike Hero: An Analysis of the Literary Devices Employed in Tolstoy's Trilogy, "Childhood," "Boyhood," and "Youth."* The Hague, 1971.

War and Peace

Berlin, Isaiah. *The Hedgehog and the Fox: An Essay on Tolstoy's View of History*. New York, 1953.

Bocharov, S. *Roman L. Tolstogo "Voina i Mir"* [Tolstoy's novel *War and Peace*]. Moscow, 1963. Short, perceptive, and original.

Carden, Patricia. "The Recuperative Powers of Memory: Tolstoy's *War and Peace*." In *The Russian Novel from Pushkin to Pasternak*, edited by John Garrard, 81–102. New Haven: Yale University Press, 1983.

Christian, R. F. *Tolstoy's "War and Peace": A Study*. Oxford, 1962. Largely a study of the rough drafts and variants and some analysis of the language and style.

Debreczeny, Paul. "Freedom and Necessity: A Reconsideration of *War and Peace*." *Papers on Language and Literature* 7 (1971):185–98. Consideration of Tolstoy's theory of freedom.

Farrell, James T. "Tolstoy's *War and Peace* as a Moral Panorama of the Tsarist Feudal Nobility." In *Literature and Morality*. New York, 1945. This volume contains a number of essays on Tolstoy: "History and War in Tolstoy's War and Peace," "Tolstoy's Portrait of Napoleon," "Leo Tolstoy and Napoleon Bonaparte," and "Historical Image of Napoleon Bonaparte."

Lehrman, E. H. *A Guide to the Russian Texts of Tolstoy's "War and Peace."* Ann Arbor: Ardis, 1980.

Leontiev, Konstantin. "The Novels of Count L. Tolstoy: Analysis, Style, and Atmosphere." In *Essays in Russian Literature. The Conservative View: Leontiev, Rozanov, Shestov*, 225–356. Athens: Ohio University Press, 1968. Originally published in 1890; a Russian classic. Detailed analyses of *War and Peace* and *Anna Karenina*.

Neatrour, Elizabeth. "The Role of Platon Karataev in *War and Peace*." *Madison College Studies and Research* (March 1970):19–30.

Saburov, A. A. *"Voina i Mir" L. N. Tolstogo, problematika i poetika* Moscow, [Tolstoy's *War and Peace*: Problems and poetics]. 1959. A 600-page study of the formal elements of *War and Peace*: language, style, genre, character, structure, themes, and ideas. Difficult to read but important.

Sherman, David J. "Philosophical Dialogue and Tolstoj's *War and Peace*." *Slavic and East European Journal* 24 (1980):14–24.

Shklovsky, Viktor. *Material i stil v romane "Voina i Mir" L'va Tolstogo* [Matter and style in Leon Tolstoy's novel *War and Peace*]. Moscow, 1928. Important study during the period of Shklovsky's accommodation of formalism to Marxism. Of special interest is listing of contemporary reviews in the appendix. Basically a study of Tolstoy's use of sources and how he deformed them.

States, Bert O. "The Hero and the World: Our Sense of Space in *War and Peace*." *Modern Fiction Studies* 2 (1965):153–64.

Wasiolek, Edward. "The Theory of History in War and Peace." *Midway* 9, no. 2 (1968):117–35.

Anna Karenina

Arnold, Matthew. "Count Leo Tolstoy." In *Essays in Criticism*, 2d ser. London, 1888. Early English review of Tolstoy, with emphasis on *Anna Karenina*. First published in the *Fortnightly Review* (December 1887).

Babaev E. *"Anna Karenina" L. N. Tolstogo* [L. N. Tolstoy's *Anna Karenina*]. Moscow: Khudozhestvennaya Lit., 1978.

Blackmur, R. P. "Anna Karenina: The Dialectic of Incarnation." *Kenyon Review* 12 (1950):433–56. Intelligent but not always clear. Provocative argument.

Call, Pau. "Anna Karenina's Crime and Punishment: The Impact of Historical Theory upon the Russian Novel." *Mosaic* 1 (October 1967):94–102. Links Anna's fate with Tolstoy's theory of history in *War and Peace*: the individual is free to act but cannot determine the outcome of his choices.

Christian, R. F. "The Problem of Tendentiousness in *Anna Karenina.*" *Canadian Slavonic Papers* 21 (1979):276–88.

Ermilov, V. E. *Roman L. N. Tolstogo "Anna Karenina"* [L. N. Tolstoy's novel *Anna Karenina*]. Moscow, 1963. Short and sensible reading by an orthodox Soviet critic.

Gifford, Henry. "Anna Lawrence and 'The Law.' " *Critical Quarterly* 1 (1959):203–6. Argues against Lawrence's thesis that Tolstoy betrayed Anna.

Jackson, Robert L. "Chance and Design in *Anna Karenina.*" In *The Disciplines of Criticism: Essays in Literary Theory, Interpretation and History*, edited by Peter Demetz, Thomas Greene, and Lowry Nelson, 315–29. New Haven, 1968. Detailed analysis of the scene in which Anna first meets Vronsky. This scene is seen as a microcosm of the novel.

Jones, Peter. *Philosophy and the Novel: Philosophical Aspects of "Middlemarch," "Anna Karenina," "The Brothers Karamazov," "A la recherche du temps perdu," and of the methods of Criticism.* Oxford, 1975.

Leavis, E. R. "Anna Karenina." *Critical Quarterly* 2 (1965–66):5–27. Also available in *Anna Karenina and Other Essays*. London, 1967. Sensitive and sophisticated reading.

Mann, Thomas. "Anna Karenina." In *Essays of Three Decades,*" translated by H. T. Lowe-Porter, 176–88. New York, 1965. First written in 1939 as preface to a Random House edition of the novel.

Trilling, Lionel. "Anna Karenina." In *The Opposing Self*. New York, 1969. Original published by Viking in 1950. Graceful and readable essay, but shows a limited knowledge of Tolstoy.

Studies of Late Works

Bilichenko, N. A. *"Obraz Simonsona v romane L. N. Tolstogo "Voskresenie": K voprosu o prototipe."* [The portrait of Simonson in Tolstoy's "Resurrection"; the problem of a prototype] *Russkaya literatura* 15, no. 4 (1972):161–65.

Dayananda, Y. J. "The Death of Ivan Ilych: A Psychological Study on Death and Dying." *Literature and Psychology* 22 (1972):191–98. Comparison of Tolstoy's short novel with Kubler-Ross's five stages of dying as expressed in *On Death and Dying*.

Fanger, Donald. "Nazarov's Mother; On the Poetics of Tolstoi's Late Epic." *Canadian-American Slavic Studies* 12 (1978):571–82.

Halperin, Irving. "The Structural Integrity of *The Death of Ivan Il'ich.*" *Slavic and East European Journal* 5 (1961):334–40.

Hardwick, Elizabeth. "Seduction and Betrayal, Part II." *New York Review of Books* 20, no. 10 (14 June 1973):6–10. Discussion of *The Kreutzer Sonata* and *Resurrection*.

Hearn, Lafcadio. "A Note upon Tolstoy's Resurrection." In *Life and Literature*, 300–307. Freeport, N.Y.: Books for Libraries Press, 1969. Reprint of 1917 publication.

Hirschberg, W. R. "Tolstoy's *The Death of Ivan Ilich.*" *Explicator* 28 (1969), item 26. Explication of the black bag symbolism.

Holquist, James M. "Resurrection and Remembering: The Metaphor of Literacy in Late Tolstoi." *Canadian-American Slavic Studies* 12 (1978):549–70.

Howe, Irving. "Leo Tolstoy; *The Death of Ivan Ilyich.*" In *Classics of Modern Fiction*, 113–78. New York: Harcourt Brace Jovanovich, 1972.

Jahn, Gary R. "The Role of the Ending in Lev Tolstoi's *The Death of Ivan Il'ich.*" *Canadian Slavonic Papers* 24, no. 3 (September 1982):229–38.

Karpman, Benjamin. "*The Kreutzer Sonata*: A Problem in Latent Homosexuality and Castration." *Psychoanalytic Review* 24 (1938):20–48.

Myshkovskaya, I. I. *Tolstoy, rabota i stil'* [Tolstoy, work and style]. 1939. Mostly on *Hadji-Murad*, but some analysis of *Khozyain i rabotnik* and *Kholstomer*.

Shestov, Lev. "The Last Judgment: Tolstoy's Last Works." In *Job's Balances: On the Sources of the Eternal Truths*, 83–138. Athens: Ohio Univ., 1975. Discussion of *The Death of Ivan Ilytch, Father Sergius,* and *Master and Man*.

Sorokin, Boris. "Ivan I'lich as Jonah: A Cruel Joke." *Canadian Slavic Studies* 5 (1971):487–507.

Trahan, Elizabeth. "L. N. Tolstoy's *Master and Man* — A Symbolic Narrative." *Slavic and East European Journal* 7 (1963):258–68.

Wasiolek, Edward. "Tolstoy's The Death of Ivan Ilych and Jamesian Fictional Imperatives." *Modern Fiction Studies* 6 (1960):314–24.

Woodward, James B. "Tolstoy's Hadji Murad: The Evolution of Its Theme and Structure." *Modern Language Review* 68 (1973):870–82.

Zhdanov, V. A. *Tvorcheskaya istoriya romana L. N. Tolstogo "Voskresenie."* [Creative History of Tolstoy's novel *Resurrection*]. Moscow, 1960. Introduction to drafts and variants of the novel.

INDEX